FOREVER IN
THE SUNSHINE

FOREVER IN THE SUNSHINE

The Story of Morecambe & Wise
as Only Family Can Tell It

GARY MORECAMBE

SPHERE

SPHERE

First published in Great Britain in 2023 by Sphere

1 3 5 7 9 10 8 6 4 2

A CIP catalogue record for this book
is available from the British Library.

ISBN 978-1-4087-3110-9

Typeset in Bembo by M Rules
Printed and bound in Great Britain by Clays Ltd, Elcograf S.p.A.

Papers used by Sphere are from well-managed forests
and other responsible sources.

Sphere
An imprint of
Little, Brown Book Group
Carmelite House
50 Victoria Embankment
London EC4Y 0DZ

An Hachette UK Company
www.hachette.co.uk

www.littlebrown.co.uk

For Michael Fountain, family friend and chauffeur to my father, who drove off into the sunset on 15 May 2022. What great memories of all those hours spent on the road together.

For Michael 'Wiggy' Threlfall, family friend and first cousin once removed of Eric Morecambe. Visits to Morecambe are never the same without your beaming face and wonderful sense of humour to greet me.

For my former literary agent and friend, Jennifer 'Jen' Luithlen, who finished her final page and passed peacefully away in the spring of 2023.

And remembering the actress and politician Glenda Jackson, who left us in 2023, and who played such a big role in the success of the *Morecambe & Wise Show* at the BBC.

NAM-MYOHO-RENGE-KYO

INTRODUCTION

Christmas! It's always about Christmas with *The Morecambe & Wise Show*. As the actor–director Kenneth Branagh once told me, 'Eric and Ernie hijacked Christmas, but it was the most wonderful bit of hijacking . . .'

Christmas in the Morecambe household was no different from that of many other households across the UK. The focal point was a family Christmas meal that in essence was both lunch and dinner combined at around 5 p.m., which fitted in with the arrival of our uncle, aunt and cousins, who drove over from North Finchley, once they'd closed up their pub.

We didn't talk about Morecambe and Wise at all during the day, from what I recall. Christmas Day was always about the family being together. It was very important to my father, perhaps because he'd grown up as an only child. He liked a family gathering.

We would have had the Christmas dinner, and about fifteen minutes before the show started, my father would gently propose that anyone who wanted to watch it should grab a glass of something and find themselves a seat. This was a suggestion rather than an instruction, as he and Ernie had already seen the show back at the studios, and almost always knew when it worked or didn't. Mostly – though not entirely – the younger family members would end up at one end of the house in the TV room, and the adults in the living room. And that's how we spent the next hour, all of us – my father included – falling about laughing. Because that's the thing about Morecambe and Wise: they were, and continue to be, incredibly funny.

After the show, Ernie would phone up, and he and my father would do a gentle analysis of it all. I know Ernie and his wife Doreen would often watch the show on their own in their house near Maidenhead. Ernie, who was pretty much a non-smoker from his late twenties, would allow himself one large cigar to be enjoyed throughout the Christmas show.

While the ancient theatres and the less ancient TV studios of Morecambe and Wise's working days have lost their past glory through a gradual but discernible fading of their once mesmerising aura, M&W themselves continue to entertain. They remain a prime-time Christmas fixture, waving to us from festive seasons past. If Charles Dickens created what we came to accept as the modern Christmas – of snow, family unification, merriment and generosity – then with quiet efficiency, Morecambe and Wise took up residency there, and never left. And no one has appeared to object. We enjoy their annual visitations, as much as Ebenezer Scrooge loathed his own. As for my family, we welcomed Morecambe and Wise's Christmas appearances in our household as much as any other.

Was it a little strange to be watching the seasonal event with Eric Morecambe himself? Perhaps, if we'd thought about it long enough, which possibly we didn't. It was just how it was.

And he always laughed the loudest and longest, which was as amusing as anything they did on television. I remember my younger brother, Steven, turning to him one Christmas and saying, 'Why are you laughing? You know what's coming!' These are the memories that I focus on today, rather than the fact we were watching *Morecambe and Wise* with Eric Morecambe.

No one has come close to displacing them, despite lots of other annual Christmas 'event' television. Seeing André Previn bemused as my father plays all the wrong notes is still as great a festive treat as witnessing the annual rebirth of Scrooge through his epiphany.

I've been a Morecambe and Wise fan since turning five, which is when I started at primary school and discovered everyone else knew who my dad was. My being a fan has lasted pretty much uninterrupted from that memorable day. But despite my closeness to the subject, my memories are my memories, and those are the only ones I can deliver.

My sister, Gail, on reading one of my M&W-related works some years back, told me that she found it fascinating how my memories of conversations and events didn't quite tally with her own. I'm writing this book as a Morecambe rather than a biographer, and Gail is here to help this final time around, her additional personal thoughts about her dad and 'Uncle' Ernie peppering the text.

I've never objected to other writers' biographies of this double act – and there have been a few. If I've had a concern of any sort, it is the obvious unavoidable one: that none of them were actually there to experience it; they are outside looking in and not inside looking out. Or, as my mother likes to put it: 'There's nothing particularly bad with any of the books written about Eric and Ernie, it's just that they don't somehow get it quite right.'

My father always light-heartedly complained that his mother, Sadie, kept embellishing tales of his childhood with each rendition. He made the point that she never meant to, it was just that she had come to believe them herself through so many retellings. That's the difficulty any author faces – what is genuinely a fact and what is a 'fact' honed over countless years of presentation? To that end, my mother, Joan, has been a great support in putting a book of this nature together by adding authenticity. She can spot an embellished anecdote or one built on a fictional tale a mile off!

It wasn't a given that I'd involve myself as much as I have with Morecambe and Wise. Up until I was in my early forties, I'd for the most part opted to keep the double act at a relative arm's length. Yes, I would talk about them if asked to, and write about them very occasionally; I'd even crop up in one or two interviews. But the path I was following involved quite a few other interests and distractions: working in hotels, bringing up a large family when in my late thirties and forties, and also moving to France for a period of time in the late 1980s.

As time passed, not only did I start to write a good deal more about Eric and Ernie in various ways and for various media outlets, but radio and TV documentaries began beckoning on quite a regular basis – they still do to this day. All at once I had to have a voice and, unlike my sister, I've never been very good at dealing with full-on attention and public speaking. But instead of diminishing with the passing of time, the M&W story has been developing, and thus so has my involvement. While Eric and Ernie's longevity isn't altogether unexpected – certainly not in my family or to those who have been close to the double act over the years – the sheer scale of the joy they continue to bring into people's lives perhaps is.

Morecambe and Wise are a combination of both the past and the present, making them a unique phenomenon: a comedy pairing that transcends what they did, to become something lodged in the public psyche more for who they were.

I've always said that it's difficult to date two men who seem forever middle-aged, sharing barbed conversation interlaced with big doses of affection for each other, and while mostly wearing identical suits. Perhaps that is also key in understanding the staying power of this remarkable duo, as they have essentially morphed into one life force, and have somehow become timeless.

And here I am again talking about Morecambe and Wise, entering their surreal world for one final adventure, because I fully intend this to be my last book about them. I want to end all my writings of them on the publication of this work – coincidentally falling exactly forty years since my first book – by returning to their whole remarkable story from beginning to end: a reappraisal of their magical career together.

In the blink of an eye, I'm not far off being a decade older than my father was when he passed away. But with age comes a sense of freedom – one of a few benefits, alongside my state pension, senior railcard and free bus pass! That freedom impacts what I've written in this book, without concern about what people might say or think, and discarding restraint that has in the past made me guarded about telling certain stories.

An editor of a large publishing house once told me that when you write a biography, you should always write it like it's the first thing that's ever been written about the subject. Sound advice. I'm adhering to that while also writing it knowing it will be my last chance to say what I feel I want to say. I'm also comfortable in the knowledge that there are elements herein that can only come from inside the family.

Writing now, I'm conscious too of the absence of almost everyone else who populated the M&W story. My mother is currently ninety-six, my sister seventy and I am sixty-seven – it's time to deliver something from within the family, while we're still here to deliver it! I've never written anything that has so involved my family; in fact, there have been occasions when I've published a book and they haven't even known about it until after it was out. Including my family when deciding to take this project on now was the decisive factor in turning an idea into an actuality.

There's a track on a Morecambe and Wise album from the early–mid 1960s, in which you hear Eric and Ernie apparently scaling a mountain. Pickaxes are chipping away, and eventually my father says, 'It's tough at the top, isn't it?' It's obviously a metaphor for their journey from obscurity to fame, and it has stayed with me all these years chiefly for that reason. And on an album otherwise filled with comedy, it was clearly a point they felt the need to make. There was an underlying seriousness to this short piece that had no sense of comedy in it, just a nod at where they'd come from, where they were heading, and what stresses and strains the journey thus far had created and would no doubt continue to create.

Scaling a mountain is exactly how I reflect on their long and wondrous partnership. They entertained as child performers in the 1930s and '40s, and were still entertaining right up to the very end of their partnership decades later.

But let's head back to those earliest of days one final time, as we re-enter the company of Messrs Morecambe and Wise, and journey into their sunshine. It's a place that I'm forever willing to visit.

Gary Morecambe
January 2023

PART ONE

HOW TO CLIMB TO THE TOP OF A MOUNTAIN

ONE

Comedians are a bit like class-A drugs: they entice you into thinking they're worth the attention, hook you by how they make you feel, and when you're addicted they're almost impossible to give up, always lurking somewhere in your psyche demanding a return visit.

One question has followed me down the years: what on earth motivates someone to decide on becoming a comedian? Comedians have it tough. An actor acts a part, and is dependent on the quality of the film or play they are in. But a comic has to stand in front of an audience, be it theatre, television or cinema, and make an audience want to laugh out loud. They have to provoke a visible physical reaction to create any kind of success. Bearing in mind that laughing releases endorphins in the brain, increases your intake of oxygen-rich air and stimulates your heart, lungs and muscles, we can assume that the desire is, biologically speaking, already there and just needs tweaking by the talent of the comic in question.

Over to my sister:

GAIL: I have always thought that it must be an advantage to perform comedy on stage as an unambitious youngster. You mind less if you fail or 'die on stage'. It is pre the

11

excruciating teenage embarrassment years, and I imagine at that age you barely care what people think or say. After all, you didn't find the gig, book the gig, think about if an audience doesn't show up, doesn't laugh, or that a future career may depend on it. Dad certainly cringed a bit in front of his friends, but I don't think an audience of strangers would have bothered him at all. A fantastic time to experience it – hearing the laughs, getting the timing right, getting used to not getting the expected laugh, without any of the associated stress. I doubt Dad the child ever thought, 'What if they don't like me?' or, 'What if they don't laugh?' All of that creeps in later.

My father spent almost his entire life being described as a 'natural comic', which he surely was – he thought funny at all times about every subject. If he found after a few minutes he was sounding serious, he would pull the rug from under his own feet and come up with a punchline – something his closest friend, the musician–actor–presenter Roy Castle told me when I interviewed him back in the early 1980s. When my father awoke each morning, the last thing on his mind was breakfast, the first thing was always what would he find funny during the day. Even so, to be a natural comedian takes work, and a journey of self-discovery.

He always claimed that he wasn't interested in the entertainment game until it started to pay big money. I've never fully bought into that. Yes, I'm sure he enjoyed not having any serious money worries as time went by, but inevitably he really couldn't help himself when it came to comedy – it was his whole *raison d'être*. He was probably asked so frequently about his past and his motivations that it became inevitable to tweak it just to have something different to say. But be under no illusion that it was comedy that got him up each morning.

My father was without doubt the most quick-witted man I've ever known. If we were ever out and about and it coincided with his having a rare quiet moment, people would ask him if he was ill! Inevitably that led to him being more and more 'on' all the time, as the one thing he hated was not to fulfil public expectation. He was so abundantly aware that his success was through their approval.

As a young boy, I'm sure my father was more interested in the idea of becoming a footballer, and I know he was slightly resentful of being dragged away by his mother, Sadie, from the after-school kick-about with his schoolmates, which was a regular event on Christie Avenue, Morecambe, where he lived. A heavy brown leather ball, barely pumped up – few people had the luxury of a pump back then – that would leave lace marks on your forehead if you were foolish enough to try to head the thing, was the centre of their young universe. His friends would chuckle whenever Sadie made her inevitable appearance: they knew that, for young Eric, it was game over – off with his everyday clothes and on with his song-and-dance outfit, consisting of top hat and tails, shiny shoes and a bow tie. Plus a fair coating of make-up, which was possibly the most embarrassing part.

According to my mother's notebooks, Sadie was an

usherette at the Central Pier, Morecambe, and a part-time waitress at the Café Royal. These two jobs financed my father's dancing lessons at Miss Hunter's Dance School.

My father would walk away from his mates, head down, ignoring their whistles and jibes, as he trudged across the open spaces to his extra-curricular lessons. He would get a cheery, sympathetic smile and wave from a girl working in a shop near Miss Hunter's, a girl who would later become known to the world as Thora Hird.

It's interesting he never resisted Sadie, even if he went through the whole rigmarole of pretending that he was resisting. This was for two reasons: firstly, his respect for his mother, as he recognised that without her drive he was, to use one of Sadie's own expressions, bone idle. He once told me that he was quite torn as a child between loyalty to his mates and loyalty to his mother's dream for him to have a bigger future. And secondly, linked to Sadie's 'bigger future' notion, I sense he felt he knew he needed these diversions from what was only local, everyday life as a youth of the 1930s. Sadie was offering him a hint of glamour – of 'something else out there' – that made the whole palaver he was going through somehow, perhaps only on a subliminal level at this point, more palatable. Once he understood the concept of the bright city lights, I believe he wanted them to be part of his own reality. The film star Cary Grant used to watch the boats leaving the harbour in Bristol, America-bound, dreaming – more literally perhaps than Eric Morecambe – that one day he would be on board one of them. Some people just aren't suited to being a permanent part of their native upbringing; they need to take a real or imagined journey over the horizon.

Some years ago, I met up with a lady in Morecambe who had been a friend of my father's during their school years. She described Sadie as being quite hard on him. But I'm not sure she fully understood their relationship. Where she saw hardness, my father saw encouragement and purpose. He occasionally talked about those early years to me, and it was the mutual love and affection between my father and grandmother – possibly never vocalised, because such was how things were in that era – that was the foundation on which dreams could be made reality. And he and Sadie spent a lifetime bantering and making barbed comments about each other, in spite of this strong shared love and affection. My favourite one of their exchanges occurred when we were all walking down a Morecambe street, and Sadie told my father he should spend some of his money as he couldn't take it with him when he was gone. He said, 'Not where *you're* going – it'll only melt!'

> GAIL: I am sure Nan, Sadie, knew he was a truant, knew he was bright and knew he was very mischievous. So, at the start she was probably keeping him off the streets, occupied and out of trouble.
>
> We've said many times that Nan was shrewd and even that perhaps she should take the lion's share of credit for the existence of Morecambe and Wise. But I don't think she had a plan as such. I don't think she would ever have dreamed of the extraordinary success her son and his partner went on to have. She could never have imagined in her wildest dreams that there would be a statue of 'Our Eric' on the seafront in their hometown. Nan was one of

15

those people that had an uncanny ability to understand what makes someone tick — she could work people out very quickly, including her own son and his partner, Ernie. As a younger lad, Dad was already in a double act with his cousin Michael, aka 'Our Sonny'. Only it wasn't comedy, it was mischief! And poor Sonny always got the blame. Even then Dad could look like butter wouldn't melt in his mouth. Also, being skinny and pale faced played to his advantage when standing next to his cousin. Sonny, compared to Dad, looked chubby, pink cheeked and always wore a big smile on his face. He was the same in adulthood and I have very fond memories of him.

I remember a story Nan told me of the time she was looking out of the kitchen window while washing up, to see Dad dangling from a long scarf, turning blue. The two boys had been playing Cowboys and Indians apparently, and she went running down the garden to the rescue! Or the boys regularly being thrown out of the cinema during Saturday matinees, where they would go to the front row of the circle with peashooters, to fire down upon any bald heads below.

While I am sure Nan knew that Poppa [her husband, George] was very happy with his life, very contented, she recognised that with the same life this probably wouldn't be true of her son. Ernie must have seemed like manna from heaven to her! I think she understood Ernie and realised he was the perfect personality match for Dad, but I don't think that, at the beginning, she thought he was much more than a companion for all the hours of travel. She possibly hoped that Ernie's good qualities, like his manners, his being good with money

and his drive to succeed in show business, might rub
off on her son.

At some point the double act got a life and energy of its
own. Nan was ready to let go, but even so, given how much
of her life it had become, she might have felt left behind in
some way. I know I would have.

Sadie also recognised, extremely early on, that her son not only liked being funny and entertaining people at any given opportunity, but that he was rather good at it. And she was right, because my father's humour and general ebullience, despite his being plagued with heart disease from a relatively young age, plus an increasing dropping off in watching and performing comedy in his later years, never fully left him. He couldn't stop being funny, even when he eventually tried quite hard not to be. And there is nothing funnier than a renowned comedian attempting to be serious. Tommy Cooper would walk into a busy room believing he was James Bond, while every else there looking at him would start to laugh.

The late Ronnie Corbett of *The Two Ronnies* – arguably Eric and Ernie's closest rivals in the 1970s, though in fact they were very different performers – loved my father for his natural humour and 'sparkling' company, as he put it. 'As far as being socially funny, Eric was wondrous,' Ronnie told me in a letter he sent me in 2008. 'He couldn't help himself in a way, and I often wondered if there was a strain which eventually took its toll . . .'

Picking up on Ronnie's comment, I notice the tears-of-a-clown theme is a strong one with me in anything I've written about my father. The late, great comedian

Les Dawson even called his autobiography *No Tears for the Clown*. And it interests me that a comedian as notable as Ronnie Corbett should have sensed an air of melancholia in his relationship with my father. Which doesn't for a moment mean that Eric Morecambe was melancholic, dark, often depressed or generally haunted by his art and talent. He really wasn't. But it's the fact that purveyors of comedy still have that air floating beneath the surface. Even the funniest, most natural comedy performers partially hide behind a mask. I sometimes have wondered if it's a necessity – a pause button while they recharge before their next onslaught of humour.

Young Eric emerged in Morecambe, Lancashire, on 14 May 1926, into a situation that couldn't have offered much potential: a life virtually mapped out in advance. School, part-time jobs, followed by full-time employment with the corporation like his dad, or one of the factories scattered around the region. And as he said himself, there is nothing at all wrong with any of that, 'it's just not as good as being a really famous comedian!' And I do wonder if that motivation – and by his twenties he had been teamed up with Ernie Wise for some time, so clearly it *was* a motivation – had actually begun to take root when he was very young, no doubt encouraged by his mother. Though it is fair to say that his respect, if not undying love, for his hometown stayed with him throughout his life, he wasn't especially in need of it. When I was a child, I noticed he was happier talking about it rather than visiting it.

Sadie was always able to think outside the box, and once she observed an ounce of talent in her only child, she was determined to nurture it. Not in a theatrical mum type of way, living vicariously through her son, but in a manner that prevented the waste of potential talent. 'She didn't want him tied to a whistle like his father,' as my mother puts it. 'Once she saw he had some talent, she wanted him to have the chance to better his station in life – improve his opportunities. It was that simple.'

Sadie's thinking was very brave, and would require hardships of her own, and also for her husband, my grandad George. Sadie would end up on the road a lot of the time in those early years of struggle, and George would be left to fend for himself at the family home. Fortunately, Sadie and George had a surprisingly modern outlook for a couple living in 1930s Lancashire.

George severely broke his leg playing in a local football match, and he took a year off, so becoming a house-husband before the expression even came into being. Sadie got a job, and George did all the domestic chores, including looking after young Eric.

George worshipped Sadie in his own quiet, unassuming way. Although he was a man's man in so many guises – not least in his work for the corporation (council) – he was visibly content to be at Sadie's beck and call. I can still picture him around meal times, serving up food Sadie had prepared, wearing an apron over his jumper, shirt and tie. It's hardly surprising that his last word should have been shouting out her name as he collapsed and died on their living-room floor in 1976.

GAIL: I too have very affectionate memories of Poppa in a pinny. In my memory he always did the hoovering. But back in the day the Hoover was rather big, and Sadie was rather small. It was probably the same size as her.

I do occasionally wish that as a mother, I had been more like Sadie. I find myself thinking that it would have been of great benefit to my children if I had been! Sadie would never confuse her role of Parent with that of Friend. I think she had a very clear vision that her job was to help her son make something of himself. The showbiz path was the route she took only because of the innate talent she saw in her son. If he had been academic, then that is the road they would have travelled down: a doctor, solicitor or accountant might have been the target she would then have aimed him towards.

Sadie once wrote, 'Eric has always claimed I pushed him into show business, and he's even tried to sell *me* that idea! But that's not how I remember it. Eric loved performing and show business, practically from the time he could walk, which he did at nine months!

'Whenever we took him to relatives, all he wanted to do was perform. As soon as someone sat at the piano, you'd see a blond curly top no higher than the keyboard.'

As my father grew, and his interest in entertainment became not so much a passion at this stage, but a better option for someone with little interest in almost everything else with the exception of football, Sadie came up with a strategy: she would enter him into as many talent shows as possible. It was a simple but bright move, as his efforts in getting a reasonable education were somewhat unimpressive. He always claimed he only turned up at school to have a laugh with his classmates, and to go somewhere quiet for a smoke where his parents couldn't catch him.

I remember in the late 1960s getting a very bad school report, and saying to my father, 'Well, *you* did all right after leaving school so young.' He replied, 'I got struck by lightning. It's very unlikely to happen a second time in the same family. And I regret not working hard at school. You should do your best, you really should.'

Those words, clearly not the ones I'd been expecting, must have struck home, as I haven't forgotten them to this day. And I remember further conversations, not solely with my father, but with my mother too, where it became apparent that having left school so early and with so little real education, he had to spend the next twenty years educating himself. He did this mostly through books – any book he could get his hands on. He would take advantage of the tedious train journeys around the country while touring the theatres and radio studios, to consume all this eclectic material. He never stopped loving books, and always cajoled me into reading more and more varied material. 'Read anything and everything,' I can still hear him telling me when I was in my early teens.

I have a vivid memory of him saying, 'You never have as much time as you think you have.' Those words would prove accurate in his case, and they spur me on even more these days, very aware I'm now nearer seventy than sixty.

I think it must have been someone else's expression passed on to him, because you only need to examine his and Ernie's life to recognise how much they crammed in for what by today's standards can be considered a reasonably brief period of time.

If I had to sum up my father's attitude to life, it would be to describe how he saw human existence on our planet. 'It's a privilege to be here at all,' he once said, 'because there'll come a tomorrow when you won't be here at all!'

I think that explains much about a man who became so much more than his upbringing. But the upbringing would inform the comedian, and it all began to get lively in Lancashire during the 1930s.

TWO

My father claimed the reason he won so many of the talent contests he entered as a boy — all of which he loathed doing — was because his dad had such a large family. George had twelve siblings, and there were numerous aunts and uncles from both sides who were only too willing to offer their support, turning up at talent shows incognito to vociferously cheer him on. He also claimed that the competition was not of the highest standard, and I don't think he was being judgemental here, as that wasn't his style. If he said something, he tended to mean it quite literally.

GAIL: Poppa, George, was one of thirteen children. I think ten of them were boys. Sadie was one of eleven, and ten of them were girls!

It occurred to me recently that I don't remember ever hearing Poppa talk about the early years, or life with Dad as a boy, or having a young Ernie practically living with them. Nan would recount stories endlessly, but if ever a man lived in the present moment, it was Poppa! I believe that Dad was actually more like his father than his mother, but I doubt that Dad would have agreed. Poppa had the same mischievous twinkle in his eye; he had a fantastic sense of humour and could make us all laugh. He had a lovely singing voice and could dance really well. Dad would *do* something or buy something and say, 'Don't tell your mother!' And Poppa would say to me, 'Don't tell your grandmother!' He and I would often go for long walks in the lovely countryside around Hest Bank on the fringes of Morecambe Bay. Nan would always tell him to be careful and remind him that he had me, a five- or six-year-old, with him. She'd tell me to look after Poppa and don't get up to mischief. But of course, every walk would be an adventure. We always walked across fields with cows in and I always managed to tread in several cowpats. However, on one occasion we were chased by a very large bull in the field and I actually remember Poppa picking me up and running full speed towards the hedge and literally being hurled through the air and over the hedge. As I landed on the verge I turned to see my grandfather, with a big grin on his face, bursting through the hedge with the angry bull a few yards behind him! Poppa never stopped smiling, took my hand, said, 'Don't tell yer nan' and whistled all the way home.

I did love Nan and Pop's relationship. A great example of how to make a marriage work. He never left the house without giving her a kiss, and I certainly never heard raised voices or anything resembling an argument between them.

The talent-show success led to the Kingsway cinema, Hoylake, and another talent-show victory up against nine other finalists. As reported at the time:

Interviewed by a Melody Maker *representative, 13 years old* [sic] *Eric Bartholomew, who put over a brilliant comedian act, which caused the audience to roar with laughter, said: 'My*

ambition is to become a comedian. My hero is George Formby,
another native of Lancashire. I would certainly like to follow in
his footsteps' . . .

Youth certainly took its bow: The average age of the finalists
was sixteen years!

This success in turn led to his being selected to audition for impresario Jack Hylton, which then led to his first brief encounter with a young Ernie Wise – not in a dramatic way as has often been presented, but on a rainy day in Manchester. Ernie had already broken through to a high level of child stardom. He had appeared at the London Palladium with comedy actor Arthur Askey, which in itself was remarkable. Ernie was a child star, which I think my father made him pay for during the rest of his life!

GAIL: To be honest, I think Dad would have been very happy to have been less successful. He would often comment that it couldn't last, or that there's only down now. It was always hovering in the background of his thinking. He was competitive by nature, so never getting to the absolute top would be okay, but getting there and then being knocked off by another double act was something that I think as an idea he struggled with a bit. If Dad had worked in an office, he would have been happy being part of a team, but he wouldn't have wanted it to be his own business. Probably fair to say that Ernie would happily have been the proprietor or the office boss. Ernie was ambitious, not cut-throat. More like the old-fashioned bank manager, perhaps.

Ernie once told me that my father had struck him as talented at that audition. 'He did a Flanagan and Allen piece, but somehow played both parts. It was very clever.' Ernie often came out with that line – even in television interviews years later – so it must have made a big impression on him as a young lad.

And Ernie was very much a young lad when put under the wing of Jack Hylton, yet ostensibly fending for himself in the big wide world.

It was during a trip to America in 1937 that, as an impresario and bandleader, Jack Hylton recognised that theatres were in slow decline. The focus was shifting to big bands and variety shows. Hylton took this thought with him back to the UK, and promptly set about a strategy that would prove hugely successful.

Hylton cut a big deal that took the popularity of the radio shows and essentially transported them from the studio to the stage. Part of the deal was to borrow radio stars to tour the shows. Having a band already was a big plus in achieving this, and with established contacts neatly in place, he put a variety bill together.

Jack Hylton

Jack Hylton was born on 2 July 1892 in Great Lever, Lancashire. In 1905, he made his professional performing debut in Rhyl as part of a Pierrot troupe. Prior to the start of the First World War, Hylton played the piano for a band at the 400 Club in London. With the outbreak of war, he became a musical director in the band of the 20th Hussars. Hylton then became a musical adviser in the entertainment section of the Navy and Army Canteen Board (NACB, later known as NAAFI, the Navy, Army and Air Force Institutes).

After the war, Jack Hylton and Tommy Handley started a double act together. However, they went their separate ways in 1920. The same year, he joined the Queen's Dance Orchestra in London. After Hylton was asked to leave the following year, he started Jack Hylton and His Orchestra. In 1926, they played their first Royal Command Performance at the London Alhambra, and appeared at the Royal Albert Hall. The following year, he had a lucky escape when he had a car crash.

In theatre–producer mode, Hylton toured a stage version of the BBC radio series *Band Waggon*. The second half of the show, titled *Youth Takes a Bow*, provided the opportunity for new talent to perform. Jack was responsible for giving a young Ernest Wiseman a chance to appear, and soon the newspapers were full of headlines such as 'Fame in a Night For 13-Year-Old "Max Miller"'. Jack shortened the name of his new prodigy, who he took under his wing, to Ernie Wise.

Hylton then discovered a young comedian called Eric Bartholomew during an audition. This was Bartholomew's prize for winning the local heat of a talent contest organised by *Melody Maker*. Impressed, he engaged Eric for *Youth Takes a Bow*.

Despite their huge success, Jack chose to disband Jack Hylton and His Orchestra early in the Second World War, only reuniting the musicians for the Royal Command Performance in 1950.

As well as continuing to present stage productions, including musicals and farces, and producing films including *Ramsbottom Rides Again* and *Make Mine a Million,* Hylton reformed the comedy group Crazy Gang and became an adviser to the ITV company Associated-Rediffusion.

Jack died on 29 January 1965 in Marylebone, London.

In the autumn of 1938, Hylton toured all the UK's major cities. He was a shrewd man, always checking out the local acts in case he could inveigle them into his growing team. The second half of his variety show, called *Youth Takes a Bow,* was a showcase for all the up-and-coming talent he'd collect on his journey, and that would change as and when necessary as it went along.

In early 1939, a young Yorkshire lad called Ernest Wiseman, accompanied by his father Harry, arrived at Hylton's office. Ernie went through his routine – jokes, songs and some dancing – and he and his dad also went into their double-act routine, which had been going down very well in the clubs and pubs around Leeds. 'His father would enter him into every competition, and he would always come first – which upset him!' recalled Ernie's widow Doreen in 2010. 'First prize was always money, but he wouldn't get to see it, so he wanted to come second or third, because the prizes were other things like chocolate, which he could keep for himself.'

Rather shockingly in today's world, Ernie, who was the eldest of five – one sibling died as a baby – 'became the breadwinner in the family', explained Doreen. So around the age of ten, Ernie was financing the whole Wiseman family!

> GAIL: Doreen always felt Ernie had missed out on his childhood. She was very protective of Ernie all his life, and she did seem genuinely sad that Ernie didn't get to muck about with friends his own age and just be a boy! But I would have to say that Ernie really loved it. He wasn't at all resentful towards his dad, in fact the complete opposite. Ernie probably felt saved from school, which he didn't get on with at all.

Hylton saw talent in young Ernie and gave him a contract, but turned his father down. He knew Ernie had the talent to make it big, but on his own, and his ready-made *Youth Takes a Bow* showcase was ideal for such young, raw talent.

Harry Wiseman possibly never recovered from this rejection, though he didn't stand in the way of Ernie's own dreams and journey in show business. But it marked the end of their partnership. Things would never be quite the same. And as Ernie became more of a breadwinner than anyone in his family, he ultimately was used by his parents. As Doreen Wise put it, 'He was out working at age seven. Slavery, really. Both his mother and father regarded him as a workhorse.'

Ernie's schooling was almost as limited as his future partner's was. He attended East Ardsley Boys School – a

Victorian edifice of Dickensian design and atmosphere. It was an institution that put discipline above education, and where master-to-boy cruelty was rampant. It made Ernie very wary of the educational environment, and 'showbiz' became of even greater interest and importance to him as a means of escape.

When I was away from school on one of my irregular visits to the television studios to watch M&W either filming or rehearsing, Ernie mentioned to me that he really hadn't enjoyed his schooldays and had tried as much as humanly possible not to attend, whatever trouble that might have created for him. I've often wondered if perhaps Ernie was slightly dyslexic – something that wouldn't have even been recognised back then.

Ernie took to the stage for Jack Hylton on 6 January 1939, and showed no nerves at all. The audience loved him, and he was quickly making headlines. One critic wrote: 'The show is excellent, and I am sure this boy prodigy, Ernie Wise, will justify the seven-year contract. This boy has taken the West End by storm, and I think he will become a second Dan Leno.' This was a remarkable review for Ernie, as English music hall comedian and actor Dan Leno – 1860–1904 – was revered in the business as nothing less than a legend.

Ernie's name was formally shortened to Ernie Wise on 8 January, during an interview given by Jack Hylton. 'His name is Ernest Wiseman, but he's going to be famous, so we'll call him Ernie Wise,' he remarked. Jack Hylton would become more of a father to Ernie than his own father, Harry, such was his fondness for the lad, and the fact they would spend so much time together. I expect nowadays eyebrows would be raised, but Hylton genuinely saw Ernie as a son.

Ultimately, with Harry being superfluous to Hylton's requirements, it came down to logistics – Harry was in Leeds and Ernie was on the road with and for Hylton. Jack Hylton was the one who was there, and would always treat Ernie well – made sure he always ate properly, and kitted him out in new clothes. Both Hylton and his partner would always look out for him. Hylton separated from his wife, Ennis Parkes, in 1929. Although they remained relatively close thereafter until her death in 1957, he had a long-term partner called Frederika Kogler (Fifi), with whom he had two daughters during the 1930s. Hylton would have a son, Jack, in 1947 from an affair with an actress and singer called Pat Taylor.

In Manchester, early in 1940 (and there is speculation as to the exact date, but neither Eric nor Ernie seemed able to recall for certain when it was), Ernie had sat down with Jack Hylton's right-hand man, Bryan Michie, who was the producer of the *Youth Takes a Bow* segment of the variety tour, to watch this young performer from Morecambe. Ernie didn't have to be there, but both Michie and Hylton felt that he should.

Away from his work, Ernie Wise was a quiet figure who didn't overly socialise with his peers. Had Hylton and Michie spotted something in Eric that might help Ernie? It's possible, if never stated. It's even possible that Sadie, being as sharp as a knife when trying to promote her own son, mentioned to Hylton how much she enjoyed young Ernie Wise as a performer. And we know that Michie and those around him would tease Ernie after my father's audition, telling him he'd have to watch his back, and that he'd no longer be the favourite with a new kid on the block. All this banter would become the foundations of Eric and Ernie's future together.

> GAIL: I asked Dad about meeting Ernie and he said he thought that Ernie, just because he'd performed at the London Palladium, was a show-off. He thought Ernie felt his position in the pecking order was under threat now with this 'new boy's' arrival. My take on it is that I can well imagine Sadie giving Dad a hard time, regularly mentioning how talented, sensible and ambitious that young Ernie Wiseman is. I imagine the first emotion they both felt for each other was a rather jealous wariness.

On a trip to Manchester in 1982, when my father and I were doing an interview spot on a chat show for the late, great Russell Harty, the two of us walked past what had become the Odeon cinema on Oxford Street (now demolished and the site of a Landmark office building). This was apparently the venue where he'd performed that audition for Hylton and Michie. My father said to me that he remembered very little about it, but that briefly he did meet Ernie. However, although they exchanged a few cautious pleasantries, he thinks there was nothing more to it than that. It was Michie and Sadie that did the brief conversational part, and then they were gone with the infamous parting remark from Bryan Michie: 'We'll be in touch, Mrs Bartholomew'.

Eric and Ernie's second meeting was just as brief and inauspicious as the first. Ernie joined the train at Crewe with others from Hylton's 'Youth' show bound for Swansea.

My father said, 'I didn't meet him until somebody's mother introduced him to *my* mother while I was there. He said "Hi!" in a breezy fashion and bounced off.'

For my father, the timing of his breakthrough into *Youth Takes a Bow* couldn't have been much worse. Hitler was attempting to take over Europe, and when war broke out for real, my father and Ernie would find, like so many, that their careers were affected.

For now, however, Ernie was back on the road touring, and still getting positive revues. Arthur Askey was a big star, and continually in demand to perform elsewhere, so it must have come as no surprise, though hugely disappointing nonetheless, that he had to bid Ernie and the troupe *adieu* for the time being.

From the 1950s onwards, Askey was always popping up on radio, and was a very prominent television presence who made regular appearances on the BBC's long-running music hall programme *The Good Old Days*. He became a dear friend of my father's, and on several occasions I was blessed to spend a little time with him – firstly as a child with my parents, and later in Bradford when I was assigned by Billy Marsh (Eric and Ernie's eventual agent, and my boss at London Management in Regent Street) to look after him for a tribute show for Gracie Fields at the Alhambra Theatre. Arthur was always friendly and lively and had time for you. I remember being told that when I met him in at Bradford railway station, as he wasn't a youngster any more, I was to organise a taxi and have it ready for him.

His train came in from London, and Arthur bounced up the platform with his usual verve. I pointed to the taxi and he said, 'Oh, it's only a couple of miles to the hotel. I checked. Let's walk!' The taxi was dismissed, and I caught up with his disappearing form, struggling to maintain his pace. I'm glad he was happy carrying his own suitcase!

Askey was one of my father's few genuine comic heroes. Even when I was very young, I could sense the huge respect he had for him. For a start, he was much more subdued when in his company. It was as if he recognised there was no point in trying to entertain one of the greatest entertainers the country had produced. And he laughed out loud at everything Arthur said, and with good reason: Arthur Askey was a funny man.

Askey would remain in contact with Ernie and, by association, Eric, for the rest of his days.

THREE

Askey's replacement to work with Ernie was a performer called Max Wall, who would go on to have
his own successful career. Born in 1908, he was around
for the era of music hall, before appearing in films, television and theatre. In the 1970s, he even backed new-wave
band Ian Dury and the Blockheads, Dury being a big fan
of his. No one of a certain age will forget Wall for the
bizarre walk of the oddly dressed – or under-dressed –
Professor Wallofski. Certainly John Cleese hadn't,
acknowledging Wall for his influence on Monty Python's
Ministry of Silly Walks.

'Max was a melancholy type of comedian,' commented
Ernie, many years after working with him. 'More depres-
sive than optimistic. He didn't suffer fools gladly.'

The late comedian, actor and entertainment archivist
Roy Hudd once recalled, 'Max's association with the
opposite sex always gave him trouble, and I remember
standing next to him in the gents in Grosvenor House.
Looking down, he muttered in that unmistakable voice,
"You, you little swine – you're the cause of it all!"'

Ernie now had the opportunity to learn from another
brilliant stage performer in Wall, and would continue

to tour with him until the show came to its end in June 1940.

The next year or two were surprisingly life-changing ones for Eric and Ernie. Too young to be actively involved in the war, and just about able to continue working while those around them disappeared for the duration, it was during this time they started to develop their double act.

Entertainment history rightly records how Sadie, on a train between Birmingham and war-damaged Coventry, with Eric and Ernie in the compartment – both fourteen years of age by now – came up with the idea they should form a double act.

She'd already taken Ernie under her wing on the *Youth Takes a Bow* tour. She had always been troubled that Ernie had been touring unchaperoned. I would agree with Gail that Sadie, being no fool, probably played one against the other a little bit to get the best out of the two of them. While never expressing guilt at her son being an only child – and why should she? – she would've been aware that he had entered a lonely profession with ostensibly no peer support. What better than to have a perpetual mate on hand on that lonely road, and one as unencumbered as young Ernie Wise, who had until this point a reputation for being notoriously independent? So when we get to the time and place the double act idea was 'casually' introduced by Sadie on a train journey across the war-scarred landscapes around the Midlands, it's tempting to believe she had been planning this suggestion for some time.

It was certainly a light-bulb moment for both the

young lads, who had genuinely – according to conversations with my father decades later – never considered it as an option. 'We were two separate acts, you see,' he told me. 'We hadn't thought about doing something else for Jack Hylton. We were employed individually.'

Part of comedian, writer and actress Victoria Wood's 2011 TV film called *Eric and Ernie*, which covered their early years, focused heavily – and realistically – on their developing friendship. How by chance they met up in Oxford when the boys were no more than thirteen. Ernie, with no place to stay, went house to house in the black-out that was war-time life, knocking on doors to find somewhere to sleep. He stumbled across Sadie's digs, and she let him in to share a bed with her Eric. I do wonder, and alas never asked their writer Eddie Braben, if it was less Laurel and Hardy and more their own digs-sharing days on the road touring that inspired him, years later, to have them share a bed as a regular part of *The Morecambe & Wise Show* on television. His widow, Dee, thinks it was a combination of both those influences. Eddie was certainly keen that whatever their situation on TV, they must perform side by side at all times. With that in mind, the shared double bed seems as appropriate as the shared apartment. And as boys touring together, it was no less appropriate for them to share a bed.

SIDENOTE: Steve Punt, comedian, writer and half of double act Punt and Dennis, reminded me of one of these many train journeys Eric and Ernie took. It would have been after this initial one, probably when the double act was newly formed, so more likely during the endless touring of the early 1940s. 'They met another variety hall performer in their compartment,' says Punt. 'He was about to retire, and said they could have all his props if they wanted them. What wonderful imagery that creates, and so of its time. I think of that quite often. And also Eric saying, while reflecting on the disappearance of this specific era, that there aren't any funny men any more – just funny lines! That's an amazing observation, as it holds true to this very day. You can watch a load of comedians, who on the surface might not be intrinsically funny, but they say funny things. And that works the other way around, too. Funny people saying funny things that on paper don't read as that funny.'

GAIL: Sadie told me that they [Dad and Ernie] used to drive her mad on train journeys, fooling around, annoying or amusing the other passengers, and that out of desperation she said, 'If you boys can't stop mucking about, why don't you work on a double act of your own?' She made it sound like a throwaway comment, but I agree, and wouldn't be at all surprised if the double act idea hadn't been bubbling away for quite some time for her. Considering her love for Ernie was equal to her love for her son, it isn't unlikely.

Sadie assuredly wore rose-tinted glasses, but I really liked that facet to her personality. She might well consider the half-empty glass, but inevitably would always pick up the half-full one. She made everything seem hopeful and optimistic. There was a naivety there that I firmly believe Eric and Ernie caught like some airborne virus, and brought into their act. As with Sadie, my father only recounted his past with a smile, and confessed to me that he wouldn't have changed anything. Not many of us can claim that.

The connection between Laurel and Hardy and Morecambe and Wise was clearly going to be more than a young Eric and Ernie occasionally doing a passable impression of Stan and Ollie. Their love for that double act, which would supplant a love for anyone else in show business, not only remained with them until the very end, but influenced the direction of their careers.

It's of course easy for Gail and me to relate to Stan Laurel's daughter, Lois. She passed away in July 2017 at the age of eighty-nine, having spent a solid part of her life promoting the legacy of her father and his partner. She would appear in documentaries about the duo and worked diligently to preserve their legacy. Snap! She also said on camera that Laurel and Hardy were closer than brothers – very similar to writer Eddie Braben's comment made in the late 1960s, when describing Eric and Ernie's relationship.

M&W have often been referred to as the television equivalent of Laurel and Hardy, and I think that's a fair observation. And there is, of course, a certain irony in Stan hailing from Ulverston, which lies directly across from Morecambe Bay, all of about twenty miles in distance as the crow flies.

For me, the key connection between the double acts is in the way they are both instantly remembered by what became their own signature songs. For Laurel and Hardy it was 'The Cuckoo Song'. For Morecambe and Wise it would be 'Bring Me Sunshine'.

28 August 1941, and through Bryan Michie, Eric and Ernie convinced Jack Hylton that they could do a small double-act piece, 'which was terrible,' my father claimed many years later. But Hylton trusted my father, and adored Ernie, so after they did an audition of sorts for him, he let them have their way. The one proviso: they still had to do their solo spots. People came to see Ernie Wise as a solo performer – the young star of London's glittering West End – so that made sound sense. And I like to think that Michie and Hylton were no fools, and perhaps were among the first to see the glimmer of a spark between these lads that Sadie had certainly picked up on. Who's to say that Sadie wasn't even in quiet talks with Hylton? I wouldn't have put it past her. In an innocent, serene way, she could be very wily.

Thinking of these young lads doing yet another audition reminds me of the time my father told me that for many years he and Ernie continually had to prove to people they were 'good enough', as he termed it. In fact, that requirement didn't really cease until they were big stars at the BBC.

At the beginning of their notable journey into

entertainment history, Ernie saw himself as a singer–dancer who happened to do some comedy. My father, of course, very quickly came to see himself as a comic who happened to do some basic dancing and had some minor musical skills.

What struck me with Ernie, during our spasmodic times together over many decades, was that the style of crosstalk comedy he would be remembered for was not his natural preference. Being part of a double act was nothing more than myriad events conspiring to that out-come: what made it a wonderful outcome is that he was so good at it.

As a kid aspiring to be something in the entertainment world, the 'something' for Ernie had to be music based. And the comedy he loved was of the more physical type. He loved Chaplin, and as a child had a fair reputation for impersonating him. As he once told me, and many others both before and after, he liked harder comedy – the sort where a performer is on stage, and his partner strides on, slaps him on one cheek, and says, 'How dare you have the type of face I don't like!' Both he and his wife, Doreen, would become big fans of television's *Spitting Image* – political, edgy, satirical comedy, cleverly disguised as family entertainment.

Appearing for the first time together as fifteen-year-olds, Eric and Ernie were 'Bartholomew and Wise'. At this point, my father hadn't dropped Bartholomew for his soon-preferred stage name, Morecambe. But that moment was fast approaching.

FOUR

Let's take young Ernie Wise back to before Eric Morecambe, before Jack Hylton, before Arthur Askey.

It's odd to be writing anything about Ernie Wise from my office in central Leeds, a stone's throw from St James's Hospital. The site has gone through phenomenal changes since 1925, but it's undeniably the location where Ernie Wise was born.

Ernie lived his first days in Bramley, at 6 Atlanta Street, before moving swiftly on. Sadly, most of Ernie's childhood homes were in extremely poor areas, some even referenced as slums. Because his father was a railway signal light-man, they tended to shift to properties near a station, or at least the tracks. Next up was 35 Warder Street, destined to be demolished in the slum clearance of the mid-1960s, which was not restricted just to Leeds, but was a national undertaking. The nomadic Wisemans ended up staying at Warder Street for the surprisingly long period of five years. Their biggest move would take them to the village of Kinsley, a fair distance from where they'd been living, and south of Wakefield.

Not quite visible from my office window, but only a very short drive away, the Wiseman family would soon move to Station Terrace, East Ardsley, which is the town most associated with Ernie. It was the final move for him. The house stood on the embankment near to Ardsley station, so that his dad could, of course, work more easily. And it's also where his dad and Ernie would do the local pubs and clubs as *Carson and his Little Wonder!* That last family address is now part of the M62 motorway.

In terms of education, Ernie never much liked to talk about his schooling. He simply hated it, and always explained that it was because he'd had difficulty with words, especially learning them. This is the clearest sign, perhaps, of mild dyslexia.

Despite his struggles with education, Ernie – and my father, too – would have to continue studying while they were child performers. Whatever city they found themselves in, they had to join a school-room class. As my father commented in 1973, 'I was always just handed a book and put at the back of whatever the class was that I'd joined, just to keep me out the way!'

'Me too!' agreed Ernie. 'And at the end, you just handed the book back.'

'Yes. And it was the same book!' joked my father.

In 1938, Ernie also made an early stage appearance in nearby Morley, when he performed in, and won, a talent competition at the long-since-departed Pavilion Theatre.

SIDENOTE: I have huge reservations about the stone statue of Ernie that's in Morley. Why Morley and not East Ardsley, or central Leeds? The Morley link is a tenuous one. And why not carry on fundraising until there was enough money for a bronze statue, after a Lottery bid was turned down?

This isn't about the artist, very talented she is, no doubt, but the location and material used for this particularly subject matter seem inappropriate.

The statue isn't easily visible for a start, and there's hedging growing around it, giving the air that someone left it there by mistake. This is a dispirited statue trying to escape town as fast as possible, but it hasn't as yet worked out the quickest route. A stone statue caught in indecision!

Ernie deserved bronze, just as artist and sculptor Graham Ibbeson created for my father in his home town. It's a huge source of comfort that the Winter Gardens, Blackpool, erected a vast bronze work of the two of them together in 2016, another amazing creation by the hands of Ibbeson, who came into the Morecambe and Wise story after both comedians had left us.

Adelaide Louise Hall – an American-born but UK-based musician, singer actress and dancer – would have more than a fair bit to do with Eric and Ernie in the early years of their double act. Indeed, my father often referenced her as one of the few who proved to be a pivotal person in the creation of Morecambe and Wise – as significant as Jack Hylton, Winifred Atwell and later Stan Stennett (of whom more later) were. But mostly it was Adelaide Hall's husband, Bert Hicks, who gets the credit. It was Hicks who gave Eric Bartholomew his new name.

Adelaide Hall

It is usually reported that Adelaide Hall was born on 20 October 1901 in Brooklyn, New York. However, there are other reports that suggest she was born between 1895 and 1909. Hall's career got underway when she joined the chorus line of the hit Broadway musical *Shuffle Along* in 1921. She then went on to appear in revues including *Runnin' Wild* and the *Chocolate Kiddies*. She married Trinidad-born Bert Hicks, who became her business manager, in 1924.

The performer's first visit to England saw her appear at the London Palladium in 1931. In the same decade she also performed at the Cotton Club in New York. During the 1936 Olympics in Berlin, Adelaide sang jazz at the Rex Theatre. This was despite Hitler's ban on jazz music being played.

Hall and Hicks made London their home in 1938. In the same year, she appeared in the musical version of *The Sun Never Sets* at the Theatre Royal, Drury Lane.

The couple opened the Old Florida Club in Mayfair, which sadly became a victim of a landmine. However, refusing to be downhearted, Adelaide continued making recordings for Decca; performing on BBC radio, accompanied by the Joe Loss Orchestra; touring theatres; and entertaining the troops with ENSA (Entertainments National Service Association). Her husband, meanwhile, joined the Merchant Navy.

Hicks's death in 1963 was a personal and professional tragedy, but Hall picked herself up and continued to perform live, and to record.

The release of the 1985 film *The Cotton Club* saw renewed

interest in Adelaide due to her having appeared at the legendary Cotton Club back in the 1930s. Suddenly, she was heavily in demand for interviews and performances.

In 1991, her ninetieth birthday was marked with a star-studded show at London's Queen Elizabeth Hall. Adelaide died two years later on 7 November.

In an interview referring to that time, my father said: 'My mother was talking to Adelaide Hall and explaining to her how nobody liked the name Bartholomew and Wise. Adelaide's husband, Bert Hicks, overheard and said that he had a friend who called himself Rochester, because he came from Rochester in Minnesota.

'He asked my mother where she came from, and she said, "Morecambe," to which he replied, "That's a good name. Call him Morecambe."'

Without further ado, Bartholomew and Wise became Morecambe and Wise, though my father always liked to joke that his real name was Blackpool!

SIDENOTE: Television presenter, producer, actress and writer Yvette Fielding recently (2023) appeared in the scary black chair of *Celebrity Mastermind* answering questions on her chosen subject – Morecambe and Wise. She did rather well, though one question was: what stage name had Ernie Wise contemplated giving himself? The answer supplied was 'Leeds'.

The problem we have here is that it is based on a joke and not a fact, as seemingly assumed by those doing the programme's research. My father often joked that they considered calling themselves Morecambe and Leeds, but it sounded too much like a cheap-day return, so they didn't bother. And Ernie would nod his head in feigned agreement.

In reality, Ernie had always been happy with abbreviating Wiseman to Wise, which pre-dated any involvement with his would-be partner. There never was another name genuinely up for consideration. Yvette gave an incorrect answer to an incorrect question.

One of my favourite tongue-in-cheek lines written by my father on his early meetings with a young Ernie Wise always makes me laugh. 'I remember what I thought of him then. The only word for it was "strange". But now I know him so much better I've changed that. He's "very strange".'

My dad, like all of us close to him, knew that Ernie was invariably very easy-going, whereas he himself was somewhat lively, restless and full of nervous energy, all fundamental in making him the comedian we came to know and love. But Ernie, in his calmer approach to life, was such a good influence on him, and probably during these early years of their partnership played as much the role of big brother as anything else. Ernie certainly felt a great responsibility for him, particularly after my father's health suffered during the war years following the period he spent working down the mines at Accrington as a Bevin Boy. Ernie's sustained easy-going manner was the yin to his partner's yang. They possibly needed each other, and I would agree with Gail that Sadie was the only one – certainly the first one – to fully recognise that.

There were some forty thousand Bevin Boys in total as part of a programme orchestrated by politician Ernest Bevin. Some were chosen by lot, and others volunteered as an alternative to military conscription. It was described at the time as vital and dangerous civil conscription service in coalmines.

Though my father claimed never to have experienced it, many Bevin Boys were the target of abuse from the general public, who mistakenly believed them to be draft dodgers or cowards. They were often stopped and questioned by police as possible deserters. They were not awarded medals for their contribution to the war effort, and official recognition wasn't conferred until 1995, eleven years after my father had passed.

For my dad, the mines represented the moment that bad health would begin to plague him. I'm not for a minute suggesting that the mines killed him – I think sixty cigarettes a day and living on his nerves contributed quite definitely to that – but they surely set him back many years. It was a slow process returning to anything like the full health he had enjoyed prior to the war years.

GAIL: I tried on many occasions to get Dad to talk about his time as a Bevin Boy. He always pulled a face and changed the subject. I sensed it was a tough time – certainly not one he cared to conversationally revisit. I also *wonder if he felt vaguely guilty he wasn't being shot at! It's ironic that the actual miners themselves had been sent off to fight, leaving nobody behind to dig up the much-needed fuel.*

The names were taken from a hat every twenty months, and if the number drawn matched the last digit of a lad's service number, he was sent down the mines. So, it really was a complete lottery as to whether you went down the pits or didn't. Mum told me that the mine Dad was sent down was in pretty good condition. However, she thought it would be much nicer for Dad to visit one of his aunties regularly, who lived in Accrington. So he was transferred to the Accrington mine. Unfortunately, this mine had previously been condemned and closed prior to the war, reopening as part of the war effort. I think that just made the whole experience even harder.

My father said of that time: 'When the war was on, I went down the mines as a Bevin Boy. My height was no handicap, as I worked lying down! Happy days? Yes, the days were happy indeed – I was working nights!'

Fellow Bevin Boy Gordon Jay, who would form a double act with his brother Bunny, and who would find great success in countless panto seasons over the decades, told me my father would talk constantly about his parents, often wondering what they were doing at any given moment. These conversations usually took place back at their digs between shifts down the mine.

It's pretty clear, therefore, that when my father found himself back home in Morecambe recuperating after his experiences in Accrington, he was delighted to be pampered by Sadie. I don't know what his dad made of this sickly return home, because it was he who had encouraged his boy to take the job in the Accrington mines. George himself had briefly worked as a collier at Accrington at the end of the First World War, and I think it's fair to say he was made of sterner stuff than his son when it came to physical labour.

This period of Eric Bartholomew's life – he was sixteen years of age – has little info accompanying it. It isn't a period either Sadie or my father talked about in any detail, as Gail points out. My mother can shed no further light other than to emphasise how much he would have loved leaving the 'nightmare' of the mines for the comfort of home, and some 'mollycoddling'.

It's highly likely this was one of the periods when he went fishing with his dad on a frequent basis, which formed many of our conversations during my sister's and my own childhood. George made his own fish hooks. He and his son would regularly fish in the big basin of deep water next to the old bridge at Hest Bank, when my father was aged eight to twelve. I know the area well, as my dad would one day purchase his parents a house in Hest Bank, and we would often walk the riverbank as a family, getting bitten to death by midges. My grandparents and my father seemed oblivious to them. George, wonderfully daft old bugger that he could be, would swear he knew them individually and that he'd warned them off! My mother would wrap a silk scarf over her face, as she seemed a prime target, but the real secret, I've since discovered as a keen hiker, is to keep moving.

The house he bought his parents was a long way from

his first home in Morecambe. 'When I was eight months old,' he once wrote, 'we moved to Christie Avenue into a new council house with three bedrooms and an outside loo.' Certainly some way short of luxury.

Hest Bank is always a nostalgic return for me, just as it must have been for my father all those years later. It was near that Hest Bank bridge that as a kid Sadie had made him promise her that when he was rich and famous he would buy them a house there. He had nodded dumbly, saying, 'Yes, Mam!'

Around thirty years later, he paid up on his barely remembered promise!

Ernie's time separated from my father during the war years was mostly spent in the Merchant Navy working for the Gas, Light and Coke Company. Ernie admits himself that he saw little of the big, wide-open seas. Most journeys were spent around the estuaries shipping coal from Newcastle and South Shields to Battersea Power Station. Although the work was tough, he had plenty of time off. This he would spend either in Leeds visiting family or with Sadie in Morecambe. Presumably the two spent a fair bit of time together during my father's rehabilitation period. Ernie would show up with bacon or silverside he'd acquired from the ship's engineers – a useful perk of the job during a very tough time with rationing, although I can't quite picture Ernie as a 'Walker'-type character from *Dad's Army*.

Despite their brother-like friendship, it's interesting – perhaps understandable considering the upheaval and stress of the war years – that when the war was over for Ernie, and he was back on Civvy Street looking for work, he'd just about given up on the idea of them performing as a double act. It had '... somehow lost its appeal,' he said. 'I felt happier relying on my solo routine for my professional survival.'

SIDENOTE: While war stopped play for Morecambe and Wise, in August 1944 my father, much to my own personal envy, got into the Bedford Corn Exchange to see the great American band leader Glenn Miller performing with his orchestra. Said my father to me of that event, 'We all sat on hard benches jogging our knees up and down. I was only a teenager. One of the most memorable occasions of my life.' Four months later, and Miller would be missing, presumed dead when his plane disappeared in the fog over the English Channel.

In 1946, there came along one of those moments where fate intervenes, and you begin wondering if Eric and Ernie were destined to be a double act whatever anyone might have thought or wanted.

My father and Sadie were walking along Regent Street in London's West End. According to my father, they were somewhere near the huge Liberty store, as famous now as it was then, when quite literally they bumped into Ernie. Sadie quickly suggested to Ernie he share their digs in Chiswick, which were owned by a Mrs Duer.

'Since resisting one of Sadie's suggestions was like

fighting against fate,' recalled Ernie, 'I found myself once again bound up with the Bartholomew family.'

Fate is what it seemed to be – three different personalities that when combined appeared destined to make this doubtful double act work.

SIDENOTE: Almost opposite Liberty in Regent Street is where their third and final agent, and the man who helped turn them into a television institution, Billy Marsh, would be based. Regent Street would therefore become a familiar location for Eric and Ernie. One day, I found myself walking along it with them either side of me (and for a reason lost in the mists of time) – a very surreal, and not unpleasant, moment. People looked gobsmacked to see the nation's biggest act walking together on a London pavement! Somewhat different from their first meeting on the same street.

I spoke with Ernie about this post-war reunion on Regent Street, some years after my father had died. The interesting part to me is that Ernie said that if he'd just bumped into my father, he would have had a nice chat, a few laughs, then wished him well and moved on. But, 'Sadie was made of sterner stuff.' She clearly wasn't going to let either of them escape giving it a real go. Certainly not now she'd got her hands on Ernie Wise once more, and the compulsory separation brought about by the war was over.

It would take a long time before Ernie would think

they'd made the right decision, and his partner was surely having doubts of his own, too.

'Eric was very temperamental, which I call sheer bad temper,' Sadie said when recalling the early years of their partnership. 'When he and Ernie first started doing their double act, they often used to alter their gags. But if Ernie made a slip on the stage, Eric would go mad. "You're not a bit of good, Ernie. You're meant to have learned all this," he would say.

'One day I got furious with him. "Eric," I said, "don't you ever let me hear you speak to Ernie like that again. Go straight upstairs."

'When Eric had stomped up to his room, Ernie turned to me. "You shouldn't have interfered y'know," he said quietly.

'"But I was sticking up for you," I said.

'"Don't you see? Eric's only trying to make me the best feed in the business. And I'll tell you something else. He's going to be the best comic in the British Isles one day."

'Later, I told Eric what Ernie had said, and there was no more temperament from him again. Never another cross word, never any more argument . . .'

From my own experience I know that my father's respect for Ernie was immense, and what I like about that anecdote from Sadie is that Ernie became more than the best straight man in the country, which he said his partner was trying to make him. Back then, maybe Ernie even more than Sadie sensed that something rather massive was going to occur through his close friendship with my father. Perhaps Sadie wanted to believe it too, but Ernie really *did* believe it.

Eric and Ernie had seen other double acts fail through fallings-out, and they didn't want that to be their undoing. There was enough out there to battle against, so they had to remain a team fighting it out together. And they really did, which is both wonderful and remarkable. I know Ernie particularly recognised the benefits of having a partner, and therefore never being alone in the big wide world, an expression he came to use a lot.

Lord John Sanger's Variety and Circus Tour – a bizarre combination of the two genres – was the first real post-war work for Morecambe and Wise. Surprisingly, it was the one and only time that Eric and Ernie would switch roles: Eric became feed to Ernie. The show stuttered along, finally petering out in Nottingham in October 1947.

Although it was a somewhat unusual idea, my father never resented that period on the road. All part of the learning curve, as he saw it. Their life together at that time was well covered in *Eric and Ernie*, the 2011 TV biopic. You got a real sense of the lacklustre audiences, and the awkward combination of animals, mud and manure mixing with the naive shine of a variety show. 'Dinner jackets and wellington boots,' as my father once referred to it.

Ernie wrote of that time: 'Sanger's idea was a novel one. It was to combine two worlds of show business and take it to places where the occasional visit of the big top was the only form of entertainment. We had a tent that covered half an acre with a stage instead of a ring and seating for seven hundred.' He added, 'If the original idea was good, it was killed by the belief that country people were so starved of entertainment they would accept any rubbish.'

'One night,' wrote my father, 'we went through the entire performance for six kids who came in at half-price and were shown up to the cheapest seats at the back.'

SIDENOTE: It was on the Sanger tour that my father discovered the paper bag trick, which he made famous and which would become a staple of their 1970s touring show. A clown calling himself Speedy Yelding did the trick – the imaginary ball being caught in an empty bag and making a noise as it supposedly lands inside.

Lifted and logged for the future. Such was the accepted thievery in the entertainment world back then.

For Ernie, the tour would have huge significance on the rest of his life: it was on this tour he met his wife-to-be, Doreen Blythe.

It would be a few years before my mother came on to the scene. It's fair to say that Doreen and my mother, Joan, were very different people, who had nothing especially in common at all, but it was nonetheless disappointing that while I was working on this book, certain tabloids reported that the comedians' wives didn't get on. This stemmed from a comment made to author Louis Barfe by a veteran ventriloquist who had worked with Morecambe and Wise in theatre way back when.

My mother, still ticking on at ninety-six, was quick to

point out that they couldn't have remained a successful foursome had anyone 'hated each other'. 'We were two very different people thrust together by the partnership of our husbands,' she points out. 'But you don't hate someone because you are different, and who might have different interests and opinions.' Both she and Doreen knew that their role was to support their husbands, because in doing so they were supporting the double act. Right up to Doreen's death in 2018, these, by then, widows were sending each other birthday and Christmas cards, and appeared at countless events together that were related to their husbands' work.

GAIL: Sadie was such a good judge of character. She knew, and really understood, both her son and Ernie. I think her desire for Ernie to stick with Dad and work on the double act came from the fact that she knew Dad needed someone beside him. He was a team player. She often said he was lazy on his own. I don't think he was lazy, but he was a daydreamer, and actually not personally ambitious. Sadie also saw that Ernie was the right man for the job. He was personally ambitious, very organised, and very talented. And they made each other laugh. I think Sadie absolutely believed in and trusted Ernie, and felt that he could quickly take over her role.

Interestingly, Ernie told me as much himself following Dad's funeral. He said he had let Sadie down. 'What do you mean?' I asked him.

'I promised her I'd always look after him, but I didn't go to Tewkesbury with him [where Dad died], so it was my fault.'

It was quite a shock to me, because until that moment I could barely recall Ernie ever mentioning Sadie's name. It was very moving, and I did my best to reassure Ernie that it wouldn't have made any difference: by then Dad's heart was knackered.

When Eric and Ernie married Joan and Doreen respectively, the duo became a quartet, and it was imperative they all got along, however diverse their personalities.

Mum and Doreen had the most important thing in common – the drive to support M&W's success. They both put their husband's talent first. The obvious real difference was Ernie and Doreen's decision not to have children, compared to our parents having two of them, and later adopting a third. I've been asked if we went on holidays together. That would never have worked for many reasons, the two key ones being that the men worked together constantly, so needed a break apart, and that Ernie and Doreen could have grown-up holidays. Our family holidays were very much geared around us, the children, and only being able to do so during the school holidays.

FIVE

Ernie may have been the more responsible, grounded one of the pair, but he also possessed a wonderfully sharp and wicked sense of humour, and immense vibrancy and energy. Much of their success was born out of this shared energy, because if you are constantly around that energy but don't possess it yourself, you will ultimately become exhausted by it. To put it another way, when the two men were together it was inherent in them to switch to their 'A' game.

During the 1950s – their mid-twenties to thirties – they all but merged into one life force, bouncing lines and ideas off each other, and finishing the other's sentences without hesitancy. This never ceased throughout their lifetime together. It was a joy to behold, and privileged was I that I often did, mostly in the 1970s, usually when hanging around their dressing room at theatres and the TV studios. This was particularly the case when I started working for their agent's London-based company, London Management.

Eddie Braben reckoned their almost telepathic reading of each other meant the 'and' could have been cut to make it MorecambeWise.

As is often the case when one examines more closely

Eddie Braben's throwaway comments, he has hit the nail on the head. They were two opposing parts of one life force. They were brothers in all but blood. Former television host Sir Michael Parkinson described them as a joy to interview together, as both men knew when to let the other have their moment, and when to rein in or interrupt. He also said that their 1972 appearance on his show, *Parkinson*, was one of the wittiest he ever conducted. When I met up with him in 2022, we both talked so fondly of that particular appearance, and for me it was wonderful to hear Sir Michael, who sadly passed away in August 2023, recount the occasion with such heartfelt delight.

That show – and it's the one people fondly recall, when my father went into the whole spiel about his first heart attack, but completely filled with humour and borderline fantasy that Sadie would have been proud of – is a further example of where their relationship was at a specific time. 1972 was possibly the beginning of their absolute peak years, which arguably would last until 1979. Everything was coming up roses for them. Their health was good, their popularity immense, their shows arguably the best they would ever produce, their relationship beautifully engineered to work around the need for the private lives they chose, but with that unbreakable bond from youth that shone through whenever they were together. It always made my father scratch his head when people were curious to hear that they didn't meet up outside of work. 'We're almost always *at* work,' he said, 'and if we're not, then we meet up at functions. We all but live together!'

Meeting at such a young age, and forming a double act against the backdrop of a world war, must have been intensely unifying. One can only imagine how much they came to depend on each other.

As the Sanger show abruptly ended, Eric and Ernie, still in their very early twenties, found themselves back at Mrs Duer's in Chiswick, West London, with no prospect of work.

It was my father and grandmother who had found them digs with Mrs Duer at 13 Clifton Gardens, Chiswick. I believe a NatWest Bank now stands on that site. Ernie would have appreciated that!

My father recalled, 'The idea was I should break into variety, and she [Sadie] and Ernie shared the belief that I possessed some gifts as a comic. Also, I am sure, she had seen no hope at all for me at anything else. For her only child, it looked like variety or the dole.'

It would be the longest period they would be out of work in their lives. I think my father's lack of interest in holidays, or sustained breaks from work, can in part be attributed to this uninterrupted period of inactivity. Once they started on the treadmill of success, we'll see they barely took a break at all.

But back in Chiswick, at least there was always a show-biz vibe. 'Being near the Chiswick Empire,' reminisced Ernie, 'Mrs Duer accommodated a succession of variety acts, and whenever paying guests (by that I mean guests who paid) arrived, Eric and I would vacate the front room we normally occupied, and our "guest" chairs by the fire, and muck in with the family.'

Sadie had left them to fend for themselves, as husband

George was beginning to think he was a widower! 'Out-of-work acts would converge on an Express Dairy café that used to be near the Leicester Square tube station,' recalled my father. 'The place would be filled with pros sitting over cups of morning coffee, from about ten till four, all saying how well they were doing and how this agent or that had a marvellous job lined up for them. Everything seemed to depend on the agent, who must be wooed and placated, whereas to my way of thinking it should be the other way about.' He added further to his ambivalence over agents: 'I never carried a torch for agents. In our early days there were more than there are now, but none of them ever bothered to do anything for us until we managed to get a booking for ourselves and appeared on a stage . . .'

It is very true that my father – and Ernie, to a lesser degree – never enjoyed discussing the days of finding an agent, and it was always brushed over, in any article or discussion. In fact, both men retained an air of suspicion towards agents, other than their own. And when I say 'their own', I mean their final agent, Billy Marsh.

In their more prosperous years, both Eric and Ernie would acknowledge having a good relationship with each of their various agents.

'We were lucky with the three agents we had,' recalled Ernie back in the early 1970s. 'Gordon Norval, Frank Pope and Billy Marsh. But agents are largely a strange fact of life in a performer's career . . .'

I don't think Ernie ever truly understood the purpose of an agent. I mentioned to M&W agent Jan Kennedy that, in conversation with Ernie in the early 1990s, he suddenly had the notion he could be the agent for Morecambe and Wise all by himself. Jan and I shared a smile, and thankfully Ernie never mentioned it to me or anyone again, or possibly we wouldn't still be discussing this remarkable double act.

Mrs Duer had clearly taken pity on the pair of them, keeping costs low and treating them as almost family.

Apparently, in or around 1970, my father dropped in to see Mrs Duer after all the passing time. He said she was just the same as she'd been all those years before. Not particularly giving the impression of being surprised or impressed at what they had gone on to achieve, or even especially interested. 'She was still completely devoted to her now slightly expanded, much older family, and continuing to take in guests, though on a much-reduced level now.'

These early partnership years represented some of the best and worst times of my father's life. Best, because of the kindness of Mrs Duer and her family, and worst, because they had virtually no work and no money. One can see where Ernie's astuteness with money came from. It wasn't all just an act in their later TV shows, when my father continually ribbed Ernie about his meanness, and his general obsession with money. Having had a little bit of the stuff as a child star, to pretty much zero in their partnership – plus having been the breadwinner for the Wiseman family for much of the time building up to this lean period – must have created some distortion in his relationship with his finances.

Being in someone else's home – albeit most willingly – and knowing what my father was like in regards to privacy, he would have found these early years 'on the road' very tough. I'm sure being young and desperate took away any choice, but he would have settled into life under someone else's roof with a degree of both uncertainty and difficulty.

GAIL: In terms of privacy, he would not only announce when he was going to the bathroom, we were all therefore supposed to stay downstairs to leave him in peace!

'As young lads,' recalled Ernie, 'we did everything together – touring, chasing girls, going to the cinema and, of course, performing. When we got married, our private lives diverged, but so hectic was our working life that we saw a lot of each other in the course of any week. We were, I suppose, like brothers who rarely, if ever, quarrelled and could cope with what was an intense partnership without fear of its overheating.'

And once they were married, their own relationship matured. Ernie is alluding to the fact that from that time onwards they could never again 'hang out' with each other.

Looking from the outside in, one could suggest they – perhaps unconsciously – agreed early on to have mutual accountability, the bedrock for any partnership.

Their aim was to become a double act in the mould of, to begin with, Abbott and Costello. As their confidence grew over the years, their personas would fall much more in line with those of Laurel and Hardy. The edges of what both of them were supposed to be in their act started to blur. From the late 1950s there would be a slight, though possibly not rapid, shedding of the traditional variety-hall double act. My father would remain the classic clown – an idiot and a fool, almost in an abusive relationship with his tough-guy partner. Ernie, therefore, was the classic straight man – brash and confident, though not much brighter than his partner, but that never concerned the straight man, as the partner was so stupid as to beggar belief. That would all completely change when Eddie Braben arrived on the scene.

Double-act partnerships in the entertainment world have been with us for ever, and if not infinite in number, they are difficult to tally. Pairings, both fictional and real, have attracted our attention since entertainment first began as stage appearances, the written word, radio, cinema and then television. And they cover all genres. Holmes and Watson, Burke and Hare, Wilbur and Orville Wright, Bill Hewlett and Dave Packard, Simon and Garfunkel, Ben Cohen and Jerry Greenfield, Randall and Hopkirk, French and Saunders, Chas and Dave, Dolce and Gabbana, Romeo and Juliet, Martin and Lewis, Marks and Spencer, Antony and Cleopatra, Fey and Poehler, Starsky and Hutch, Thelma and Louise, and so on ... And that paltry, random list doesn't even scratch the surface. While reading it, you've probably trebled its size.

But it is already evident that the old axiom 'Two's company' is a truism. What I suppose I'm saying is that Eric and Ernie were not unique in getting together to entertain the public, but were fitting comfortably into an already popular format that continues to this day, and will do so into all our tomorrows.

'It's wrong to suggest their success depended entirely on them having been in variety,' said writer–comedian Ben Elton, back in the 1990s. 'Their success had nothing to do with variety. It was simply because they were the best double act in living memory and, in particular, a stunning live act.'

'[We were] two comic characters: the one with the glasses, and the other one with the short fat hairy legs,' said Ernie.

The hairy legs and the glasses might have been there now, but the journey had only just begun.

I began watching Eric and Ernie on stage from around 1964, when they were appearing in summer season at the Wellington Pier Pavilion, Great Yarmouth. At least that's my earliest recollection.

How I wish, though, I could have seem them in the 1940s and '50s – witnessed that embryonic period when all they had to offer was immense energy and self-belief, as they rolled through these early years seemingly just about able to keep the wolf from the door. And while they struggled and then made some headway, others tried and failed, and some did so well Eric and Ernie could only look up to them in wonder.

It would be in Billy Marsh's Regent Street offices where one day I would go to work in a vague and futile attempt to fill an impossible gap left by that young departing employee of Billy's, a certain Michael Grade.

SIDENOTE: Billy Marsh, while taking me out to lunch in Oxford Street, London circa 1978: 'Show business is a fantasy. The whole business is based on nothing true, just performers and made-up stories. It's all imaginary, but also fascinating, and creates work for many thousands of people. But none of it's real.'

Back at Mrs Duer's Chiswick accommodation, they didn't have an audience to play to, and certainly not some large theatre.

Recorded as their only genuine variety date, which they accomplished by approaching the bookers direct, was a week at the Walthamstow Palace. This was March 1948, and they were billed as Morecambe and Wisdom, because there was another 'Wise' on the bill.

They flopped badly and were quickly dropped. You have to hand it to them, they took the endless knocks remarkably well. It's back to what my father had always said about having to constantly prove they were good enough, clearly even to themselves.

The Windmill Theatre, Soho, notorious for its nudes – somewhat mild by today's standards, and probably a show you might now feel comfortable taking your kids to – was the next port of call for these young men who had just shed their teen years.

Though it had a reputation, it probably wasn't the right reputation for a budding double act of the 1940s.

Vivian Van Damm owned the theatre, and everything was overseen by him, including the hiring and firing of performers – including Eric and Ernie, in both those instances! Clearly the audiences there weren't at a show containing statuesque nudes to see a new double act attempting to emerge on the theatrical scene.

After this latest setback, they went about contacting every London agent out there. Just one agent – Gordon Norval – came along to see them perform on what was to be their last appearance at the Windmill. He liked them and was possibly the first person other than Sadie to recognise their talent.

'We called round at Gordon Norval's office at 18 Charing Cross Road, on the Monday,' recalled my father.

He offered them opening spots at the Grand, Clapham, for the following week.

The problem was material. Ernie assured Norval they could do the two spots he needed – twelve pounds each spot.

Outside his office, my father was somewhat jumpy. 'What have you done?' he asked Ernie, whom he always let handle the business side for the double act. As he said, 'The act has to have one bastard who can say no, and it might as well be him.'

'We'll have to work something out,' replied Ernie.

Ernie would always say it was the best thing that could have happened to them. Under pressure, they returned to Mrs Duer's and started writing.

What came out of it was something my father would often reference at home in the years to come. It was the 'Woody Woodpecker Song', which was doing the rounds at the time, and had a trill at the end of each phrase, which he adapted into a very comic sound of his own.

Possibly desperate to drag out the humour in it, Ernie suggested they put a little bit of patter around the song, in which he plays up to his partner's ego by suggesting it's the bigger part. In reality, of course, my father just gets the little trill at the end of each phrase.

As Ernie said, 'After some padding and fooling, we built it up into ten minutes, but we didn't take it seriously. Our real act, the hotchpotch we had stolen from all and sundry, was our big turn . . .

'We opened with our "real act", thinking it would give us a springboard for the other. We died and went off, followed by the "Clapham silence", which in variety at that time was the next thing to the death knell.'

To their utter shock, the second spot with the tweaked Woody Woodpecker number went down a storm.

Smartly, they switched the spots, so Woody Woodpecker got the audiences on their side straightaway, and their less original material was received more favourably on the back of it. Word got around very quickly in the industry in those days, and now other regular work and appearances – after a year of absolute struggle – started to come in.

SIX

Many years later, when they were stars, both men had a tendency to underplay the hardship of those bleaker times. They would often refer to it as just being the way things operated back then, and talk about how they used it to learn, and generally hone their act.

Mind you, back in 1948–49, as a new decade beckoned, getting regular work was a long way from a rise to the top of the tree. They were witnessing the death of variety, and it would almost take them with it.

After a week performing at the Kilburn Empire, they were back again to the Clapham Grand. A week after that, they were back at Kilburn, but now as top of the bill. Their money had increased, and Gordon Norval had become their agent. Ernie's girlfriend, Doreen, who was appearing in a touring show run by Reggie Dennis, then managed to get Dennis to take a look at Eric and Ernie. He saw them at the Grand and booked them, offering a year's continuous work. Working for Dennis marked the beginning of a successful period. As well as reasonable earnings, they were getting noticed, occasionally cropping up in the local press.

The Woody Woodpecker routine was still the glue keeping their act together. 'And by now, the publishers of the song had done us a special arrangement,' recalled my father. Their second spot was a more relaxed, standard crosstalk affair, constantly being tweaked to improve it.

It's not so surprising that their careers should have really launched on the back of a song. You only have to think of 'Bring Me Sunshine', and also both men's childhood musical upbringing, to appreciate the importance music would have in their comedic work – how they would for ever be inexorably linked with music.

SIDENOTE: At the height of their stardom, they released an album in 1971 called *Morecambe & Wise Sing Flanagan & Allen*. A comedy duo presenting an album of songs! It must be unusual, if not unique. My father always claimed he did it mostly for Sadie, what with her being such a big fan of Flanagan and Allen and their songs as, indeed, were Eric and Ernie themselves. But there is a joy to this collection – 'Underneath the Arches', 'Run Rabbit Run', 'Strollin'' and countless more – that makes you fully recognise where they came from, and who and what influenced them. Also, it demonstrates that the performers they became were slightly different from who they were when they began.

GAIL: *Sadie only ever sang to us at bedtime, and never included a nursery rhyme. Flanagan and Allen songs, or wartime marching favourites, like: 'It's a Long Way to*

Tipperary' and 'Pack Up Your Troubles' by Felix Powell. I assumed they were bedtime nursery rhymes!

Back in Chiswick, what they now worked on, and discovered made an enormous difference, was worrying less about the material and more about its delivery: little looks here and there, a slowing down of delivery followed by a sudden speeding up. 'It was all in a subtle change of emphasis or our facial expressions,' said Ernie of that time. And an increase in volume, something my father was keen on even in the later years, and at home he was never the quietest person in the room! If he and Sadie started exchanging lively conversation, you couldn't hear yourself think!

How interesting it started so far back in their careers, this way of performing that would be the defining method of their comedy for the rest of their working lives. Just think of André Previn's extraordinary appearance, or Glenda Jackson and the Cleopatra sketch. The material, if read off the page – and I've read it off the page many times – is nothing much more than vaguely entertaining. Get Eric and Ernie performing it, and it soars.

Glenda Jackson told the *Radio Times* in 2022, 'In all these years, the best advice I've been given by a director came from Eric. He just said, "Faster and louder!" And that was it: we did it faster and louder.'

My father always said to me that what they performed throughout their career was high-class rubbish. While I still think that to be a little dismissive, I can begin to understand what he meant: take something ordinary, and through extraordinary comedic skills transform it into something forever memorable.

The two Empires of Kilburn and Chiswick supplied courtesy of Gordon Norval had set them on their way. And now Reggie Dennis was giving them even more. It must have felt quite a family affair, Reggie Dennis doing a xylophone act, while his wife Sylvia sang along. And Eric and Ernie feeling quietly chuffed just to be in regular work.

Dennis's revue, called *Front Page Personalities*, was the opportunity M&W needed to learn their trade. As Ernie put it, 'We learned how to go on and do a few extra minutes off the top, the very thought of which had previously scared us rigid. We learned how to compere and introduce acts, to go out and get a laugh on just local gags and chat.'

They spent eleven months in Reggie Dennis's show, at last earning some regular money. Their act wasn't only sharpening all the time, it was building pace. When you think of the TV shows that would make them stars, that fast-pace crosstalk approach to their comedy never faltered; it was established in the act's infancy. As my father put it when recalling that tour with Reggie Dennis, 'We never waited for a reaction from the audience.'

That's such an important observation, as it became the method of how they would work from then onwards. It was the audience's job to keep up. My father told me that as far as he and Ernie were concerned, every show they did they were having a party and the audience could either join in or not.

73

Eric and Ernie modelled themselves on Sid and Max Harrison, billed as Syd and Max Harrison. Interestingly, they were the fathers of another double act to come along some years later: Hope and Keen.

'We owe a lot at this stage,' said Ernie, 'not only to Reggie Dennis, but to the Two Pirates [from panto], Jock Cochran and Reggie Mankin. When the show was coming to an end in the autumn of 1950, they mentioned us to an agent named Frank Pope who booked for two of the top variety circuits, Butterworth's and the Moss Empires.'

Frank Pope went to watch them in Grimsby, and agreed to take them on. He came to a satisfactory arrangement with Gordon Norval, and the next phase further up the ladder began for M&W.

They were now earning thirty-five pounds a week. That's slightly over one thousand two hundred pounds a week in 2022.

Eric and Ernie appeared at the Grand Opera House, York, on 12 March 1951, and this was when they visited the house of the father of the great film composer-to-be, John Barry.

SIDENOTE: Barry's dad – Jack Xavier Prendergast – owned several local cinemas in York during the 1950s. I never discovered from my father or Ernie quite what they were doing as fresh-faced young comedians paying him a call at his home. It's possible that he'd seen the show they were in, and maybe even liked them. But I do remember my father telling me that while they were there, Jack's son John, looking like the lanky schoolboy he still just about was, came bounding in. This was still some years from his composing 'Goldfinger', and many other great film scores, and collecting numerous awards to go with them.

Fast forward to the 1960s, and by a bizarre twist of fate, the two people who would become my parents-in-law in 2015, George and Pat Reed, purchased the property from Jack Prendergast.

Through this purchase, George was invited to one of the theatres owned by Prendergast, during which he announced to George and the audience gathered that at the interval, as a treat, they could watch the first ever performance of his son John and his group, the John Barry Seven. As a big fan of John Barry – as was my father – I consider that quite a historic moment.

As a further point of interest, George was one of the first story-line writers for *Coronation Street*.

Morecambe and Wise had come a long way, both creatively and financially, since Mrs Duer's. The 1950s began a new and partly fruitful decade, though they still hadn't become what you could call well-off performers. It would be many years, and comfortably into yet another decade, before they could claim to be that.

By 1952, Eric and Ernie, now in their mid-twenties,

were flitting around the country, constantly on trains and often bumping into their contemporaries at Crewe station, which was a big interchange for all points of the compass: Birmingham for the Hippodrome, the Empire at Dewsbury, the Shepherd's Bush Empire in London, the Empire Theatre in Edinburgh, the Empire in Glasgow and all points in-between. They also managed to get guest radio spots on *Workers' Playtime*, *Variety Fanfare* and *Variety Bandbox*. Lots of train travelling, but as my father would often tell me, it was where he got the chance to read and read and basically self-educate. As for the radio, it represented the beginning of their arriving in people's homes. As my father put it, 'People hearing us on the radio are rarely the same ones that would go to the theatre to see us. This meant we reached a whole new audience.'

It was in June 1952 that my mother, Joan, met my father. This was at the Empire in Edinburgh, now the Festival Theatre. 'Your father knew the moment he saw me that I was the girl he was going to marry. He told Ernie that. I thought he was very presumptuous. That made me keep him at arm's length at first. "What's going on here?" was what I asked myself.'

My mother wasn't exactly enamoured of my father on their first meeting, but he managed to get her to agree to at least go out for a coffee, and then the cinema, which is what happened a lot during those touring dates.

GAIL: I asked Dad once, 'What was it like when you first met Mum?' And without missing a beat, he said, 'It was Monday-morning band call, Gail, and this beautiful woman glided up to the piano. I thought, "I'm going to marry you!"'

Later that day, I asked Mum the same question. She raised her eyebrows and rolled her eyes, let out a big sigh, and said, 'Well, he was very funny.' I said, 'Yes, but what did you marry him for?' Again the eye-roll, and she replied, 'He was a difficult man to say "No" to.' Clearly very persistent. She told me he would pop up behind the counter in a shop when she'd go to the till, and say, 'You are going to marry me, you know!'

It took him six months to get his way!

My mother was filling in for another girl who was unwell and couldn't do the show. I have a personal reason therefore to be hugely grateful for her unfortunate health issue, though naturally I hope she made a full and speedy recovery!

My mother knew little about Morecambe and Wise as a double act. 'I guess I thought they were a couple of pianists, or something like that.' But once she saw them performing, she says without a moment's hesitation, she could see their talent would take them to the top. 'Your dad was a funny man, as we all now recognise, and Ernie was a brilliant complement to that.

'Ernie and I got on from the very beginning,' she reflects. 'We were two like minds coming together to watch over Eric. I think Ernie was pleased of the support. He'd probably found it quite hard work looking after his hugely talented and mercurial partner. But he was the right personality to deal with that.'

My father was no gambler, but my mother says that

back then he loved a flutter on the horses. 'He once put a bet on with a complete stranger in the pub. I remember being a bit shocked. And straight after he agreed how stupid it was to have done it. He didn't even have a number or an address for the man. He'd simply given him his own address. "You're right," Eric said. "It was really silly of me. Well, that's that." It was an accumulator bet, and it won thousands. The stranger duly contacted him and gave him his large winnings!

'Fortunately, he rarely had a bet after that. I think he recognised how lucky he'd been in several ways, and was somewhat overcome by the whole event.'

As a youngster, I well recall his playing card games with us for loose change. And if he could get away with it, he'd cheat! That was about as adventurous as it got.

GAIL: My memory of playing any game with Dad when we were children was that he'd rather cheat than lose! And he'd bet me on anything at any time. On one occasion, there was condensation running down a window. He pointed to two drops of slowly descending water and said, 'Pick one!' I did, and we watched as these two drops of water trickled slowly down the pane. Mine won, not that I or the drops knew it was a competition. Instantly, he said, 'Double or quits?' I had no idea what that meant, but it seemed we were competing again. I won again, so he said, 'Best of five!' I rolled my eyes and walked away victorious.

After Edinburgh, and into Christmas 1952, Eric and Ernie were appearing as Captain and Mate at the Sheffield Lyceum. By now my father had convinced my mother

78

that she loved him – it must have been the humour! As Sadie put it, 'It can't have been his good looks or money!'

They announced their engagement, and for Ernie and Doreen, who had been dating each other for some time by now, the news must have come as something of a shock. 'I think it left Ernie stunned,' my mother told me recently. 'It wasn't the most sensible thing to do, with hindsight, and to get married just before Christmas not the best timing, either. But we both felt it was a good opportunity, as work was fairly constant at this point so you weren't sure when the opportunity would next arise. I certainly would never have wanted to stand between the two of them, or cause any friction. Both Doreen and I were bonded to the double act as much as Eric and Ernie were.'

The knock-on effect was that Ernie and Doreen got married very soon after, in January 1953. Eric and Ernie, unsurprisingly, were each other's 'best men'.

'When we got married,' recalls my mother, 'you couldn't really buy anything. I managed to get some sort of outfit and feather hat, but that was about it. We were still on rationing from the war years.'

When I chatted to Gail about this time, and about Eric and Ernie in general, she concluded that the strongest marriage in that group of four was in fact Eric and Ernie to each other. It was the closest two people could be without the physical aspect. I was going to express some uncertainty on this observation, but genuinely found I couldn't. These two men really loved each other, and were so conscious of each other's thoughts and emotions in a way that possibly did go beyond what you could term a conventional marriage or friendship.

GAIL: I have thought about this quite a lot over time. I do wonder if their relationship is tricky to define, because it was born out of so many childhood experiences and some very tough times, not least living through a war. Then add Sadie to the mix, who always encouraged that bond, the 'you're in this together' attitude, and the idea that they must look out for each other always perhaps seems inevitable.

Mum did point out to me that Sadie really loved Ernie, he very quickly became a second son, and anything 'our Eric' had, Ernie had to have, too.

SEVEN

The 1950s was the decade that consigned Morecambe and Wise's past to the history books – and books like this. It was unofficially the start of a different game – not one of survival, but one of seeing how far they could take their act. And now comedian and singer, and later brunt of many a Morecambe and Wise gag, Des O'Connor – fresh from being a Butlin's Redcoat – would crop up in their lives on various variety bills.

> ERNIE: I've just finished a play about an old man in his eighties who had lost everything. He'd lost his voice, his dignity – all gone!
> ERIC: Great. But will Des do it?

The first time the three men met was at the Regal, Hull, in 1953. 'They were very good even then,' recalled Des in the 1990s. He went on to describe my father as a good faller. 'He did a fast and funny dance routine kicking his legs to one side while just keeping on going . . .

'Eric also had the ability to genuinely ad-lib witty repartee or responses. I don't think I've ever met that many who have this ability, and in my career I've met all the big names: Jack Benny, Phil Silvers, Groucho Marx. I think there were strong similarities in style between Groucho and Eric.'

In terms of the double act, Des said, 'Eric Morecambe was always there, solid as a rock. Ernie Wise, too; always there, and just as solid ... And Ernie didn't seem to mind – though privately perhaps he did – that Eric was getting seventy-five per cent of the limelight and ninety per cent of the laughs. You've go to give Ernie great credit for that. He would set Eric's lines up like a golf ball on a tee.'

It is an interesting point Des raised back then, and one I've often thought about myself – did Ernie Wise mind the dubious honour of being Eric Morecambe's straight man? Indeed, *was* he a straight man by the time they became national treasures? I don't think so on either point. Pursuing the idea they were more Laurel and Hardy later on than anything from the variety halls, you'd have to say there was no straight man or funny man in the accepted sense. They both, at times, played straight man and funny man, especially once Eddie Braben got his hands on them and gave them specific characters and characteristics. And Ernie was first to acknowledge that his partner was one of the funniest men ever to perform comedy. He told me that several times over the years.

Des O'Connor

Des O'Connor was born on 12 January 1932 in Stepney, London. Suffering from rickets as a boy did not stop him from playing football professionally for Northampton Town.

He was 'ordered into show business' and told to take part in a talent contest by his commanding officer, who caught him impersonating him, while he was doing National Service in the RAF.

Like many comedians, O'Connor had a baptism of fire by becoming a Redcoat entertainer. In his case, he worked at Butlin's holiday camp in Filey, North Yorkshire. But his first theatre performance was at the Palace Theatre in Newcastle.

Des O'Connor continued with live work throughout his career. He performed in variety shows, summer seasons, pantomimes and concerts. Particularly noteworthy were his runs at the London Palladium, where he appeared on more than one thousand occasions, and touring with Buddy Holly.

His prolific television shows included *The Des O'Connor Show*, *Des O'Connor Tonight*, *Take Your Pick*, *Today with Des and Mel* and *Countdown*. Des's appearances with Morecambe and Wise, meanwhile, included their Christmas specials in 1975 and 1979, not long after Eric had had heart surgery. Movingly, O'Connor paid tribute to Eric on Thames TV's *Bring Me Sunshine* on Christmas Day 1984.

The entertainer's achievements also included recording thirty-six albums. In 2001, he was presented with the Special Recognition Award at the National Television Awards for his contribution to television, and in 2008 was awarded the CBE.

Des died on 14 November 2020 in Buckinghamshire.

I vividly remember Des telling me that he, Eric and Ernie hit it off straightaway and became great friends. After a while his suspicions grew, as it became evident Eric and Ernie were making an extra special effort to be nice. It transpired they'd worked out that Des was the only one in their show they knew with a car.

The gag with Des, which started out as personal ribbing, grew so far beyond its origins that it made a much-loved appearance in a 1970s Morecambe and Wise Christmas show, with Des supposedly complaining about all the gags they did regarding his singing skills. And it reached the stage where, as Des told me, he began phoning in his own anti-Des gags.

Des was fine with the ribbing, even claiming, quite truthfully, that the more the boys ribbed him, the more record sales he achieved.

Years ago, while interviewing Des, he explained to me that it all began when he and my father were having a coffee together, and he told my father that he wanted to do less comedy and become a singer. My father famously replied, 'And I want to have an affair with Brigitte Bardot, but some things aren't possible!'

GAIL: Dad told me that in their early days, Des was a comic who would sing a song during his act, as was pretty much the norm back then. Dad and Ernie were drinking a coffee in a café at the end of the pier, when Des burst in and joined them at their table. 'I've made a decision, boys,' he told them. 'I'm going to give up the comedy and just be a singer.' Dad's immediate reply was, 'Well, that's the funniest thing you've ever said!' And so it continued for ever after.

I did say to Dad something about the whole country joining in the gag. He said that Des loved it, of course, and that they couldn't or wouldn't do it were he really a bad singer. Des had a great voice and a wonderful career. Let's not forget, he sold over sixteen million albums in his lifetime!

The downside for Des from this running gag was that others exploited it – other comedians as well as members of the general public. He must have begun having doubts of his own. The worst downside, however, and one my father went to his grave not knowing, was the continual bullying his daughters faced at school. As my mother put it to me on learning this: 'If Eric and Ernie had known about it back then, the whole thing would have immediately stopped. Never another comment or gag about Des would they have made.' One of his daughters was very generous in her attitude to this when, in a documentary a few years ago, she pointed out that it is rather better to be looked over than overlooked. But the fact remains that what once started as a gag between three friends came to negatively impact the upbringing of the family's next generation.

And Des himself didn't always find the gag quite as hilarious as he made out to the public. He took the mock criticism in good spirits for the most part, even by appearing on a *Morecambe & Wise Show* in a sketch that was designed to mock him (though in fact it was written in a way to mock Eric and Ernie). My father, Des once admitted, 'made out I was a terrible entertainer and I was really worried the jokes would do me damage and ruin my career. But I've kept selling records, kept selling out theatres and being on the television. I'm happy with the way it's kept going. The jokes did hurt, but only because we sometimes take ourselves too seriously. I've since laughed it off.'

Getting on the radio was a really big deal in the 1940s and '50s, as it would take the Queen's coronation in 1953 for television to really present any notable competition. Eric and Ernie had first appeared on radio in 1942, before moving on to *Workers' Playtime*, which gave them a much bigger listenership. From this they got an audition from a London producer for *Variety Bandbox*. This was a big breakthrough, and led to their own series, broadcast from Manchester, called *You're Only Young Once* – or *YOYO*, as inevitably it became known.

Listening to what survives today, I'm struck by just how good they already were. These were men in their twenties, and yet the energy and timing that would mark them out so clearly in later years was already evident. The material might have been somewhat thin, but I've always believed that Morecambe and Wise were never purely about material. The key to them was always their relationship and their timing. They had what Kenneth Branagh once described to me as sing-song voices that all the great comedians have. And it's true. As you listen you're pulled in and along by the quick rhythm of their style, and find yourself smiling and even laughing out loud – and this on old 78 rpm vinyl copies of work recorded over seventy years ago.

86

Radio and occasional variety spots were their staples during the 1950s, but the biggest push to their career at this time was meeting, and joining, the entertainer Stan Stennett.

I've gone on record for saying how fundamental Stan Stennett was to the success that would follow for Morecambe and Wise. I have no intention of changing that opinion. Stan is absolutely one of the key figures on their remarkable journey – as important even as Billy Marsh would be. While I genuinely feel Eric and Ernie would have been a big success anyway, I know Stan's involvement and supportive recognition of their burgeoning talent played a huge part, not only in speeding up the process in achieving that future success, but in giving them paid work and a profile during this era when they were really honing their skills. And with variety shows looking less likely to have a great future than a decade earlier, all work was desperately needed and appreciated.

Stan Stennett

Stan Stennett was born in Rhiwceiliog, near Heol-y-Cyw, Bridgend, Wales, on 30 July 1925. His mother, Doris, died when he was young, and Stan was thereafter brought up by his grandparents, Richard and Annie.

In a career lasting more than sixty years, Stennett could rightly claim to have worked in all aspects of show business. However, he was primarily known as a comedian, musician and actor. He shared the stage with names including Bob Hope, Danny Kaye, Johnny Ray, the Marx Brothers, Laurel and Hardy, Max Miller, Ronnie Corbett, Ken Dodd and Morecambe and Wise. Stan also ran venues in Tewkesbury, Hereford, Caerphilly and Porthcawl.

When not serving his country in the Army, Stennett's time in the Second World War saw him playing guitar as part of a jazz quintet. With a band called the Harmaniacs, radio bookings came along in the form of popular shows including *Workers' Playtime*. Eventually, he began to make a name for himself as a solo stand-up comedian and musician. He attracted positive attention performing on a radio variety show called *Welsh Rarebit*.

Among Stan's stage credits were more variety shows, summer seasons and more than fifty pantomime appearances. In the latter, he tended to play an amiable character called Billy, who was accompanied by a white, black and brown prop St Bernard dog called Bonzo.

As well as a time working on the television version of *The Black and White Minstrel Show*, Stennett gained exposure appearing in other programmes, including *The Good Old Days*, *The Golden Shot* and *Celebrity Squares*. Most famously, he played Sid Hooper, a likeable garage mechanic, in the soap opera *Crossroads*.

In May 1984, during his tenure of the Roses Theatre in Tewkesbury, Stan interviewed Eric Morecambe on stage. It had a fateful outcome.

Stennett continued performing into his eighties. He was a member of the Grand Order of Water Rats and a Fellow of the Royal Welsh College of Music and Drama. He was awarded an MBE in 1979, and died on 26 November 2013 in Cardiff.

My parents struck up a lifelong friendship with Stan. I've never been fully sure how pleased or not he was by M&W's burgeoning success. While hopefully pleased with his own part in their success story, it must have seemed strange that these two young comics he gave such a leg up to would go on to outshine every other entertainer on television.

In the 1950s, Stan was calling the shots with his summer seasons and pantos, and he, Eric and Ernie got on famously from the get-go. Liking them therefore as people as well as performers, he put them in both his summer seasons and his panto seasons. 1953 saw Morecambe and Wise in Stan Stennett's pantomime at the Lyceum, Sheffield, a big and very successful show, and one often referenced in the history of Morecambe and Wise.

I vividly recall my father saying to me, 'You have to have luck as well as talent,' and then his listing the key moments in his career. Obviously the first was meeting then teaming up with Ernie Wise through Jack Hylton. The second, getting an agent who believed them to be funny, and that was Gordon Norval. The third, getting radio appearances and expanding their audience. The fourth, meeting the woman he would marry, who would support him through thick and thin. The fifth was meeting up with, and being taken on by, Stan Stennett. The list would continue, but to the point we're at in their story, these were the five big moments.

> GAIL: I have often had it said to me, especially when doing talks on M&W, that my father was a comic genius. While I agree with that statement, I don't think you just wake up one morning a fully fledged genius. To my mind, I think the stars aligned and gave his genius potential the best opportunity to develop and thrive. I would point out that the stars aligning in Dad's life included five very important people: Sadie, George, Ernie, Mum and Michael Fountain [his chauffeur]. Dad's parents were particularly exceptional at a time in history that somehow you wouldn't have expected them to be, and proved integral to his life's path and ultimate successes. The rest came into his life at exactly the right moment they were required, and were the perfect mixture of personalities that enabled him to really be the Eric Morecambe we all came to know and love. If Ernie had wanted more of the limelight, or more say in the actual comedy they performed, that would've been difficult, and possibly doomed them to failure. If our mother had put pressure upon him to conform in some way to being a more standard husband and father – running the finances, and a useful handyman with a balanced work–life ethos – that, too, would have doomed their double act to failure. The timing of Mike

90

*Fountain entering Dad's life as his chauffeur was per-
fect, and Mike's own personality and temperament was
ideal. These people all made it possible for Dad to focus
on what he needed to do and be, surrounded by people
who fully understood what that took.*

The downside for Morecambe and Wise in the latter
part of the 1950s was the elephant in the room – television. Certainly, post Her Majesty the Queen's Coronation
of June 1953, the variety hall receipts began to dwindle
as television sales increased.

Britain's once-thriving variety hall industry was not
quite dead but it was showing signs of terminal illness.
It was not just the threat of television, but also cinema,
which had been ringing the changes since the talkies
became the norm in the 1930s. What made television
much more threatening was that you no longer had to
get dressed up and leave the comfort of your house to be
entertained.

That once-adored theatrical arena of packed, cheery
'houses', watching a stage filled by wonderful acrobats,
singers and comedians, was beginning to look old-
fashioned. And Eric and Ernie – and possibly very few
others at this time – recognised that they had to change
or be left by the wayside.

But amid all of this brewing turmoil, they were getting
regular work, and the key to anyone's success in show
business in the UK during the early fifties was appearing
in Blackpool.

*

Morecambe and Wise had first experienced Blackpool in 1940, as teenagers appearing at the long gone Palace Theatre on the seafront for Jack Hylton. The Palace was a beautiful theatre both externally and internally. It was a 1904 redesign of Wylson and Long's theatre on the same site, which had opened in 1899. The renowned theatre architect Frank Matcham was charged with bringing it in to twentieth century glory, which he certainly achieved.

Eric and Ernie were again in Blackpool in April 1949, but it was in 1953 they got their big spot, billed third to American singer Allan Jones and Lancashire comedian Ken Platt. It was also during this run that Gail was born.

GAIL: Mum told me that Dad hung on around the house for as long as possible for my delivery. I was born at our grandparents' home [Sadie and George]. But in the end, I didn't arrive when expected, and Dad had a show to do. At some point during this show, Allan Jones came on to the stage and completely confused the audience by announcing that Eric Morecambe's wife had just given birth to a six-month-old baby girl!

I am amazed at the foresight of a piece written at this time by a reviewer called Bill Burgess, for the *Gazette*. He wrote: 'Particular mention must be made of Morecambe and Wise. How do we define their act? It is an adroit blend of wry humour and the unexpected comeback, launched on immaculate timing and likeable personalities.'

Little did Bill Burgess realise just how perfectly he had described what, in my humble opinion, has been the key to Morecambe and Wise's eventual iconic status – that being their timing, and 'likeable personalities'. That likeability would develop into a shared love between them and their audience that would transcend their comedy. My father often commented on the fact that much of his fan mail – which was prolific – focused on his health and not his comedy. It was as if people came to care more about the man than the performer. That has to be unique, I imagine. People would write in to say how much they enjoyed one of their comedy dance routines, but please don't do too much of the dancing, it might be a strain on your heart.

Blackpool was referenced by both Eric and Ernie as the foundation stone of their success. Their repeated successful appearances in the town propelled their careers forward like nothing before. It's no coincidence that the giant bronze statue of Morecambe and Wise by Graham Ibbeson is located in the foyer of the Winter Gardens, Blackpool.

Morecambe and Wise always went down a storm in Blackpool, but the most successful double act to appear there was Cannon and Ball.

It should never be forgotten just how huge Cannon and Ball became in the 1980s. As Tommy Cannon recently told me, 'The biggest thrill Bobby and I had was when your dad said he considered us their competition.'

Cannon and Ball own the record for business at the North Pier, Blackpool. Nearly four months of selling out twice nightly. That is an utterly mindboggling achievement. It will never be equalled, particularly when one considers how seaside entertainment has altered over the years.

Tom and his wife Hazel have become personal friends in recent years, and live fairly near to me and my wife. I so enjoy catching up with him and chatting about those glory days of Blackpool, and the successful TV series that would follow for both them and M&W. It's so good to see a growing interest and recognition in their work, and their incredible achievement as a double act. As Tom is always quick to say, 'I still haven't worked out how I got from being a welder in Oldham to a television star! I really wasn't interested, despite Bob's determination. He always made directly for me on any working site. It was almost as if he knew something – knew that we had to be working in the entertainment industry together.'

SIDENOTE: Tom told me of the time they were working Caesar's Palace, Luton, and a call came in from my father telling them to come to the Luton football match the following day as his guests.

'Bobby literally had to run to the toilet, he was so bowled over,' says Tommy. 'We just couldn't believe it. Morecambe and Wise were our heroes. Then to be told by your father how good he thought we were, and that we were the ones to watch out for, was beyond everything.'

Bobby Ball tragically died in hospital in October 2020 after contracting Covid-19. In its obituary, the *Guardian* made the following comment: '[Cannon and Ball] fulfilled the prophecy made by Eric Morecambe just before his death that [they] would inherit Morecambe and Wise's crown by becoming television's most popular double act of the 1980s . . .'

I told Tom how I once ribbed my father after watching one of Cannon and Ball's television shows with him. 'You've got serious competition now,' I said with a wink, and he replied, 'Good! It's what we need.' And he genuinely came to admire them as a double act. Not at first, it's true to say. At first he was a little wary and unflattering. To say he was suspicious of them may be a better way to word it. But slowly he came to see what they were about, and liked the way they worked.

Tommy Cannon says, 'When we went to the Luton game on the Saturday that he'd invited us to, we were so nervous. I'd never seen Bob like it. But your dad was wonderful. One of the first things he did was roll up his trouser leg and show us the scars, which were there from his heart by-pass surgery he'd recently undergone. He pointed at those scars and said, "Whatever you do, don't let them do this to you." I wasn't sure what he meant, and then on the way home it suddenly struck me. He wanted us to be successful but without killing ourselves in the process. Your dad gave so much of himself to his audience, there was nothing really left for him to give.'

Back in the 1950s, long before my father was causing other comedians to have bowel movement issues, working life was more about getting an audience to watch them. With Stan Stennett, that was now being achieved.

Ernie struck me as enjoying the summer and panto

seasons marginally more than his partner. Mostly this was because he and Doreen made a conscious decision not to have kids, whereas my father understandably was separated from us for long periods, and also from his wife as she was looking after us back at the family home. We would visit for long periods during the school holidays, but we certainly weren't there for the whole season.

I have fond memories of those years, whether Torquay, Blackpool, Bournemouth or Great Yarmouth; they all hold memories of those summer seasons. I'm sure the endless sunny days are no more than a figment of my imagination, as I recall my father being thrilled when it rained. 'Ticket sales always go up when it rains,' he would say gleefully. 'Gets them off the beach looking for something to do.'

SIDENOTE: One other memory of pantos and summer seasons jumps out at me – singer Matt Monro bringing to my father's dressing room a recording of a demo he'd laid down for 'some film or other'. He wasn't sure it was any good. He played it to my father who loved it. 'You've got to do it,' he advised him.

'You think it's good enough?'

'It's wonderful.'

The song was 'From Russia with Love', by that composer again – John Barry. It was the title track for the second James Bond film.

I remember asking my father – possibly during Morecambe and Wise's summer season in Yarmouth,

96

1967 – if I could watch them perform from the side of the stage. He was rather chuffed by that. What it was I'd intended to do all along was endlessly watch the amazing guitarist Bert Weedon from the wings of the theatre. I'd stick around for a few minutes of M&W, before sneaking off. Ernie thought I was either mad or very bored, and with a laugh would say as much. My father would tease me that he was going to drag me on to the stage with him one day!

This routine rolled along for some while. My father would cheerily say to me, 'You were watching the show again from the wings yesterday. That's good.' Then with this continuing to occur with suspicious frequency, he got talking to Bert and discovered the truth. He fell about laughing, and so did Ernie, who had already sussed there had to be a reason behind this ritual. As the older man I now find myself to be, I would of course give anything to be back there watching the whole of the show with every single performer in it, every night.

GAIL: *The panto and summer seasons were very long in those days. Really, if you had a panto and summer season lined up, you basically had a year's work.*

I have the best memories of our childhood when Eric and Ernie were doing summer season. What a perfect life for us, the children. Mind you, exhausting for the grown-ups. I think Dad found the repetition of the shows tough. I also tend to forget that once we were school age, we joined Dad for the school summer holidays, and he had already been doing the shows and living by himself till we all arrived. Therefore, I think it must have been rather lonely

97

*for him without any of his family around, and especially
without his wife. Yet on a personal level, when I think of
those times, the memories are in glorious Technicolor.
They were honestly the best of times.*

Ernie told me he especially enjoyed the camaraderie
over the Christmas season. They all would have a day off
on Christmas Day, and that was pretty much it. On occasion they'd share a makeshift Christmas dinner together,
all the artistes piling in like one happy family. For Ernie,
it must in a sense have represented the happy family he'd
been denied in his childhood. By his own admission, life
at home was something to be avoided: lots of arguments
and tension. He certainly grew up with an 'anything-for-
a-peaceful-life' attitude in his personality. 'Ernie wanted
everyone to be happy around him,' my mother tells me.
'He couldn't cope with any upheaval of any kind. He'd
experienced too much of it. Too much constant arguing
between his parents. It was too painful for him.'

Ernie is perceived as having a lack of involvement with
the scripts of Morecambe and Wise, always demurring
to the writers and his partner. I never sensed that was
about a lack of creativity – Ernie, after all, came up with
the breakfast stripper routine – but because sharing ideas
can be confrontational. Ernie, as my mother points out,
wanted to avoid upheaval. He wouldn't have wanted to
argue any creative point. I had witnessed him first hand
in casual conversation with my father, producer John
Ammonds and writer Eddie Braben, when his point
about something in the script would be over-ridden
before he'd even finished delivering it His reaction was

just to nod his head and go along with what the more vociferous colleagues around him decided upon. It might be reasonable to suggest that Ernie was somewhat put-upon by his partner and work associates, but if he was then he still became a wealthy television star, and I think he rather appreciated that as being fair compensation.

Away from Blackpool, though directly because of it, in 1954 along came what was supposed to be their big TV break.

EIGHT

A lot has been said about *Running Wild*. Suffice it to say it wasn't very good, and wasn't well received. It would be their first television series for the BBC. As my mother points out, though, 'They themselves never actually saw it as their big break – their big chance. While they were understandably excited about doing it, it was never going to mean everything to them. They already had a very successful career on the stage and radio – this was just something new to try – perhaps the icing on the cake.'

That it damaged their careers, or at least set them back, is a myth – indeed, in those early days of television it was becoming clear that there's no such thing as bad publicity. Hence on making a return to their more familiar work in the variety theatres following their 'disastrous' television debut series, they would now get billed as 'those stars of television'. But it possibly hadn't felt that way at the time. At least not to my father and Ernie. Or at least not to my father, if we're going to be honest about it.

'The series was corny, old-fashioned,' recalls my mother. 'But it was still mostly funny. I think the press were just looking to jump on something as the only other big TV star was Bob Monkhouse. Bob was the blue-eyed boy at that time, so perhaps in desperation they turned their attention to Eric and Ernie, being newer on the scene. But they would learn from all this. One thing they learned when returning to television is how *not* to do it.'

In a nutshell, a BBC producer called Ronnie Waldman, who had seen Eric and Ernie in Blackpool and loved them, felt the North–South divide in comedy could be bridged with their brand of humour.

Sadly, Eric and Ernie themselves would not have any creative control over the proposed project, and were told what to do, where to stand and what to say. Waldman was also experiencing undue pressure from above, being advised that a national audience wouldn't take kindly to two northern comedians. What in fact the audiences didn't take kindly to was the paucity of decent material the double act was given to deliver. I don't think my grandmother Sadie quite saw it that way to start with. 'What the devil are you two playing at?' she said. 'I daren't show my face outside the house.' But Sadie was always negative and positive in equal measures, and could be marginally over-the-top in both directions.

A reviewer, Eric Littler, who was working for the same *Lancashire Gazette* as the earlier reviewer Bill Burgess, and who had had to stop watching *Running Wild* on TV as he didn't like what he was seeing, wrote a piece that pretty much nailed the whole problem with the show.

Referencing their appearance at the Palace Theatre, Manchester, following the TV series, he wrote: 'I am left wondering if they can possibly be the same two artists who were in that television studio. They are, of course, but whatever the BBC did to them they have left it behind, and instead we have two performers whose slick humour had last night's first house audience rocking in their seats.'

This BBC commission could have been damaging to them, but considering the good the BBC was to do them some years later, no one can complain – it was part of the learning curve and the wonderful story of Morecambe and Wise. They certainly never intended to work in TV again if all they could perform was other people's words with no input of their own.

My father carried the negative *Running Wild* reviews in his wallet to his dying day. 'A reminder of where we came from,' he would say. He would also say that 'you're never as good or bad as they say you are'. And, as mentioned earlier, 'You never have as much time as you think.' Both these mantras have had occasion to come to mind over the years, and the latter can be directly applied to us all.

Ernie pointed out on numerous occasions that no one really noticed the reviews other than agents and bookers. All the public now knew were that these two young comics they could see in theatres had also been seen in their sitting-rooms on the television. And Ernie shrugged off the TV failure with his usual cheery ease.

GAIL: I remember Mum saying that only the critics hated it. There are loads of examples of that happening to this day. Mum believes that the viewers rather enjoyed it. Mind

102

you, not too many viewers, as hardly anyone owned a TV back then.

SIDENOTE: My father was enamoured of the television set from the mid-fifties onwards. Interestingly, he would at first watch anything and everything. What became apparent quite quickly to him, and lasted throughout his life, was his inability to watch any scene that involved people eating food! It made him feel sick, as did any medical programmes if they happened to be screened while he was having a TV meal.

I enjoyed the rare times I'd sit down and watch a film with my father, usually with the feeling that for him even this was an extension of his working life.

On one occasion we were watching some corny comedy-drama from the 1950s, and after a scene that was supposed to be funny, he suddenly stood up and said, 'Well, that's it. They've lost me now. I can no longer believe in it.'

'Why?' I queried, genuinely perplexed.

'It's forced humour,' he explained. 'It's telling you it's funny without actually being funny. Good comedy doesn't work like that.'

While my father claimed they would be fine so long as they steered well clear of television from now on – oh, the irony! – they still had guest spots on others' shows, not least that of their friend and erstwhile supporter, and if not mentor then saviour, the successful pianist Winifred Atwell. Both Eric and Ernie talked very fondly of Atwell whenever her name came up in conversation. And it often did when they found themselves in the company of others who had graduated from the Variety-hall era M&W had travelled.

Winifred Atwell

Winifred Atwell's birth date cannot be confirmed. It's claimed she was either born on 27 February or on 27 April 1910 or 1914 in Tunapuna, Trinidad and Tobago.

Early piano lessons were courtesy of Winfred's mother, who owned a pharmacy with Atwell's father. By the age of just five, she was already proficient enough to play the works of Chopin. Three years later, she began playing the organ at St Charles's Church in Tunapuna.

She played for American servicemen at the Air Force base before deciding to move to America to study the piano with Alexander Borovsky, a Russian-American pianist, in the early 1940s. Further study came Atwell's way when she moved to London in 1945. There she attended the Royal Academy of Music. She also began playing ragtime in clubs in the capital. But it was while performing at the Casino Theatre (now the Prince Edward Theatre) that producer Bernard Delfont spotted her.

Like Adelaide Hall before her, Winifred was signed by Decca Records, and her successful recording career of boogie-woogie and ragtime hits, in which she reportedly sold over twenty million records, began. She was the first Black person to have a number 1 hit in the UK Singles Chart. At the time of publication, she remains the only female instrumentalist to do so. Her numbers included 'Black and White Rag', 'Let's Have Another Party' and 'The Poor People of Paris'.

Winifred enjoyed her biggest success in England and Australia, the latter being where she eventually moved to with her husband, the one-time comedian Lew Levisohn, who died in December 1977.

Morecambe and Wise appeared on Winifred Atwell's shows in the spring of 1956 alongside acts such as Teddy Johnson and Pearl

Carr (close friends of Ernie and Doreen Wise), The George Carden Dancers and Jennifer Jayne.

Atwell continued to perform until she was forced to retire following a stroke in the early 1980s. Following a fire at her home, she had a heart attack while staying with friends. Winifred died on 28 February 1983 in Sydney, Australia. Despite the uncertainly of when she was born, her gravestone states that she died at the age of seventy-three.

In 1956, Dicky Leeman, on behalf of ATV, invited Morecambe and Wise to perform a regular spot on *The Winifred Atwell Show*. Their material was to be penned by Johnny Speight, best known for creating the character of Alf Garnett and writing his various vehicles, such as *Till Death Us Do Part*.

Their first appearance on the show was to be on 21 April 1956. My father had just enough time to see me after I'd been born around 3 p.m. that day, before going to the Wood Green Empire for the broadcast at 8.15 p.m.

My arrival must have been a further strain on my father! The biggest strains, however, were the ever-decreasing variety audiences and the slow but sure closure of some of the venues.

I know from conversations with him, and more recent ones with my mother, that the act was literally saved from splitting up by the dramatic arrival of a telegram to their dressing room in 1957, offering them six months' work in Australia during 1958 – their time to be evenly split between Melbourne and Sydney

A bit like the arrival in the lives of Morecambe and Wise of Jack Hylton, Adelaide Hall, Winifred Atwell and Stan Stennett, this invite to Oz was right on cue. I wouldn't say Eric and Ernie had started arguing – they had always agreed they would never stoop to that. Instead, to Ernie's concern as much as anyone's, my father said they should break up the partnership. He was fed up with the struggle. Like Ernie in the earliest years, he was beginning to feel he could go solo.

It was that plain and simple, and apparently was voiced about ten minutes before the career-saving telegram arrived in their dressing room.

My mother and Doreen were there when it happened, and in a second they went from tears of despair to tears of joy. But there was still a lot that needed sorting to make it happen.

The six months' work in Australia was for none other than their saviour, Winifred Atwell. 'Whether Winifred had sought out your father and Ernie for this work, I'm not sure,' says my mother. 'But if her people had said that they were thinking of putting Morecambe and Wise on the bill, she'd have been supportive and very pleased. She really liked the boys, as they did her.'

'But there were no real winners in accepting the Australia trip,' recalls my mother nearly sixty-five years later. 'You were much younger than Gail, and I knew therefore you'd be less resilient. This wasn't the era of big jets getting there in a matter of hours. This essentially was a slow trip around the world. To leave my two kids for six months was very difficult. But Eric said he wouldn't go without me, and the work was extremely important to them at this time. We had a few tricky days between us when we were tetchy with each other.'

And so it was that our grandparents, Sadie and George, came to the rescue. 'From the beginning they'd both doted on you,' says my mother. 'Also, you were both very used to being there. The visits, and the summer seasons in nearby Blackpool, and so on. You became their children. They literally grew to see you as theirs, which is understandable after such a period of time. And while Gail was fine and completely understood the situation, you were more suspicious, as we had become strangers compared to George and Sadie by the time we returned.'

I have little memory of that period, though my sister will have plenty, being a couple of years older than me, and even spending two months at the same local school our father had attended – Lancaster Road Junior School.

GAIL: Apparently Sadie told Mum, 'You can't possibly have your husband the other side of the world for six months – George and I can have the children.' To me, this is Sadie again being amazing. She knew they needed the work, and Ernie and Doreen were definitely keen to go. And she knew that Dad wouldn't really cope without Mum there. She knew that having you and me was the only sensible option. As a grandmother myself, I now realise what an incredible offer that was to make. As much as you love your grandchildren, the perk is you hand them back! But six months? A long time. And during that half year, I would start at 'big' school, and would require more than just being looked after at Sadie and George's house.

I think my experience was very different to yours, Gary.

This is mainly because you were so young, and as you say yourself, the more shy and introverted of the two of us. All I can say is that I loved it. I understood what was happening, and looking back I was well prepared by the grown-ups to take it all on.

I had many friends of the same age living nearby, and so much freedom. I absolutely adored both my grandparents, and feel very grateful to have had those childhood experiences. I honestly feel that the time living in Morecambe, living a very normal northern way of life, became an integral part of my personality. I often joke that you and Mum are the southerners, and Dad and I are the northerners of the family.

It's perhaps a sad thing to say, but I'm not sure Mum ever fully got over leaving us behind for so long. Some pain can run very deep. Being so young, there are a lot of changes in a child in half a year. It must have been very hard for her to miss that period of our growth.

I love that my first school, aged five, is where Dad also started school. I'm guessing I was only there for the one term. I recall my first day vividly. I remember early that first morning, Poppa was going to take me on the bus. He usually cycled to work. Nan plonked a hat on my head and said, 'Don't lose it!' Naturally, I left it on the bus, but found it still there the next day. Poppa and I then walked up the road, and as we rounded the corner, there was a huge bright red double-decker bus, packed with men like Poppa going to work. There was nowhere to sit, so he grabbed the dangling handle with one hand, and wedged my head between his knees. As we approached our destination, he said in his strong Lancs accent, 'Gail – look out winda. See them kiddies? Follow them! And when you come out after, get someone to see you over t'road. You want the number thirty-two bus.' I don't actually remember the number of the bus, but you get the gist. So, I jumped off the bus and followed all the other children. Once at the entrance, a teacher greeted me and took my hand, and we walked along what seemed a big corridor. And to me, she was at least twelve feet, eight inches tall!

She then bent down and whispered in my ear, 'Your daddy came to this school.' If I'd been a little older, I might have thought that to be a tough act to follow. But knowing his school reports, that never was going to be the case! The best line in one of his reports: 'Handwriting . . . Would comment if I'd seen any' . . .

Just after we must have waved Mum and Dad off for Australia (I actually don't remember that moment), I was halfway up the stairs and facing the front door when Nan, who had a new dress for me in her hand, which Mum had probably given her, said that we were going to keep that dress for the day that 'Mummy and Daddy come home'. I thought no more about it. Then, one day, she said she thought I should try it on and see if it still fits. I put the dress on and within a few minutes Mum and Dad arrived home. Brilliant – no over-excited children anticipating the return of their parents and no time to make the new dress dirty before their arrival!

My mother's quick to point out that we didn't have the communication back then that we have today. No Zoom and video calls – barely a telephone connection. 'So when we got back,' she says, 'you didn't particularly want to know us. Even when we were away in Australia, sure I enjoyed it all, and the boys were hugely successful over there, but I never quite came to terms with it. I was always homesick, or homesick for my young family. And each day you had to tell yourself you had to accept it, and that it would come to an end. Equally, it's hard to look back and say that we did the wrong thing. I don't think we did. We did a tough and painful thing, which is very different. The strangest thing was discovering how many people from Morecambe had settled in Australia. We joined a Morecambe set!

'But it was a great experience, and it was a fundamental move in keeping Eric and Ernie working as a successful double act.'

Eric and Ernie's then agent, Frank Pope, had them booked at the ABC Theatre back in Blackpool for the summer season of 1959, so a late 1958 trip to Australia slotted in perfectly.

In 2003 I made a visit to Australia, and I was staggered that so many Australians remembered Morecambe and Wise. It wasn't just from stories handed down from their parents and grandparents, though there was that, too. But the BBC TV shows went down very well in Australia. Morecambe and Wise and *The Two Ronnies* series were still relevant on the other side of the world. In one store there were Morecambe and Wise DVDs in the window!

Eric and Ernie returned from Australia to discover that during their successful six-month tour for Winifred Atwell, the variety theatre scene at home had faded away at shocking speed. Furthermore, six months was a long time to be out of the public eye. They had the summer season of 1959 at the ABC Blackpool, booked through Frank Pope, but after that there was nothing. 'It was worse for us,' remembered Ernie, 'because the Butterworth circuit of theatres – for which our agent Frank Pope had the sole booking – had closed down. This left him with virtually nothing to offer us.' And this made the competition stiffer as the many variety acts out there vied for the same gigs. Morecambe and Wise found themselves offered second- and even third-grade dates to which they were now unaccustomed. Television was going to be their only route for survival.

By 1960, the variety halls that had flourished in the nineteenth century and the first half of the twentieth were essentially gone. It would be pop stars and actors from TV that would give the remaining halls any lifeline at all.

Pantomime and summer season continued successfully, but not quite in the traditional sense of years before. Again, it was the new names from radio, pop and television headlining these two distinct calendar seasons, rather than the old pros who had successfully trod the boards unchallenged through winter and summer.

It had been early entrepreneurs who had tapped into the commercial potential of variety entertainment, and who had created status-symbol theatres to provide a 'home' for acts and punters alike. Venues with names like Apollo, Empire, Palace, Regal and Grand all gave gravitas to what they were selling the consumer. This was part of the project for these entrepreneurs of their day: creating great wealth out of the recent empire-building era, with all the perceived glories that accompanied it. There was no subtlety in these grandiose theatrical constructions, magnificent though many were.

The music hall became the mass populist form of entertainment: indeed, there was no other mass entertainment at its outset. And every town had its own venue. These enabled artists and audiences to share a symbiotic relationship, and it was the beginning of creating star names − artists separated from the general populous by the stage upon which they performed.

Now, with competition increasing, these decaying theatres were on their knees, and Eric and Ernie, in their mid-thirties, realised very quickly they had to find a new agent − one who could get them the one thing my father had been so wary of since *Running Wild*: regular television work.

The decision was the right one. Executing it was the painful part. They had enjoyed a great relationship with Frank Pope − he was my godfather − and didn't in any way want to end that personal connection, but they were equally determined to further their careers. As my mother puts it: 'This was make-or-break time in their careers and there could be no room for sentiment. It was very hard, because we had even been abroad on holiday with Frank and Marjorie Pope. Now the boys had to explain to Frank just why they needed to go their separate ways.'

113

SIDENOTE: While Frank Pope was my godfather, both Ernie and Doreen Wise were Gail's godparents.

Founded in 1880 by Charles Carson, *The Stage (and Television Today)* was, and possibly still is, the main trade paper for all that is UK show business. Eric and Ernie put an advert in announcing the termination of their association with Frank Pope by mutual agreement and that they were looking for representation.

This got a very good response from many major agents, but the one they chose to join, and who would transform everything, was of course the legendary Billy Marsh.

The fact I used to work for Billy Marsh, and that he would remain a personal friend till his passing in December 1995, always makes me feel on comfortable ground when talking about him. Within the business, he is indeed a legend.

Billy Marsh

Billy Marsh was born on 19 June 1917 in Whitfield, Kent. He entered show business working as a secretary for a touring show, lived in a caravan and earned just a pound a week. Before striking out on his own, Marsh worked for Bernard Delfont's London Management company for thirty-five years. His clients included Bruce Forsyth, Frankie Vaughan, Tony Hancock, Norman Wisdom and Morecambe and Wise, gaining the latter a come-back television series – *Two of a Kind* – with ATV.

In 1987, Billy, who himself once trod the boards as a straight man and impressionist, founded Billy Marsh Associates. He then started a show business promotions company in 1991, with Johnny Mans working as his managing director and partner.

Marsh was the subject of *This is Your Life* on ITV and *Great Lives* on BBC Radio 4. Described as 'a man of great humility' by Michael Grade, he was proud that he owned the record for being associated with more Royal shows than any other agent or manager in entertainment history. Billy, who died on 19 December 1995 in London, received the accolade of having his ashes interred under the stage of the London Palladium, a theatre where many of his clients had appeared.

Former M&W agent Jan Kennedy says there was a board displayed at Central Television saying: *Beware of Billy Marsh!* That was because he had the ability to gently sweet talk people into agreeing to his terms.

'Billy was so good at dealing with the stars,' Jan goes on. '"Let's go and tell them what they want to hear, and tomorrow they can tell us where it went wrong." This was Billy's wonderfully gentle touch when dealing with acts like Eric and Ernie, because he knew that after a performance the last thing they needed was to hear what went badly, and what, therefore, needed changing. But come the next day, in his office and just chatting, they themselves would come up with the observations, and Billy could just softly agree, and maybe even at that point make a few observations and suggestions of his own.'

I was in my early twenties when I joined London Management, which was Billy's Regent Street office. In the evening, when most had sensibly departed for home, Billy would summon me and get me to pour us both a drink, and then we'd talk M&W. And he did so with such affection, because Eric and Ernie were two artistes that he not only represented as performers, but genuinely loved as people. I think this almost daily ritual was his way of chilling out after the madness of each day. Essentially, Billy had stumbled across a double act that had become living legends. It doesn't really get much better than that if you're an agent.

Billy Marsh was all of five feet four inches, and had a slight frame. In shape and height, he looked like Mr Burns in *The Simpsons* – someone who might get blown over by a gentle gust of wind.

On the rare occasions he was spotted away from his desk, Billy was led by a cigarette that managed to support a long tail of ash perpetually on the brink of falling away, but never quite doing so, like he'd trained it to wait for the ashtray. Much of my first year working for him was spent rushing out to an Oxford Street tobacconist to pick up his Player's Navy Cut cigarettes. As Michael Grade recalls of his time there, 'We shared an office and half a dozen ashtrays,' which sums up nicely office life in Billy's Regent Street block in the 1960s and '70s.

'Your father came into the office one day,' says Grade, 'and, in front of Billy, he said to me, "I'm now going to do my impression of Billy Marsh!" He got a little box of talcum powder out of his pocket and sprinkled it on his lapels. Billy always had cigarette ash all over his lapels! We both fell about at that.'

In Billy's later years, I often chatted with Jan Kennedy, who by then was the agent for Morecambe and Wise. An excellent agent, and arguably the best the double act ever had, even if in my father's case it came posthumously. Although Jan would disagree, claiming all she learned she learned from Billy.

'On my first day working for Billy,' she chuckles, 'he said to me, "Welcome to London Management, and your first day as an amateur psychiatrist."'

SIDENOTE: Billy Marsh's former office block in Regent Street now houses a giant Apple Store. All the many floors, and with them the elevator, have gone. All that remains is the marbled front entrance – now a window – where the main, solid wooden door once stood. I was getting an issue with my iPhone sorted out there quite recently, and I told the man working on it that the building was where I had worked back in the 1970s. 'Really?' he said. 'I wasn't born then!'

Billy left Regent Street and his London Management company in 1987. He formed a new agency, Billy Marsh Associates, which for years after his death was run by Jan Kennedy. Jan would take over all business responsibilities for Ernie Wise and Doreen, and the Eric Morecambe Estate, and effectively became agent to me, my mother and my sister.

'Billy had a great sense of humour,' Jan recalls. 'For Billy, it was all about comedy. It's easy to see why he would have got on so well with Eric and Ernie as people as well as clients. It was the shared humour.

'His smoking could be overpowering,' she goes on. 'I thought the best thing to do was to buy an Xpelair for his office window, so we could all breathe again. After installing it, I had an internal call from Billy to come into his office at once. He sounded a bit serious, so wondering what I might have done, I walked over to his room straightaway. When I got there, he was on his windowsill standing with the glass behind him. His arms were outstretched, and he said, "It's that Xpelair you bought. It's sucking me out the window!"'

And Billy was once on the receiving end of an Eric Morecambe line, as Jan Kennedy tells me. 'Part of a deal Billy did for M&W was for some product placement for Rolex. Out of it, Eric and Ernie got a wonderful gold Rolex each. Billy said to Eric, "But what's in the deal for me?" Eric replied, "Nothing, but you can call us up every ten minutes and we'll tell you the time!"'

Billy Marsh once said something that has always stayed with me. 'If you're a comedian, you never want to analyse what makes you funny. If you begin doing that,' he said, 'you'll end up going mad. Tony Hancock started doing that, and look what happened!' Billy had at times acted as Hancock's agent. I know that both Eric and Ernie had the same opinion as Billy. My father was particularly in agreement, and would shudder at the idea of even thinking about why something works as funny and something else doesn't. He always kept any introspection focused on what he and Ernie needed to do in each show that would make their audience laugh. And if anyone ever suggested they were 'comic geniuses', he would have a look of bemusement on his face, as if they were talking to the wrong person.

NINE

Eric and Ernie had been appearing at the Princess Theatre, Torquay, in the June of 1961. I remember it well, as we lived out the summer on a caravan site in nearby Brixham, and Gail and I were free to go exploring in an Enid Blyton 'Famous Five' sort of way that wouldn't be advisable for today's kids. Bernard Delfont was presenting the show, with Joan Regan starring, and supporting her were Tommy Cooper, Edmund Hockridge, Morecambe and Wise, and many other performers from singers to speciality acts. It was a big show and a brand-new and impressive theatre.

SIDENOTE: Actor Kevin McNally – *Pirates of the Caribbean, Valkyrie, Conspiracy* – a big M&W fan, told me that he saw them live as a five-year-old boy, as he was in one of the audiences at Torquay that season.

GAIL: Torquay and Brixham caravan site. More fabulous memories. This was most definitely one of my most favourite summer seasons. It wasn't an easy one for Mum, though. I think the caravan was quite small for a family of four, and it was made smaller after we badgered Mum relentlessly, as only children can, to buy a puppy. We won in the end, and the infamous Border terrier Chippy arrived on the scene. We got him from a highstreet pet shop. He was in a cage in the window, and I think Mum took pity on him. He was lively and opinionated. He instantly claimed our mother for himself, and everyone else became the enemy. Especially Dad, who years later would walk past his dog basket and say, 'Die, Chips, die!' Despite being run over at least three times while trying to bite moving car tyres, he lived a long life.

I also have fond memories of making friends with the local farmer – a lovely 'old boy', who would let me bring the cows in with him and help with the milking (in a bucket by hand). I spent a lot of time on that farm, far more preferable to me than the theatre and the show, and having to dress up!

'One day Billy Marsh rang me up,' recalled Ernie of that time. 'He said that Leslie Grade had been on the phone. "He's quite impressed with the spots you boys have been doing on television, and he's offering you a live television series for ATV ... starting in October to run for thirteen weeks. Isn't that great? Now, you go and talk it over with Eric and let me know."'

Ernie knew, as did my father, that Michael Grade's dad Leslie was fast becoming a big fan of their double act.

My father was still sceptical when it came to making a TV series. Doing successful spots on other people's shows, such as Winifred Atwell's, was more than fine, but it would require a big step to return to the ground where they'd buried *Running Wild*. However, he also knew it was the only future they would have. Both Eric and Ernie always kept up with the way the entertainment industry was and where it was heading. Indeed, they would try to keep just ahead of it. While sceptical, they wouldn't just hope the 'old days' would last for ever. They had travelled together too far, and were too savvy to fall into the nostalgia trap.

Colin Clews, Dick Hills and Sid Green. This would be the team to launch Morecambe and Wise to huge success – not the ultimate success that would follow, but a vast leap from near the halfway mark of the showbiz ladder to just approaching the top two rungs, to use that as an analogy.

Colin Clews was regarded as the best comedy producer in British television. It was Ben Warriss – one half of a double act himself, with Jimmy Jewel – who not only rated Clews and convinced Ernie of his merits, but also talked up Hills and Green. (Note that Jewel and Warriss preceded Morecambe and Wise as the first major northern double act to get their own series on British radio and television.)

Warriss being right about the team behind Morecambe and Wise didn't mean that at first it all went swimmingly. While unlike *Running Wild*, Eric and Ernie were pleased with the scripts, they still found themselves lost amid 'a cast of thousands', as my father put it.

Sid Green and Dick Hills – always known as Sid and Dick – went down to Torquay to pay a visit to their new act. They had a vinyl record with them by Johnny Mercer called *Two of a Kind*. It became the theme song and subtitle to the series, though Eric and Ernie always felt the title best suited the writers.

'There were too many people in the sketches,' commented my father, and he was still commenting about this at home many years later whenever we were sitting around musing over their earlier days. But it was a key observation, and one overlooked by those in command. Eric and Ernie both knew that the success they'd so far mustered had arrived through the intimacy of their crosstalk. The show needed to be about them and their relationship, not the similar background hustle and bustle that had populated *Running Wild* so unconvincingly.

Eric and Ernie recognised that the jokes were there, and that Sid and Dick were capable writers with a good track record, but each week the sketches continued to be thickly populated, and that was adding nothing to the comedy or what M&W were about.

It seems extraordinary all these decades later that those supposedly in the know just didn't get what Eric and Ernie were about. There was certainly a sense of authority figures of the day not just overruling the creative people, but almost patronising them. Perhaps they believed Eric and Ernie's theatre audiences just appreciated them for telling gags, but M&W were never about telling gags, as I keep commenting.

At home, I can barely recall my father telling a single joke. They observed and brought their observations – however ludicrous, childish or pointless – to their relationship, and it was those observations that they shared with their audience. Admittedly, in the early 1960s that relationship was incomplete, and still underpinned by variety hall traditions: they were a double act, so they had to be comic and feed, the feed being slightly know-it-all and aggressive, the comic somewhat dull-witted, if not stupid, and ludicrously gullible.

Although Eric and Ernie were already softening those edges, they wouldn't rid themselves of that formulaic partnership until they'd left ATV and teamed up with Eddie Braben at the BBC. And through Eddie and their own talents, they would eventually – inevitably – transcend the comedy itself. They virtually became Eric and Ernie, no show title required, no explanation as to who they were, just Eric and Ernie appearing as nothing more than Eric and Ernie, who could read out the dictionary or a shopping list and still sound funny. But that would be about familiarity, and the love of a nation that years of honest hard endeavour and genuine engagement with their audiences would create.

Sid Green and Dick Hills

Sid Green was born on 24 January 1928 in Becontree, Essex, and Richard 'Dick' Hills on 17 January 1926 in Eltham, London. They first met when they attended Haberdashers' Aske's Hatcham Boys' Grammar School in south-east London.

After the Second World War, in which Green was in the Army and Hills was in the Navy, both men decided to form a writing partnership. Their first professional client was the comedian Dave King. When King found success on television, with the aid of their writing skills, he engaged them to contribute material for his appearances in America on the *Kraft Music Hall* series. They went on to contribute scripts to the Sid James sitcom *Citizen James*.

The writing partners wrote for Morecambe and Wise on their ATV series *Two of a Kind* throughout each run, often appearing in the sketches. They also wrote the screenplays for their three Pinewood cinematic ventures, which also had contributions from other writers. Other names Sid and Dick wrote for included Bernard Cribbins, Bruce Forsyth and Frankie Howerd. In 1967 they were given their own series, *Those Two Fellers*, which they also penned.

Post Morecambe and Wise, they worked at ATV for two years before heading to America, where they wrote for *The Johnny Carson Show*.

When Dick moved himself and his family back to England, Sid stayed on to continue working as a solo writer before he too returned home. In the following years Green wrote for performers including Michael Barrymore, Freddie Starr and The Krankies. He also created and contributed episodes for the LWT sitcom *Mixed Blessings*. Hills, meanwhile, hosted editions of Southern TV's chat show *Tell Me*

Another and wrote material for Tommy Cooper, Smith and Jones and Jasper Carrott.

Certain material written by Sid and Dick in the 1960s for Morecambe and Wise was later used by fellow double act Cannon and Ball. While at Thames, Eric and Ernie occasionally re-used items written by Hills and Green in the same decade.

Sid died on 15 March 1999 in Essex, and Dick on 6 June 1996 in Sussex.

Back in 1961, their new television series, this time at ATV for Lew Grade, threatened to do only marginally better than the *Running Wild* series had. Then fate happily stepped in, and everything changed for ever.

The actors' union Equity went on strike, taking with them almost everyone appearing on *Two of a Kind*. Sid Green thought they were done for, but Eric and Ernie pointed out they weren't with Equity, they were with VAF – Variety Artistes' Federation. They weren't affected by the strike. And as Michael Grade puts it, 'What developed then was the intimacy. The shows, by good fortune, had to be stripped down, so you had Eric and Ernie really talking to each other. Essentially, this came about because the strike meant it wasn't possible for the show to book anyone else. The chaos of before – big and brash, lots of people running in and out of doors – all that was gone.'

Suddenly they could do it all by themselves and appear in front of camera just as they appeared on theatre stages year after year. It made all the difference, and with the strike lasting around twelve weeks, it was long enough for them to establish a successful format and create Morecambe and Wise as television personalities, if in embryonic form.

My father would sometimes watch the ATV shows at home on video years later. He was never fully comfortable with the traditional comic persona that he was encouraged to deliver back then. 'I talk stupid as well as act stupid,' he'd complain, and then go into a fascinating impression of himself, delivering lines from those ATV shows with exaggerated nasal tones and stereotypical northernness, which really emphasised how far they would take their comic personas after bidding farewell to ATV. One could almost claim that the Eric and Ernie of the 1960s (to round it up) were the same as the Eric and Ernie of the 1970s in name only. They had not only matured, they had radically changed as performers.

SIDENOTE: One of the guests to appear on *Two of A Kind* during the ATV years – who would reappear many years later on one of M&W's Thames TV shows – was the musician, presenter and entertainer Roy Castle. The reason I'm singling him out is he was arguably my father's best friend. My father also introduced him to Fiona Dickson, who would become his wife. Roy always joked that he'd throw stones at my father's windows whenever he and Fiona had an argument!

People have asked me if lots of showbiz figures used

to crop up at our house, and I have to explain that they did not. It wasn't how my parents operated. Home was something very separate from show business. With the one exception of Mr and Mrs Roy Castle!

My father and Roy also spent time together in America when he and Ernie were over there at the same time as Roy. My father and Roy had to 'bunk up', which according to Fiona brought about much amusement and constant giggling.

As a family, we are still in touch with Fiona Castle and her family – indeed, for a short while, my wife and I lived about a mile away from Fiona. Gail was a bridesmaid at the Castles' wedding, and their daughter, Julia, a bridesmaid at Gail's own wedding in 1975.

GAIL: Also, Dad was Daniel's [Roy and Fiona's eldest son] godfather, and Fiona went on to be Amelia's [my eldest's] godmother. Fiona was my favourite babysitter. I remember, in my teens, being on my own in the house one evening when the phone rang. It was a strange rather scary voice, like something out of *Doctor Who*. I couldn't make out much, just what seemed like some numbers being quoted, so I quickly put the phone down. I later learned that it was Roy, calling to tell us that Fiona had given birth. The numbers were the date, time and weight of the baby!

Roy Castle

Roy Castle was born on 31 August 1932 in Scholes, West Riding, Yorkshire. The expression all-rounder could have been invented for Castle. He was a self-effacing dancer, singer, musician (with a repertoire of over forty instruments), comedian, actor and presenter. However, he was a family man first and an entertainer second.

Tap-dancing lessons as a boy were a chore for Roy, but would later pay off in more ways than one. Joining an amateur concert party also gave him early experience of being an entertainer. After he left the world of education, Castle toured the northern music halls as a song and dance act.

Early breaks came in the form of being a stooge for the comedians Jimmy Clitheroe and Jimmy James. To this day, the famous 'box sketch' he appeared in with the latter and Eli Woods is still fondly remembered and repeated in documentaries.

In the 1960s, Roy starred in *The Roy Castle Show*. Radio work included Roy's own series *Castle on the Air*, while his film credits include *Doctor Who and the Daleks*, with Peter Cushing, and the original version of *The Plank*, with Eric Sykes. He also joined the *Carry On* team for *Carry On Up the Khyber*.

In 1972, Castle began hosting the children's series *Record Breakers*, even breaking his own records during his long involvement with the show. This didn't stop him from continuing to perform on stage. As well as cabaret and summer seasons, he appeared in the musicals *Singin' in the Rain*, with Tommy Steele, and *Pickwick*, with Harry Secombe.

A committed Christian, Roy was diagnosed with lung cancer in 1992. Despite knowing his remaining time was limited, he helped to raise funds for the Lung Cancer Fund to build the first research centre dedicated to that disease. His *Tour of Hope* followed in July 1994, which saw Roy and Fiona Castle travel 1,200 miles across the country on a specially chartered train to spread the message and meet fans and well-wishers. This raised a million pounds in just three days.

Roy, who was awarded the OBE for services to Charity and Show business in 1993, died on 2 September 1994, aged sixty-two. Since then, the Lung Cancer Fund has gone on to be named the Roy Castle Lung Cancer Foundation in his honour and as a mark of gratitude for his help and support.

When I look back on our family's early days during the budding success of Morecambe and Wise, and my own growing interest in their shows, I must admit that I was temporarily distracted, as many were, by the arrival of the Beatles.

I had my own Dansette record player – no doubt I still have it somewhere in my mother's attic. Whenever my father was away working, he'd return bearing vinyl gifts. Buddy Greco was high on my list of favourites, Matt Monro, some classical albums and even some spoken stories. All enjoyed and gratefully received. Such a magical day it was when he returned home with a single called 'She Loves You', by a group called the Beatles. That was the beginning of a new world, and not just for me but for everyone, whether they cared to admit it or not. Nothing would quite be the same again.

American actress Whoopi Goldberg has spoken about

this in Ron Howard's film *The Beatles: Eight Days a Week – The Touring Years.* She expresses clearly how her life changed the moment she heard them, and from that time on, her life, her decisions and how she's operated in the big wide world has come through discovering them. They changed everything for her for always.

I was too young to claim I was a part of the sixties vibe, or of what the Beatles began and others followed in changing our attitudes and our ways of seeing things, and even the way we behaved and interacted – certainly the way we dressed. But I can still think back and recall that there was a definite divide created between a pre-Beatles time and a post-Beatles time, something my own mother recently recognised.

Earlier this year (2023) we were chatting about the time the Beatles made a memorable appearance on *The Morecambe & Wise Show,* and my mother remarked, 'We hadn't heard anything quite like them before. It was as though a light had been switched on. And from then on we all had to change to keep up.'

Which would explain why instead of remaining on the 'wrong' side of that divide, M&W embraced it, and rather cannily secured the Beatles for that famous appearance on their show. Recorded for ATV in Studio C, Elstree, Hertfordshire, in the winter of 1963 – transmitted at a later date, it should be noted – it still resonates to this day.

This was just ten days after the Beatles had released their second album, *With the Beatles,* and it was possibly an early music-TV example of how a symbiotic arrangement can benefit all parties concerned. M&W were big TV by that time, and the Beatles a massive phenomenon

131

in the pop-music world. However, being musical meant they had few appropriate places to show their humour and general likeability. Cue two other northern lads in Eric and Ernie, loved and respected on television for their comedy, and one can sense what a great idea it was to put the two acts together. In fact, so good was it that you'll still find headlines online today saying: 'When the Beatles made a legendary appearance with Morecambe & Wise'.

My memories of those times bounce around my ever increasing love of both the Beatles and Morecambe and Wise, and their momentary blending together on that show, and of a developing sense of what the Fab Four and Eric and Ernie were beginning to mean to people beyond the music and the comedy they were producing. And what they were beginning to mean beyond the north of England.

The link is a tenuous one, even if both acts started their careers in Liverpool. Soon Morecambe and Wise and the Beatles had no further connection other than a quiet admiration for each other over the passing years. I know my father really admired the *Sgt. Pepper* album, and that in the 1970s, Paul McCartney once rang M&W's then producer, Ernest Maxin, about perhaps appearing on a Christmas show. I wish that had materialised. I'm not sure why it didn't happen. McCartney also wanted Eric and Ernie to appear as two of the prisoners escaping on the cover of his album *Band on the Run*; James Coburn and Michael Parkinson ended up on it. And my father flew back from New York with Ringo Starr – not pre-planned – and said how much he liked him. I've always felt Ringo possessed a similar sense of humour to my father. Very quick, very funny. You see it in any interviews – it's mostly Ringo who gets the others going. He has funny bones, as Billy Marsh would've said.

I can't imagine what it must feel like to survive that struggling period of early youth and then actually realise your dream, and on an even grander scale than you could have thought possible. It's one thing to wistfully pursue the end of the rainbow, but entirely another to reach its end and claim the pot of gold.

My father told me his idea of big success as he was growing up was for him and Ernie to be able to continue getting enough work to keep going, and never having to look for other employment. From that, then maybe he'd acquire enough money one day to own a small terrace house with a patch of lawn out front and back. That they would become living legends wasn't on their wish list, and was beyond the realm of dreams. It just wasn't considered possible by them or, one imagines, anyone else associated with them. When it eventually happened it must have come as something of a shock.

TEN

A transatlantic interlude.

There was a TV documentary not that long ago about Morecambe and Wise in America, which us Morecambes were happy to be a part of. It jogged many memories and was a sharp reminder of how far their double act had risen from 1961 to 1964.

America came about through the powerful American TV mogul of the day, Ed Sullivan, who had caught their act at the London Palladium. As my mother puts it, 'Ed Sullivan loved English comedians, and was a real Anglophile.' He knew and worked with many over the years.

He loved Eric and Ernie's act, and he liked them as people, too. It was pretty much the accepted belief that if Sullivan liked you, then the American public would catch up in turn. It was reciprocal, and therefore a no-brainer that they'd take an offer to work over in New York, and on excellent money.

Between 1961 and 1968, Morecambe and Wise would go backwards and forwards across the pond to appear on Sullivan's show. Initially they were received in near silence – believe me, that makes difficult viewing – but as the visits increased, so too did the American audiences' understanding of who they were. 'At least by the final visits they recognised us,' my father once said to me. 'It took a long time to get to that stage, though.' But Sullivan never gave up on them, giving them so much build-up, and on one occasion infamously joining in a routine with them singing their 'Boom Oo Yata-Ta-Ta' number. Eric and Ernie were convinced Sullivan just didn't get it at all, but there's no question you can see he's really enjoying himself. And Sullivan never normally engaged with the acts – not in their actual performance – so this was a privilege indeed, and a sign of how much he liked and respected their double act.

Ernie said that in general the Americans were very kind to them. 'Once when we were booked to play in Toronto, Canada, the entire Ed Sullivan unit flew over to support us. On another occasion, Ed took us out to a restaurant and gave us a dinner, a great honour for a visiting act.'

Albeit briefly, their names appeared in lights on Broadway. 'We were completely knocked out,' said Ernie. Later they went backstage at the theatre to thank Sullivan and his son-in-law, Bob Precht, who handled the show's marketing. Precht seemed embarrassed. It turned out the names were actually coming down! 'Anyhow,' said Ernie, 'later, out of kindness, they put them back again for a while.'

Years later, after both my father and Ernie had passed away, they would be on Broadway again, with David Pugh and Kenneth Branagh's *The Play What I Wrote*, an unusual and brilliantly entertaining tribute to Morecambe and Wise, written and performed by The Right Size

(Sean Foley and Hamish McColl), and co-starring Toby Jones. That would have so tickled both Eric and Ernie. A posthumous triumph of the first order.

Eric and Ernie did about four Sullivan shows a year and for four years in total. It was a heavy workload, as my mother points out. 'If you look at the diary we kept at the time,' she says, 'it's almost impossible to believe they could have fulfilled their working obligations. Fly to America, do shows, fly back, next day straight into the ATV studios to record a live *Morecambe & Wise Show*, then get ready to do some filming for the Rank Organisation based at Pinewood Studios a week later. Plus all other "appearance" commitments – opening stores, attending functions, and so on. It was madness, really. But having struggled early on, to suddenly be in demand made it impossible to say no to anything.'

SIDENOTE: It was clearly very tough for Eric and Ernie in the States to begin with.

When they arrived in the US, they would have so little time to settle in. Within some twenty-four hours they were performing. That air of 'doomed from the start' lingered throughout their visits, though possibly for the most part they ignored it, remaining professional at all times. But as my father said of those visits, 'We were flying by the seat of our pants!'

136

While trips continued to and from the United States with slow, but increasingly more positive reactions from the American audiences, back in the UK, the ATV series with Sid and Dick rolled on unabated. That long-awaited success had finally arrived for the double act. Indeed, both Eric and Ernie were certain that they'd reached the pinnacle of what was possible in their line of work when the awards started to come in with a rapidity and regularity they could have once only dreamed of. BAFTA and Variety Club awards were particular notables in the early to mid 1960s. *Two of a Kind* had become one of the top television programmes of its day, establishing Eric and Ernie as the UK's favourite double act. And while continuing to flit to and from America, in the midst of this new routine there came an unexpected addition with an approach from the film company Rank. They wanted to make three films starring Morecambe and Wise. In terms of commitment to these film projects, they would be required on and off from 1963 to 1968.

Ernie always retained a love for 'Old' Hollywood, which he later would come to enjoy by proxy once Ernest Maxin and Eddie Braben started working together on their BBC shows. But some years before he even knew that was going to happen, the idea of doing something for the 'silver screen' really motivated him.

My mother says, 'Doing the Sullivan shows had been a great introduction to America for Ernie, and I'm convinced Ernie and Doreen would have settled out there had Eric not categorically refused. Ernie could see a future there through the Sullivan appearances. Your father saw the potential of staying with what they already knew and had proved successful with, namely British television audiences.'

There's no right or wrong, of course, as we don't know for sure what might have happened had my father proved more compliant. But I've always said that he not only saw himself as British, but specifically English. He never showed signs of seeking deviation from that. He clearly recognised what he and Ernie had as an act, and what we had as a family, so the idea of deliberately derailing to have a toe nearer Hollywood didn't overly inspire him to take any risks. I believe the only thing that might have changed things would have been if their success in the UK hadn't been as big and spectacular as it now was. The return from Australia to little or no work back in the late fifties was a very different situation from their current one. Back then they would have taken anything offered from anywhere abroad, not just America. But they were now British television stars.

It was back in the UK they now found themselves, and my father, like Ernie, was keen to make some movies. Not that he was confident about this untried genre. It was another venture into the unknown. He was very aware they were totally new to it, and I'm sure Ernie felt the same way, especially after their first forays in television, but perhaps he embraced it a little more enthusiastically. Both men had past experience of how things could go awry, so they would remain cautious throughout the project.

A few years later, with the Rank Pinewood films behind them, Ernie would still talk of their doing more. 'I have always wanted to make a film in Hollywood,' he said. That was a desire that would never leave him. 'I was a song and dance man when Eric and I met, and it is still my first love.'

Slightly more negatively, my father butted in with, 'That ambition has always been in my mind, but I suppose that has gone now.'

How many times did my father and I sit through Fred Astaire and Ginger Rogers movies? Eric and Ernie also both loved the 1930s and '40s gangster films, like those starring James Cagney, Humphrey Bogart, Edward G. Robinson, George Raft, Sydney Greenstreet and Peter Lorre. Those action-driven films, alongside the more musically driven ones, I believe were a true inspiration to both men when they started to tread the boards as a double act and they stayed in the back of their minds throughout their careers. My father loved them as much as Ernie – he had grown up on them, too. But he was marginally less influenced by them; that was the only difference between the two of them.

However, having a chance to make their own mark in films was too good an opportunity to turn down, especially as they were to be filmed over a reasonable period of time and would not interfere with their ATV series or trips to the States for Sullivan's shows. Though interestingly, they did an interview in 1964, claiming that they'd be laying off TV for at least a year while making the Rank films. 'We're giving it a rest while they still like us,' joked my father. 'We're not fools!'

Ernie added, 'Right now we're at the peak,' which in

fact wasn't to be the case, but it's understandable that he would have believed it. 'You've got to make it last as long as you can. You can't last for ever, and we haven't always been so lucky on TV.'

As my mother says, 'They were, at this stage in their careers, unable and unwilling to turn anything down. There was no blueprint as to how one should go about a burgeoning show-business career such as theirs.'

Making films is undeniably very different from performing in front of an audience, be it theatre or studio. With an audience you have immediate feedback and no retakes. My father was not a retake person at the best of times. Even when recording in the studios, he never liked it – though accepted its inevitability – when they'd have to do a retake because of a camera or sound issue. He'd turn to the audience and say, 'Just laugh like you've never heard the line before'. And then his mind would race, as invariably he'd deliver the line in a slightly different way, which then *did* get the required laugh. There is no laughter when making comedy movies – with the occasional exception of cast and crew.

The order of the three films they made for Rank was: *The Intelligence Men* (1965), *That Riviera Touch* (1966) and *The Magnificent Two* (1967). Perhaps inevitably they weren't great films. They appeased Eric and Ernie's desire to make something for the big screen, though, and they were entertaining enough. But it was apparent that M&W themselves worked best almost entirely through an invisible connection with their live audiences. They needed that audience reaction. As the late writer, director and actor Bryan Forbes once put it to me, 'For most comedians without the physical reaction of an audience, it's very difficult to time comedy.' On top of that, intimate cross-talk comedy doesn't work so well in exterior locations, mainly because said intimacy is diluted.

SIDENOTE: It's interesting that their first film was in 1965, only months after Ernie's mentor, Jack Hylton, died aged seventy-two. I questioned my father about Hylton, sometime in the mid-1970s. 'Did you ever see him again after working for him as a child performer?' was the main question I put to him.

'Oh yes,' he replied. 'And me and Ernie saw him once more. It was in his office after we'd made it big with our own series on ATV.'

'He must have been really proud of you,' I commented.

'No, not really,' he replied, a little sadly. 'I think he was slightly disappointed. He probably hadn't expected us to become so successful as we did.'

'I think the boys were out of their comfort zone, and were learning how film worked,' reflects Michael Grade. 'I believe that if they'd gone on to do some more films, they'd have got more control – control that they'd by then have known how to use. But back then, they didn't know how films worked. [In] a television studio they knew everything very well, but with film they were putting themselves in the hands of people who'd made hundreds of films, and they naturally went along with it.'

And we've come to learn that Morecambe and Wise were always best when in control of their comedy.

> GAIL: I sometimes think that these three films fall into the same category as their television series Running Wild, insomuch as the critics were not especially keen on them, particularly Barry Norman. And they would often only achieve a two-star rating. But I personally have never had a member of the viewing public say anything negative about them. In fact, they usually say how much they enjoy them, and tell me which is their favourite and why. Considering Dad and Ernie never went to drama school, or ever had acting lessons, they did come out of it all rather well. Yet again in their career, they were learning a new genre on the job.

I agree with Gail on this, and I'll attempt to explain the negativity shown towards these films. Firstly, if Eric and Ernie had been hoping to bring some magic to the big screen, in the way they were now doing with television, then ultimately they would be as disappointed as the critics. These films were very much comedian Norman Wisdom-style vehicles. Another issue that is evident is that while Sid and Dick were good TV writers for Eric and Ernie, they weren't screenplay writers. Inevitably they brought Eric and Ernie as they were in the ATV shows straight on to the big screen. That was a mistake, if an understandable one, because as you watch these films you realise they need and deserve more than transplanting from TV studio to various locations.

Having said this, it's interesting how fondly they're remembered, as my sister comments, and how frequently they turn up on television as repeats – especially *That Riviera Touch*, which has a vociferous cult following. Money was spent on them, and being shot in Technicolor added a depth and quality that belied the faults. Time has been a good friend to these three films.

Ed Sullivan had started out in journalism, and through a mix of determination and good fortune found himself presenting *The Ed Sullivan Show* for the CBS network. He was an oddball character, often lampooned for his forgetfulness, especially with artistes' names. His persona, which in fact was natural, was of this rather average man who managed to bring lots of varied talented acts to his high-rating weekly variety-style show. One only has to consider Morecambe and Wise, Elvis Presley, the Beatles, Norman Wisdom, Buddy Holly, Jackie Mason, Bobby Darin, Connie Francis, Rickie Layne, Creedence Clearwater Revival, Janis Joplin, The Rolling Stones, Wayne and Shuster, Bill Haley & His Comets, Itzhak Perlman, Milton Berle, The Supremes, and literally dozens more to appreciate just how eclectic his guest entertainers were.

GAIL: We often used to joke about Ed Sullivan introducing Mori, Cambie and Wise! He was infamous for mispronouncing the names of his guests. I was recently amused to discover that the original name for Morecambe was in fact Morikambe. Apparently, Ptolemy in AD 150

143

wrote that there was a place called Morikambe Eischusis, meaning curved bay, or salt flats, on the north-west coast of Britain. Morecambe Bay doesn't appear until 1774. Morecambe the town took its name from the bay. You're welcome. So, dear Mr Sullivan was on to something!

SIDENOTE: It's true what Gail says about the humour our father took from having his and Ernie's double act introduced as a triple act. The only problem: it's hard to find any proof from the available material that it was as evident an error as our father liked to make out. In one of Sullivan's early introductions, there is a slight slurring of Morecambe, but nothing especially obvious.

By 1971, changing styles, especially in light entertainment, saw Sullivan's ratings irretrievably collapse. In March of that year, not resting on sentimentality, CBS cancelled the show. Sullivan was incensed, but if he'd been totally honest with himself he would surely have accepted his run at the top had been phenomenal and possibly somewhat fortunate.

In early 1974, Sullivan was diagnosed with advanced oesophageal cancer. His family kept his terminal condition from him, and he was left believing that his illness was related to years of gastric ulcers that had troubled him. He died in October 1974, two weeks after turning seventy-three.

It was while Eric and Ernie plus wives visited Ed Sullivan and his wife Sylvia in 1967, that my father made a note in one of only two diaries he ever (partially) kept. He wrote that he'd felt a strange, lingering pain in his left arm, and slight nausea. Clearly this was the start of his own brush with serious ill health, which would nearly kill him a year later.

ELEVEN

Eric and Ernie didn't leave Lew Grade's ATV in 1967 for more money, though it's fair to say they were offered more money by the BBC, which was welcome, I'm sure. They left ATV because they not only felt undervalued, but they wanted colour television, which Lew Grade couldn't offer them. 'ATV at the time were only just starting to move towards colour television,' my mother recalls. 'It was mostly for the big shows, and specifically for the American market. The BBC was ahead of the game, already transmitting in colour on BBC Two. They were able to offer them what they wanted.'

They'd had the experience of seeing some of their own television material in colour for *Piccadilly Palace*, which was the name of the US version of the last ATV series Morecambe and Wise recorded. It was broadcast in the States as the summer version of *Hollywood Palace*, an American variety show, which was very popular.

'Part of the problem,' continues my mother, 'was Lew Grade himself. We all got on very well together, and always would. But Lew was not a great people person. He could easily rub you up the wrong way, and appear quite brusque and almost tyrannical. His nephew, Michael, was the complete opposite, and it was he who would instigate

Eric and Ernie's move away from ATV to the BBC, by whispering in Bill Cotton's ear.'

It was in 1964 that Michael Grade first met Morecambe and Wise 'properly'. And it would be Michael who would go on to change the history of entertainment by taking M&W away from his Uncle Lew, and over to the BBC. 'The first time I met them was in Uncle Lew's office,' recalls Michael. 'They were closing the deal to play the ABC, Blackpool, in summer season. My dad [Leslie Grade] introduced me, and I knew exactly who they were. The boys [M&W] eventually left the office, and I was left talking with my dad, who said, "I can't believe what I'm paying them!" It was about two thousand pounds a week, I think, which was huge money back in the early 1960s [over fifty thousand pounds a week in 2023].'

Michael Grade and Eric and Ernie were in contact in some way or other for the rest of Eric and Ernie's lives. 'They came to my wedding, and Eric and I would go to watch football together,' Michael recalls. 'On one occasion, Eric and I went to Caesar's Palace [in Luton] to see Tommy Cooper. We all loved Tommy. A waiter suddenly dropped a tray of drinks, making a hell of a noise. It wasn't a set-up – it was a genuine accident. Tommy stopped mid-sentence and just stared out at the waiter. Seconds went by and nothing happened. Then all he finally said was, "That's nice!" It got a huge laugh. Eric couldn't believe it. He chuckled and said to me, "I'd thought of twenty gags in that time, and not only does he just say, 'That's nice!' but it gets a huge laugh!"'

In his autobiography, *Still Dancing*, Lew Grade makes

the point that no one could have known just how big Morecambe and Wise would become. He has a reasonable point. It would perhaps have been more likely for the industry people to have a less optimistic view – that their double act had enjoyed a few successful years, and at some point, sooner rather than later, would virtually disappear, like so many acts Lew Grade had overseen in his long career.

Lew Grade

Lew Grade, originally named Lev Winogradsky, was born on 25 December 1906 in Tokmak, Ukraine. An expert Charleston dancer, he won the Charleston Champion of the World at the Royal Albert Hall in London in 1926. In the early 1930s, Grade and Joe Collins started a talent agency called Collins and Grade. After the war, in which for a time he served in the Army, Lew and his brother Leslie began a new talent agency called Lew and Leslie Grade Ltd, also known as the Grade Organisation.

Grade, Val Parnell and Prince Littler's bid for an ITV franchise with the newly formed ITP (Incorporated Television Programme Company), which later changed its name to ITC (Incorporated Television Company), was rejected because of Lew's dominance in the entertainment industry. Although ABD (Associated Broadcasting Development Company) had won ITV franchises for the weekend service in London and the weekday service in the Midlands, they didn't have the capital to meet their responsibilities. They joined forces with Grade's consortium.

ATV (Associated Television) was eventually formed and Lew became managing director. In addition to signing Morecambe and Wise, Lew's programmes included *The Saint*, *Sunday Night at the London Palladium* and *The Muppet Show*.

Lew had mixed fortunes as a film producer. His successes included *The Muppet Movie*, *On Golden Pond* and *The Dark Crystal*. However, the costly *Raise the Titanic* did not fare well at cinema box offices. After stepping down from ATV in the early 1980s, Grade sold ITC, although he returned to head the company in the 1990s, and for a while chaired Embassy Pictures, later forming The Grade

Company, which made television films including *The Lady and the Highwayman*.

Lew, who was knighted in 1969 and went on to become a life peer, Baron Grade of Elstree, in 1976, died on 13 December 1998 in London.

SIDENOTE: Talking of Lord Lew Grade always makes me think of my father's response to people constantly asking him, 'Where's Ernie?'

'Oh, he couldn't come,' he would reply. 'He was cleaning Lew Grade's Rolls Royce when his tongue ran dry!'

My time spent working with Billy Marsh only lasted for a few years, whereas Michael Grade was involved with Morecambe and Wise in a working capacity to a level – at Billy Marsh's office, at least – that I never was.

'In terms of Lew and the move from ATV to the BBC,' says Michael, 'I think Lew had dug himself in. He'd set a price. And the price had been moved up and up and up by Billy [Marsh], and then he said that his last offer really was his final offer. Lew was very much a man of his word, so that was it. Once he'd dug himself in, and the boys replied that they wouldn't accept his final offer, then it was all over. But Lew knew the game. He'd been an agent himself.'

I know my father would have kept quite quiet during any negotiations, as he felt that the business side was always Ernie's role. Michael Grade agrees. 'Ernie dealt with the business side. That was the agreement – the understanding – they had. And it worked well. Eric perhaps carried the responsibility for keeping their act shining bright, and Ernie dealt with the money.' Especially in the earlier years, I would agree with that.

'They managed their relationship incredibly well,' continues Michael. 'They had seen every double act in the history of vaudeville come to hate each other, and they decided very early on that that wasn't going to be what happened with their own partnership. And where they were smart is they didn't mix socially. Once it wasn't related to a work scenario, there was complete separation.'

Michael spent more time in their company than I'd ever realised before writing this book. 'I can remember being on the road with them, and what would drive Eric mad was Doreen was always there watching over Ernie. And Eric would turn to me and whisper, "Let's go to the casino tonight," or some such thing, "and I'll watch out that Ernie and Doreen don't spot what we're doing." It was hilarious. And also it suited Ernie. That was the choice they made as to how their life would work out best for them.'

It transpires that Billy Marsh was out of the country when all the talk in 1967 of moving away from ATV was coming to a head. 'I think he was on business in America,' recalls Michael Grade. 'He would phone me and I would phone him, and he trusted me to complete the deal, and the boys trusted me to complete the deal, and so that was that.'

I've often wondered if the situation created family problems for Michael, given that the person he was taking M&W away from was his uncle. But he says a categorical 'No' to that suggestion. 'Lew was out of the picture. He'd made his final bid. So, I was now free to contact Bill Cotton at the BBC.'

Bill Cotton had known Morecambe and Wise since his days as a song-plugger. 'I used to go round to all of the theatres,' recalled Cotton, 'and try to get the artistes to sing our songs. Morecambe and Wise were quite often on the bill with their good friend Alma Cogan ... They were both there, of course, and we used to meet quite a lot, and I got to know them. Lew Grade booked them for ATV before I thought of it!'

Michael Grade says, 'I rang Bill [Cotton] and asked if he wanted Morecambe and Wise. I'd known Bill for years, and he replied, "I know you're using me as a stick to beat Lew with, but I'll go along for the ride." I told him there and then that if we could do a deal then they were his. We met for lunch, and he still didn't believe it was going to happen. I told him what they wanted if they moved to the BBC, and he eventually came back agreeing to the terms, which included the shows being in colour. He essentially did all that was required to make sure he got them. And he did get them. And then I had to ring Lew and tell him!'

Despite the fact Lew had given his final offer, he accepted rather than welcomed the outcome. 'He could see that that was the position it had got to, and he'd been in that same position a million times over the years, so life would go on without Morecambe and Wise, even though they were a huge attraction for ATV.' But, as Michael says, 'Once you see some of those Morecambe and Wise sketches in colour, it does bring a whole new dimension.' Perhaps that was something Lew Grade hadn't quite thought about enough, or recognised as important. Michael adds, 'Going on to BBC Two was a clever move, as it was then a very small channel, so it was like trying a potential West End show out in the provinces first.'

Michael Grade

Michael Grade was born on 8 March 1943 in London. As his father was the theatrical agent Leslie Grade and his uncles were the television mogul Lew Grade and the theatre producer Bernard Delfont, it was destined that he would work in the entertainment industry.

Known for smoking cigars and his trademark red braces, Grade spent time as a sports columnist at the *Daily Mirror* before joining London Management to learn the job of a theatrical agent. During his time there, he worked with Billy Marsh and agency clients including Morecambe and Wise.

Michael gained the position of deputy controller of entertainment programmes at LWT in 1973 and subsequently director of programmes in 1977. On his watch, he brought Bruce Forsyth to the company from the BBC and green-lit the action series *The Professionals* and the long-running arts show *The South Bank Show*.

After spending time as president of Embassy Television in America, Grade returned home and became the controller of BBC One, and then two years later the director of programmes. While at the BBC during this period, Michael commissioned the then twice-weekly soap *EastEnders*, gave a thrice-weekly slot for Terry Wogan's chat show *Wogan* and gave permission for Live Aid to be shown on the channel. In 1988, Grade became the chief executive at Channel 4. Under his leadership, both the medical drama *ER* and the sitcom *Friends* were brought to the channel.

After a two-year tenure at First Leisure Corporation, Michael and Ivan Dunleavy acquired Pinewood Studios from the Rank Group in 2000. Then the following year, Pinewood Studios and Shepperton

Studios were merged to become the Pinewood Shepperton Group. Grade and Dunleavy managed the new company until 2017.

In April 2004, Michael became the chairman of the BBC. Then in 2007, he went back to ITV to become their executive chairman. He oversaw a period of great change at the commercial channel. More recently, in 2022, Grade was appointed chairman of the UK's communications regulator, Ofcom.

Michael became a CBE in 1998 and a life peer, Baron Grade of Yarmouth, in 2011.

TWELVE

In November 1968, Morecambe and Wise had squeezed a few nights at Jimmy Corrigan's club in Batley, West Yorkshire, into their hefty work schedule. James Corrigan was a larger-than-life figure, affectionately known as the King of Clubs.

Corrigan and his wife, Betty, designed the club themselves, and had it built in early 1967 on a disused sewage site on Bradford Road. Despite a few hiccups on the way, they managed to open on 27 March for Easter, which had been their plan. The headline act that night was the Bachelors, who had worked with Morecambe and Wise in the early to mid sixties on various variety shows, and appeared on their ATV television series.

Maureen Prest was in charge of promotions and PR during the club's sixties and seventies heyday, and she was probably the one who coined the 'King of Clubs' nickname for Jimmy Corrigan. 'It was Jimmy's vision that the north should have some top-class entertainment,' she said, 'and he had the vision and the drive to pull it off.'

The stars he managed to get playing at his club were extraordinary: Louis Armstrong, the Everly Brothers, Eartha Kitt, Roy Orbison, the Bee Gees, Gene Pitney, Shirley Bassey, Lulu, Ken Dodd . . . and Morecambe and

Wise. In fact, Louis Armstrong described Batley as '. . . a living aspirin'.

Maureen Prest says that the club's demise began once other venues started emulating its successful formula, and James 'Jimmy' Corrigan passed away in 2000 having made and lost a fortune.

Back in 1968, of course, things were buzzing for Corrigan. As most know, my father retold the events of that November night in Batley quite superbly on the Michael Parkinson show in 1972. I was genuinely thrilled that Sir Michael himself felt it was one of the best interviews out of the many he had done in his long and illustrious career. I re-watched it recently, and it is so genuinely vibrant and funny, and shows to a TV audience the nature of Eric and Ernie's remarkable relationship perhaps more clearly than any written words or performances on stage and in studio ever will. Just the two men sitting there with the wonderful Parky gently nudging them along. It was like sitting in a pub listening to three friends banter away together.

Suffice to say, my father was driving through Leeds in the early hours in his Jensen Interceptor, having performed at Corrigan's club, in pain and virtually unable to continue to drive the vehicle, when he happened upon Walter Butterworth. Walter was a twenty-four-year-old tyre fitter, and a cadet for the Territorials. It was Walter who took the wheel and got Dad to Leeds Infirmary.

On *Parkinson* there was quite a bit of what I like to call David Nivenisms – that thing of not allowing the truth to get in the way of a good story – which slightly grated with Walter at the time, I would later discover, but he also came to appreciate its value. You can't keep a great comic down, and Walter understood that.

Walter and I met for the first time in 2017 at the Silverstone race track, when I was heavily involved with a documentary called *Morecambe and Wise Forever*. Meeting Walter was a special moment for me. He had only been in his twenties back in November 1968, when my father had what we soon discovered was his first and very serious heart attack. What brought about our meeting was that both Walter and I were reunited with my father's Jensen Interceptor for the documentary. And it didn't end there. Walter was put behind the wheel of the car once again, and I was in the passenger seat as he took us for a ride around the track. As Walter put it, 'It was very fast. A nice motor.' And, despite my father's claim on *Parkinson* – and perhaps it was true of the time it was made – Walter proved to me he could drive more than a Territorial Army tank!

SIDENOTE: In November 2022, while out in Portugal, I met a man called John Cotterill. John, who after 1968 would work at the Leeds Infirmary as a physician, was already a friend of a Willie Whittaker. Whittaker was the senior cardiologist on the Brotherton Wing at the Leeds Infirmary, where my father was in a private room recovering from his major heart attack. 'Willie told me that one day he had to take a group of young doctors around the wards,' John recounted. 'When he reached your dad's room and looked inside, all anyone could see was a sheet over his entire body, and a pair of glasses on top of his hidden face. He never forgot that image.' Yes, that sounds so like my father. Finding humour in all situations, good or bad.

GAIL: A few years ago, I met a pleasant lady who told me she had been a nurse at the hospital where Dad had been recovering from a heart attack. She said that Dad was always being funny, and entertaining everyone. On one occasion, with Dad in full flow, the ward sister came over to him and said, in a booming voice, 'Mr Bartholomew, you do not have to be funny here!' He replied, 'Well, Sister, that would be very stressful for me.' I love that. The poor sister trying to make him stop being funny and just relax, and Dad knowing that the effort that would take would have the opposite effect!

My mother was in bed at home when the phone rang that fateful night in November 1968. 'I'd been asleep, and it woke me up. I thought it was a cruel joke when they said it was the hospital and explained Eric had had a heart attack. And I went into shock and wasn't thinking straight. I rang my brother Alan up, and he came straight around and drove me to Leeds, still with me in shock.'

What I now recognise, as my father clearly did back in November 1968, is all that really came to matter in that near-death moment was his health. This would dictate

159

his future both with his family and with his partner. It was fairly inevitable that the wheels were going to come off for Eric and Ernie before long: it was never feasible it could last for ever with their flitting to and from America with huge commitments always waiting for them back in the UK. Not unexpectedly, it was my father's health that put a stop to it, as he was this irrepressible comedian living on his nerves, still possibly slightly dazed by all that he and Ernie had achieved in an insane eight-year period, neither man possessing the necessary knowhow (and who did back then?) to sustain a successful career as part of a double act without keeping impossible hours and taking on overwhelming workloads.

This era in their careers was a long while before comedians were setting up their own production companies and taking long breaks away from work by doing the occasional panel show to keep their profile up. But one immediate result was that the thoughts of power, affluence, riches and a promising future that had once seemed of absolute importance suddenly did not.

In a way, the signs had been there the previous year while they were in summer season in Great Yarmouth. Again, as when visiting Ed Sullivan's house, through some random diary notes, we discovered that my father had complained of pains in his left arm, and not feeling quite a hundred per cent. He took himself to a doctor in Yarmouth, but other than being advised to take it easier after the summer season was over, and relax more – neither suggestion taken, or remotely feasible – he ploughed on right up to his health crash of November 1968 at the age of forty-two.

Ernie made the observation, a few years after my father's death, that some people burn through life, here one moment in glorious Technicolor, and gone in a blink, while others take greater care to mount up the years. 'No one way is the right way,' he remarked, 'it's just a personal choice.' He was naturally alluding to his partner in this conversation, and I'm not sure my father, long term at least, ever considered the latter approach of how to live his life. Once he burst on to the scene, whatever that scene amounted to back in the 1930s, there was essentially no stopping him. He was a powerhouse of energy and activity, determined, with Sadie's support, to achieve what he could with his God-given talent.

Post 1968, certain protections were put in place to ease his path back, but what no one had anticipated, M&W included, was that far from this being the pinnacle of Morecambe and Wise as a hugely successful double act, it was barely the start.

Once safe enough for him to leave the Leeds Infirmary, my father found himself back at home in Harpenden. The house was partially rearranged so he could sleep downstairs, which was an odd aspect of the whole affair for the family. This, more than anything, reminded me he was a sick man.

We all had to tiptoe around him, and keep noise to a minimum – not always easy for a fifteen-year-old and a twelve-year-old. I know that for me, personally, it was as if my father had gone off to work somewhere in the north of England one day, and then returned months later as an old man!

GAIL: I remember quite a lot about Dad's heart attack itself in Leeds. But my memories thereafter seem a little different to yours. I was living at home, studying for O levels at school. You were weekly boarding, so just home at the weekends. I remember Mum coming into my bedroom much earlier than usual, and giving me the news. I remember her leaving very early with Uncle Alan for Leeds. I sorted out two dogs, five cats and my horse and then met my lift to school at the top of the road. It was a lift with a friend from my class and her father.

I must have looked like something was badly wrong as it wasn't long before my friend's dad asked me if everything was okay. I think my form teacher had heard and called me up to his table after registration. Everyone at school was really very good about it all. Beyond that, it is a complete blank apart from one very vivid memory of Dad sitting up in bed, downstairs in the room we called the playroom. He seemed to me to be fine, no sign of being ill at all! I do remember a LOT of cards and letters arriving. Beyond that, I have nothing. That's being a teenager, I suppose!

The first thing my father agreed with Ernie was to take six months off. Three months was the recommended minimum time, during which he was advised not even to read a stimulating book or watch anything much on television. The reason he decided to make it six months rather than the advised three was that he knew he hadn't stopped being in full flow since childhood, and if ever he was to return to show business again, he needed to be a much fitter version of the person he'd been up to now. He didn't want to become what the writer Martin Sterling referred to as a victim of comedy!

Dad had to keep tranquil, walking very short amounts each day, but increasing as he felt able with each successive walk. He was very disciplined with this, and I would sometimes join him.

At the beginning of his recovery, we would walk no further than about four hundred yards, then turn back and walk home. I always found that a bit strange being so young and fit. What impressed me the most, though, was how accepting of his situation he was – there was no hint of playing the victim. He always said there had to be a price to pay for all the amazing things that had happened to him. Maybe this was it!

He stuck to this programme – exercise and diet being the two most significant elements – and began a good recovery, wonderfully supported by my mother as only a partner can do, and solidly backed up by Ernie and the head of BBC light entertainment, Bill Cotton.

Bill Cotton

Bill Cotton was born on 23 April 1928 in Paddington, London. After doing his national service in the Royal Army Service Corps., he worked for the music composer and publisher Noel Gay and then the music publishing company Chappell. His father, the bandleader Billy Cotton, lent him the funds to set up Michael Reine Music with Johnny Johnston. In 1956, Cotton joined the BBC as a producer.

In 1962, Bill became assistant head of light entertainment. He then became head of light entertainment at the BBC in 1970.

In 1977, Cotton became controller of BBC One. He subsequently became deputy managing director of television in 1981 and managing director of television in 1984. After his retirement from the BBC, he became the chairman at Noel Gay Television. Other engagements in his later years included chairman of Meridian Broadcasting, president of the Royal Television Society and vice president of the Marie Curie Cancer Care charity. He also became a magistrate.

In March 1995, Cotton was 'humbled and amazed' to be the subject of *This is Your Life*. Guests who gave their thanks on the programme included Cilla Black, Ernie Wise, Bruce Forsyth, Mike Yarwood and Terry Wogan. Michael Grade and Billy Marsh also appeared.

Bill Cotton was awarded an OBE in 1976, appointed a CBE in 1989, was knighted in 2001 and won a BAFTA Fellowship Award in 1998. He died on 11 August 2008 in Bournemouth, Dorset.

'He [Eric] slowly began to recover his strength,' recalls my mother. 'But he continued to feel vulnerable for a long time, like he was taking a risk doing anything.'

She adds, 'He gave up the cigarettes straight after that first heart attack. He went to smoking a pipe and the occasional cigar, which wouldn't be at all sensible nowadays, but it was a big concession back in the late sixties when everyone seemed to smoke.' They even had a pipe-smoker of the year award, of which my father was a recipient in 1970, two years after nearly dying! It seems utter madness now, but even my father's doctor smoked a pipe, often when he was examining my father at the family house.

Now that cigarettes were more detrimental to his health than ever before, my father simply never referenced them again. Occasionally, he'd even grimace if someone reminded him of how he used to smoke them – and how many he could get through. Sixty a day was normal.

What of Ernie during his partner's convalescence? 'Like all of us,' recalls my mother, 'Ernie was just waiting to see what might happen next. He was naturally worried, but there was nothing he or we could do but wait to see how things panned out.'

'It was the shoes I remember most,' Ernie wrote of that time. 'Eric's shoes standing marooned and empty on the hotel-room floor when I set off to collect his things . . . Why they affected me as they did, I do not know. Was it because they conjured up images of retirement (or hanging them up for good), or that they suggested phrases like "following in somebody's footsteps", or, worse, "stepping into dead men's shoes"? I know only that the sight of his shoes, which I called to mind once again when he died, filled me with more sadness than I could have imagined, providing me with yet another incentive to keep working.'

GAIL: I did a Q&A at the Roses Theatre on one of the anniversaries of Dad's death. It followed *Morecambe*, the play performed so brilliantly by Bob Golding. It was all very moving. The audience had several people in it that had been there on the fatal night, which added greatly to the poignancy. When I was leaving the theatre, an elderly gentleman was waiting to speak to me. He proceeded to tell me that he had been the ambulance driver that had taken my father to the hospital. It was a very moving conversation. He wanted me to know that Dad had been alive on arrival and because of that he really thought that Dad would be fine. He talked about the pressure of driving Britain's best loved comedian, the huge responsibility they had all felt in that ambulance. But the main thing he wanted to say was that having delivered Dad, he was asked to fetch his shoes from the back of the ambulance. He said that it had been emotionally quite overwhelming to see them there and the thing he just couldn't believe was how small they were. Almost like children's shoes. He asked me, 'What size were his shoes? Did he really have such small feet?' I laughed and confirmed that he certainly did - size 6 and narrow. Dad used to call himself Twinkle Toes, and was very proud to have dainty feet, and never had a blister in his life!

The biggest turning point in regaining his health during this period of convalescence was when his doctor turned up one day, gave him a brief examination and suggested he did six holes of golf with him that afternoon on the nearby course. My father was utterly shocked, claiming he was ill. But like most patients, he went along with his doctor's advice. And he returned from this outing feeling great, like he'd really achieved something. A big shift took place from then on.

Ernie's patience was severely tested during this period. The sheer uncertainty of everything must have been stressful. 'If the doctor had said there was no chance of him ever working again, that would have put a completely different complexion on to things,' said Ernie. 'But as it was I had to stand by him, just as he would have done for me.' And Ernie noticed the difference in their later phone calls, as suddenly his partner was talking ideas about the act, and referring to 'when we get started again'.

SIDENOTE: During this recovery period, my father resumed his lifelong love of following football. Luton Town FC was conveniently near, and so we both started going to games. He became a director and vice president, and his love for the club never faltered for the remainder of his life. And Ernie used the enforced lay-off to pursue his love of boats. Though he would undoubtedly rather have been in the studios, he was more often seen serenely cruising on his own boat around the waters of Maidenhead.

As my father began to accept the shock that sudden ill-health had completely turned his life upside down, I remember another visit to our house by his local doctor – one of the many regular ones. As he left, my father said to me, 'Well, that's good news.'

'What is?' said I.

'The doc reckons there's no reason at all why I shouldn't make it into a ripe old age.'

'Really? Oh, great, Dad.'

'Yes. Maybe even seventy or more!'

Bill Cotton had been more than obligingly supportive of Eric and Ernie from the outset, and put them under no pressure in terms of returning to the studios. Cotton wanted a fit and healthy Morecambe and Wise, not a pressured one made to feel guilty for having been away for so long. He loved the first series they had done for the BBC prior to my father's heart attack, and naturally he wanted more. He often said that whatever magic it was that Morecambe and Wise weaved, ultimately both they and their shows were just plain funny.

I clearly recall Bill Cotton visiting my father about three months after his return home from the Leeds hospital. Cotton explained that he wanted their shows lengthened, and with more rehearsal time – so taking any excess pressure off both men. Furthermore, in an act of pure faith, he offered them another contract for July 1969.

I kept in contact with Bill Cotton until his death in 2008. We didn't often see each other, but when we did we always loved talking about the BBC days of Morecambe and Wise. His face would light up at the memories. Yet it was clear he never got over their desertion in 1977, when they left the BBC for Thames Television. He regarded it as something worse than a divorce. 'Bill knew how the business operated,' Michael Grade points out. 'He might have hated their departing the BBC for Thames, but he'd have understood it.'

It was interesting to discover, decades later when talking with TV presenter, writer and comedian Paul Merton, that just prior to my father's death, Bill Cotton and my father had been in touch with each other. My father was suggesting things weren't quite working out at Thames, and that a return to the BBC wasn't out of the question. Cotton had told Merton about this in conversation. It came as such a surprise to me, because my father hadn't made any reference to this at the time. I suppose that was because time was running out for him by then.

PART TWO

HOW TO SURVIVE AT THE TOP OF A MOUNTAIN

THIRTEEN

The writers for Morecambe and Wise, Dick Hills and Sid Green, who had journeyed with them through the successful years at ATV and the first series for Bill Cotton at the BBC, had now gone. Much has been said and written about how they deserted what they saw as a sinking ship due to my father becoming incapacitated, but that's possibly a little harsh. Both men had their own careers and families to think about, and the future for Morecambe and Wise in November 1968 was far from certain. The only thing that truly hurt Eric and Ernie was how they were never directly told about their writers' exit.

Bill Cotton, who before my father's heart attack already had bigger ideas fermenting for Morecambe and Wise beyond the ATV years, including fifty-minute shows instead of the half-hours, had a meeting with Roger Hancock, agent for Hills and Green.

'Roger told me that Hills and Green would only sign a contract for Morecambe and Wise if they were also allowed to be executive producers on the show,' recalled Cotton. 'I told him that wasn't something which was even worth discussing.'

Hills and Green, therefore, signed a contract to remain

at ATV, which brought to an end a long and highly successful association.

'In any event, I think their relationship with Hills and Green would have fractured,' says Michael Grade, 'because I don't think Hills and Green ever gave Eric and Ernie full credit for what they achieved with their material.'

Michael has a vivid memory of being in the dressing room with Eric and Ernie at the recording of one of their ATV shows at Elstree. 'Sid and Dick were in the room with the boys, and holding some type of inquest of the show. They were being quite critical. When eventually they left the room, I remember Eric clenching his fists and looking so angry at their negativity. They were always so down on the boys' performances, listing all the "you got this wrong and you got that wrong", almost arrogantly negative. That really got to your father in particular. M&W were always independent by nature, and never wanted to be reliant on anybody. In my opinion, Sid and Dick thought they had the boys on a leash, really.' He does however add, 'Sid and Dick served them well. Some of those sketches they created for them are absolutely brilliant. But while Sid and Dick's sketches were clever, they weren't character-based. However, those years with them served a purpose. Eric and Ernie learned how to work on television.'

Happily, neither side of the professional divorce from Hills and Green harboured any long-term bad feelings. Although it pre-dates the separation from Sid and Dick six months later, both the writers came to my parents' house in May 1968 to watch the European Cup final between Manchester United and Benfica. This shows to me that they must have been on more than just speaking terms. Whatever the tensions, they could still have a few beers and watch football together, and exist separately from what might have been going on at the studios.

I also recall a function at the Grosvenor Hotel in the mid-1970s, where Dick Hills was master of ceremonies, and in that role had to hand my father a comedy award. I remember I felt a momentary sense of discomfort – a 'what might happen here?' type of feeling – but shortly afterwards I could see the two of them chatting and chuckling some distance away from the rest of the packed ballroom. They clearly had much to catch up on, and in a positive way.

I would agree wholeheartedly with the idea that M&W were embracing a new beginning in 1969. Even at home, I sensed my father was developing into the persona he felt he should be in comedic terms. The likeable idiot of the variety halls and ATV – which had served him and Ernie so well over the years – possibly didn't sit so comfortably with someone who had just stared death in the face. And also it was dated. It was locked more into music hall than modern colour television. And I noticed that whenever the Marx Brothers, *The Phil Silvers Show* or Jack Benny cropped up on television, he would always watch and observe them. And in the years to come you don't have to look much further than a combination of Groucho Marx, Phil Silvers and Jack Benny to see the reinvention of Eric Morecambe as the comedian we all came to know.

My father made the brave decision, with Ernie's

agreement, that to focus on quality shows for the BBC, everything else had to be jettisoned – summer seasons, pantos, the trips stateside for Ed Sullivan, the big movie ideas. They would become home-based comedians, more available to their own country, and always working from their own homes as the base for whatever they did. There would be no more months spent away, either abroad or constantly travelling here, there and everywhere for unnecessary work obligations.

In an interview at this time, my father said, 'We're going for things that produce more money, but aren't as time-consuming or hectic.' Very pragmatic.

And as Ernie added in the same interview, 'One thing Eric's heart attack showed me was that people want the team Morecambe and Wise. When there's only one of us, the appeal is different.' Prophetic words these would prove.

And so the wheels began to turn again.

There was a new edge to Eric and Ernie that the family, and those close to the double act, couldn't miss. If pressed, I would say it manifested mostly through an absence of stress and mania that had accompanied the treadmill he and Ernie had been on for the previous decade.

With a change of pace and direction, and with a new employer in the BBC, without doubt my father was more at ease than he had been for years. In the past, not only had he been physically absent quite a bit, he'd been emotionally absent, too. And living around that stress must have been exhausting not only for the man himself, but also for his partner working next to him. And it hadn't been ideal for us, the family, either.

Eric Morecambe was now fully recovered, and for the first time in a long time was really beginning to enjoy himself, and to be excited at what lay ahead.

Having said that, whatever lay ahead of them in terms of their future television shows lacked a writer or writers.

And so began the creation of a further partnership for the annals of British entertainment history with the arrival of one Eddie Braben.

Eddie Braben was a Liverpudlian with the gift of coming up with hilarious lines. He was a surprisingly shy man who never relished the spotlight, especially in the early days of his association with M&W.

Despite his inherent shyness, he had a mind that seemed to work in funny lines. He just couldn't stop himself. I recall him ringing my father up when I was a kid, and I answered the phone. This was before I'd met him and then got to know him for the rest of his life. 'How old are you?' he asked me.

'Fourteen,' I replied.

'Really? You sound very tall for your age!'

And from that moment on, I don't think I ever had a conversation with Eddie that didn't operate along those unusual lines – certainly not one you could categorise as conventional.

Eddie, who had written for Ken Dodd and would later write for countless others, didn't really want the job of writing for Morecambe and Wise. Bill Cotton *did* want

Eddie Braben, particularly on learning he'd parted company with Ken Dodd.

'I don't do sketches,' Eddie told Cotton, 'I only write jokes.'

In an interview he said, 'I worked for Doddy for fifteen years, and the rate [for gags] was something like eight per minute. They were fast.'

Eddie had never been a fan of Morecambe and Wise's *Two of a Kind* series. 'I told them this when I met them for the first time at the invitation of Bill Cotton. He asked if I would like to write for Eric and Ernie, and of course I said yes I would. But I told him they weren't really my style after fifteen years with Doddy ... I was asked to go and meet them in two days' time, and I agreed.'

And this would be the meeting that changed everything. 'I went into Bill's office,' recalled Eddie, 'and the meeting lasted for about three hours. I think, though, it took about ten minutes for me to realise that something magical had happened between the three of us. What it was I don't know, but there was something there, something inexplicable.'

Eric and Ernie would only come to recognise later how well the three of them bounced off each other, whereas Eddie saw their connection, and possibly the part he could play in developing it, almost immediately. 'The meeting continued, and I watched the two of them, the way they spoke and the way they behaved and the way they were with one another. I knew then what was missing from the Eric and Ernie I had seen on television ... It was warmth.'

What transpired from this new association was that

Eddie discovered he *could* write sketches, and Eric and Ernie discovered they could operate as something almost entirely different from what they'd been before. Eric and Ernie massively tweaked Eddie's scripts, but it was Eddie who gave them the scope to do so.

It wasn't an immediate result, though. Eddie remembered the initial reaction to the first script he had to go home and rattle off for them at speed. 'It was probably the most frantic week's writing I have ever done in my life. I went back the following week with what must have been twenty foolscap pages. It was the complete show the way that I saw it.'

Eric and Ernie read it with Eddie and Bill Cotton sitting there. 'They read it, and they laughed, and they got to the end and said they couldn't do it ... They said they hadn't done anything like it before, they had never worked like that before or used words like that before.'

Fortunately, Bill Cotton thought that they were wrong. 'I kept quiet,' said Eddie. 'You don't argue with the comedians. Bill said let's give it a try on BBC Two – there's only about thirty-seven people watching BBC Two, so it wouldn't do any harm. They did it on BBC Two, and we all know what happened after that.'

Eddie had never liked M&W's original incarnation as two music hall comics, as he saw them. 'I didn't believe in them. No one could really be that stupid as Eric was supposed to be,' he once told me, as he told many others before and after. 'And Ernie as straight man was precisely that – just another straight man.'

It is certainly true that like his partner, Ernie hadn't been able to move on from the know-it-all, aggressive feed, setting up lines for the fool, before shouting him down. That traditional format didn't allow the warmth to come through, as Eddie saw it. 'They were still Abbott and Costello by the time they'd finished with ATV,' said Eddie.

Eddie was therefore given free rein to reimagine and develop Ernie's role, to make him a character in his own right. It's important to mention that from the earliest of times in his friendship with my father, Ernie intuited every verbal digression that his partner, unpremeditatedly, went on. This in turn gave his partner great scope to be more realistic in his humour, and less the gormless fool. My father could rant, and Ernie could keep up.

This new improved Ernie was now a somewhat pompous playwright with pretensions of producing works 'Like wot Shakespeare did!' He was also made into a skinflint – similar to the way Jack Benny played his comedy.

And this was brilliant, for as Eddie said himself, once Ernie was in place, 'I didn't need to touch Eric's character at all.' And that is such genius, as the absolute natural thing would have been for a new writer to come in and go hard at the funny man and make him say lots of funny lines, and do lots of funny moves, while continuing to be fed by the straight man. But my father was now given free rein to mock Ernie's pretensions, and this allowed Marx, Silvers and Benny – masters at this persona – to merge in my father, and turn what had been the gormless fool into a sharp and knowing partner. They went from Abbott and Costello to being more Laurel and Hardy with Eddie Braben's ideas and guidance.

It worked so well that I would go as far as saying my

father became more this creation even away from the studios than he'd been before. He could suddenly breathe and show just how naturally funny he was. You could say that in creating a new Ernie Wise, Eddie Braben had created a new Eric Morecambe – or, that is, released the one that had been locked away in the genie's lamp all those past decades.

Once the ball was rolling, Eric and Ernie remained supportive of Eddie's material. I remember on many occasions my father telling me that they couldn't do what they were doing without Eddie providing the basic material. 'Without Eddie,' he would say, 'we'd be left staring at blank pages.' In later years, my father also told me his favourite Eddie Braben line of all time. It was – perhaps unsurprisingly – on hearing an emergency vehicle shoot by: 'He's not going to sell much ice cream going at that speed, is he?' My own personal favourite was when Ernie was in their 'apartment', hammering away at a typewriter, working on yet another one of his 'plays wot he wrote'!

ERIC: Ern, the Brothers Grimm were good, but you're grimmer . . .

Eddie was the master of the great one-liners, hence his long association with Ken Dodd. But it had clearly come as a surprise to himself to discover he could reinvent a double act as established as Morecambe and Wise, and in doing so create something we hadn't ever seen in terms of double acts on British television. He pretty much created, if not a sitcom, then a world entirely of its own – a fantasy that was so beguiling it enabled them, unlike almost all other performers I can think of, to remain pertinent today, and wholly entertaining.

What Eric and Ernie themselves brought to these shows was an ironic nod to their own past. The BBC studios had special curtains – tabs – made, with a bold M&W logo, for Eric and Ernie to enter and depart through, as though on a variety stage. This not only nodded to the past, but became a great comic device for my father – sometimes he'd pretend to strangle himself, or sometimes just his glasses would appear through the curtains, and on almost every occasion he'd pretend he couldn't get through the curtains.

Thus was marked the beginning of a great relationship, not just between Eddie Braben and M&W, but between Eric and Ernie and their vast army of fans. Actress Glenda Jackson, who would appear on five of their shows, said that '. . . they were loved by their audience. I don't think that's too extreme a word . . . The response the audience had towards them was such that you, as a guest star, were enveloped in that love as well.'

It's fair to say that much of this love emanated from the perfect balance of their shows, and the new format that would be tweaked a little but ultimately would take them on their journey to the very end.

Eddie Braben

Eddie Braben was born on 31 October 1930 in Dingle, Liverpool. After working in the British American Tobacco factory and undertaking national service in the Royal Air Force at RAF Kenley, he became a market trader with his own greengrocery stall, purchased for him by his father. His dream, however, was to be a professional gag-writer. Braben spent time sending a selection of jokes to comedians of the period. His first sale was to Charlie Chester. But his big break came with the toothy comedian Ken Dodd. Eddie wrote a staggering number of jokes for Dodd for fifteen years.

Having proved his ability to write the kind of material Morecambe and Wise needed for their shows, he began a long period of writing award-winning scripts for the duo, taking breaks when the stress made demands on his health. Due to their achievements together, Eric, Ernie and Eddie were nick-named 'The Golden Triangle'.

Braben also wrote books, including *The Book What I Wrote: Eric, Ernie and Me*.

Eddie died on 21 May 2013 in North Wales.

A little later, and two other key characters would appear in their set-up: Janet Webb and Arthur Tolcher. Janet, a delightful lady whom I liked enormously, would appear at the end of their shows (for several series up to 1974), to brush Eric and Ernie aside before the titles came up, and say: 'I'd like to thank all of you for watching me and my little show here tonight. If you've enjoyed it, then it's all been worthwhile. So, until we meet again, goodnight, and I love you all!'

She was a talented lady, a great singer and a capable actress, living at a time when sadly her voluptuous figure overshadowed all else that might have presented her with a more stable career. I know as a fact that she resented that enormously, and it brought a profound sadness to her life. All I can say in relation to Eric and Ernie is that both of them were always incredibly upbeat about her and hated any negative press she received. She was sparkling company to be around, and always smiling.

Arthur Tolcher also became a stalwart of the shows. It was in the days of Jack Hylton that he'd first crossed paths with Eric and Ernie. A harmonica player who never learned to read music, Arthur could retain a large repertoire and play them on request. Whenever a harmonica player was required, be it for theatre or in the studio for the likes of singer Frank Ifield, Arthur was the man to call. But he had chosen a dicey showbiz path. He had a gimmick or two – playing harmonicas of various sizes, and even pretending to swallow the smallest one – and as such was useful for pantos around the Midlands where he based himself for much of his life. But it was a tough way to make a living.

In the days of *Youth Takes a Bow*, someone would be on stage with various props, then turn to look off stage and say, 'Now? Now? . . . Not now!' Eric and Ernie were there at that time, and logged it.

By the 1970s, Arthur was really struggling to find work, and Eric and Ernie heard about this, probably through the BBC, who Arthur (and originally his mother), had been consistently bombarding with requests for work. It didn't take a moment for them to come up with the great idea of involving him as the harmonica player he was, but who was never allowed the opportunity to play. It's classic M&W – great intentions punctured at every opportunity. 'Not now, Arthur,' they would say each time he started playing. It became a very popular moment in the television shows, culminating in Arthur joining them on their live tours of the 1970s.

He was the permanent guest star, without ever being a true star. But there was a camaraderie there that couldn't be faked, as they'd all known each other from around the age of fifteen. And Tolcher's mother – Beatrice – was a friend of my grandmother, Sadie. I never met Beatrice (affectionately known as 'Beef'!). That was way before my time. But I wouldn't like to have crossed her, judging by the anecdotes and photos.

Morecambe and Wise, without ever seeming to try, managed to transcend generations. Any age could join the party, and considering this for the most part was the 1970s, there was nothing stereotypical in their shows or performances. You could be educated or uneducated; religious or not; wealthy or poor; white or black or green with pink spots; Labour, Liberal or Tory – their humour contained no agenda: no hidden message or malice; no intellectual nods and winks. They and their material existed purely to be funny.

Ultimately, they delivered their brand of comedy as two besuited, middle-aged men who had never really been able to accept becoming mature adults. They played their parts like two teenagers who had probably been kicked out of college and told to get jobs. M&W performed with such polish and perfect timing one could not help but be seduced by them.

The love for them that Glenda Jackson referenced became more evident in 1969, when Bill Cotton realised that despite the feature films and festive fare that the BBC was providing throughout the Christmas period, people were mostly talking about Morecambe and Wise.

1970 would mark the first year of a conscious M&W Christmas show, as opposed to just another show that happened to be transmitted over Christmas. As Cotton said, 'I think the second Christmas show they did for us was about the biggest thing that had happened on British television up to that point.'

And so began a new era of Morecambe and Wise – one that would smoothly move from just television series to Christmas shows without a hitch. And what became apparent from 1970 onwards was that if any great ideas came up during the course of rehearsals, Eddie would keep them back for the Christmas special. Christmas became the 'big event' show, and possibly what M&W are to this day remembered for. But as Doreen Wise once said, 'Back then there were only three TV channels, and on Christmas Day it would be the Queen's speech followed by *The Morecambe & Wise Show* . . . It was challenging work for them. And they also did many other things outside of the shows, too. Telethons, auctions and working in variety clubs.'

This new era also heralded the beginning of inviting guest stars on the show on a regular basis, not just because variety-based shows did that, but more because Eric and Ernie, through their development with Eddie Braben, could use guests to a wonderful comedic end. A guest was no longer used purely to deliver a number on the show.

Their whole attitude to the guest star, and the almost casually dismissive air they would deliberately use towards them, required their guests to be top-drawer players. They had to be big enough to subtly mock and knock – and not so subtly on occasion – because in doing it that way, it would always be Eric and Ernie who would remain looking the fools. As my father used to say, 'You can't do that to the lesser known guests, as it looks cruel.'

Other than the crosstalk segments at the opening of their shows, the guest star moments were always my personal favourite ones. Eddie Braben gave them such funny lines that delineated their BBC personas. When Angharad Rees was on a show, my father is fulsome in his praise. 'I'll tell you something, Hand Grenade. I was thrilled when I realised that you'd escaped from Colditz . . .' Ernie has to explain that Angharad was the star of *Poldark* and not *Colditz*.

Then there was the tenor John Hanson, who appeared in their 1973 Christmas show. He starts singing from one of his musicals, and Eric frowns and says, 'Get off, we don't want any of that rubbish here . . .'

Or the tall and slender actress Vanessa Redgrave. Exiting the stage, she says, 'I'll be right back.' Eric turns to Ernie, and says, 'Right back? She's tall enough to play in goal!'

And always calling their female guest stars 'young sir!' and the male ones, 'madam!'

With all this wonderful tomfoolery, it genuinely surprises me that anyone ever turned down the opportunity of being on their shows, surely recognising that the gag was Eric and Ernie making themselves look ignorant in front of their bemused guest star. But two (not mentioned here) notables did decline, and maybe there were others. One who allegedly regretted turning down the opportunity was composer Lord Andrew Lloyd-Webber.

Richard Burton was keen but then unable due to contracted work in America, which ultimately clashed. 'It was going to be *Hamlet*,' recalled producer John Ammonds, many years later. 'Burton would come on with that lovely voice, and begin with "To be or not to be, that is the question." Eric would come up behind the rampart with a white sheet over his head and his glasses over the top . . . Eric would say, "Look, sorry to interrupt you. You're doing very well, and I can see how you got where you are. It's terrific stuff. But . . . don't lose confidence. The trouble is, I've got to hear you when you say 'string and arrows'. That's my cue, you see. But I can't hear you very well behind that wall. Have you got any more voice? Can you say it a bit louder?"'

SIDENOTE: John Ammonds was rewarded with an MBE in 1975. Ernie hadn't read about it, and didn't believe Johnny when he rang him up to share his news. Ernie then rang up the BBC to make sure he wasn't having his leg pulled! 'They didn't tell me what it was for,' recalled Johnny. 'I presume it was for services to television.'

Part of my father's recovery from his heart attack was to ensure other aspects around his work were made easier. This led to him taking on a full-time chauffeur in Michael Fountain, who passed in 2022 at the age of seventy-nine.

Mike became a part of the family – certainly someone who was always there at all significant events. What my father particularly liked about Mike – who had already driven him on occasion as an employee of a car company – was that he didn't talk unnecessarily or ask repetitive, invasive questions. There was instant trust there, to the extent that Mike would even befriend Ernie, and get involved with the behind-the-scenes elements of their touring shows in the seventies.

I have a clear and fond image of Mike polishing my father's Rolls Royce just before they were due to head off somewhere, and then, when they were both settled in the car, Mike in his grey chauffeur's suit and matching cap, they would cruise up the drive with smoke bellowing out of the windows, as both men smoked a pipe.

Mike also became involved with the domestic side. During the school holidays, after he'd dropped my father at the rehearsal studios, he'd take me to Heathrow with my mate Bill Drysdale to watch the planes taking off and landing.

Gail, Steven and I kept in contact with him right up to the end, and still keep in touch with his family. They live in Morecambe!

FOURTEEN

Bill Cotton commented that the 1970s were a remarkable time for light entertainment at the BBC. *The Good Life, Dad's Army* and *Monty Python's Flying Circus*, to name but a few, bear that out. 'But I must be honest,' he went on, 'and say that Morecambe and Wise were at the heart of it all. They were the Head Prefects.'

They were now in a comfortable place, where a steady routine of sorts existed and they had the perfect team falling into place around them. Not least, of course, their writer Eddie Braben.

I think it's important to focus a little on Eddie's relationship with Eric and Ernie, which wasn't really reflected accurately in the 2017 TV film, *Eric, Ernie and Me*.

Possibly the roles of Eric and Ernie were deliberately miscast to accentuate Stephen Tompkinson, the one bright light of this otherwise fantasy drama, as he did manage to project some of Eddie Braben's spirit quite successfully. 'They couldn't have given the role to a better person,' says Dee Braben. 'He really caught Eddie's look, even the hairline. But with the story, they had to pack in a lot in a short space of time, and that's when much of it is artistic licence. And we're looking at it through different eyes from those involved, and those of the viewers, of course.'

Taking up Dee's comments, the problem those of us close to Eddie and M&W had with this film is that it didn't depict their true relationship, simple as that. I never read the script, but the writer – Neil Forsyth – read it out to me in a restaurant. That way I didn't get to see the incidentals, as I call them, where for instance my mother appears swearing and smoking a cigarette. She never swears, and she's never smoked! That is just one of many examples of a character recreated inappropriately to make the material more edgy.

Ultimately, there isn't really a story to tell. Eric, Ernie and Eddie – and all those working with and around them – got on just fine and enjoyed the hard work they were doing. 'From the moment they met, it was always the three of them,' comments Dee. 'They knew what they were achieving together, and they constantly had laughs all the way through those times together.'

Eddie Braben once stayed at my parents' house, which demonstrates how comfortable they must have all been together. Of that occasion, Dee says, 'After a while your mother told Eddie to take your father out for a walk. Apparently, your father was restless and bored being indoors. Eddie always described himself as "all bush and heath", so had no problem in taking her up on the idea. They went out for a short walk together, then Eric took Eddie to the home of the artist Gordon Beningfield, who was a big friend of Eric's. Eddie was so impressed with his watercolours, he bought two of them!'

Dee adds a fascinating point: 'I do sometimes wonder if Eric and Ernie would have been the much-loved double act they are to this day, had not fate teamed them up with

Eddie.' To which I can wholeheartedly say, No – they wouldn't have been.

That was the beauty of their coming together – and the timing of when it happened. It was an event that seems unlikely had my father's health not failed so drastically, and all at the perfect time in their unfolding story: the one time when bad health proved to be a useful thing. It certainly unified writer and performers, and that was so needed at this moment in their careers. They were instantly closer than brothers. 'It took only minutes after they first met up at the BBC Studios,' says Dee.

I've often wondered, however, what might have occurred if the writers Ray Galton and Alan Simpson had got their hands on Morecambe and Wise, what magic would possibly have occurred. But we can only speculate. I could envisage some amazing sitcoms, though, along the lines of their wonderful creation, *Steptoe and Son*.

Ray Galton wrote, 'During our long and varied career, we had the pleasure of working with most of the top-line comedians in the business, some of whom actually survived the experience! The one notable exception was Morecambe and Wise, whom we never wrote for, something we always regretted, they being one of the few double acts who were worth twice as much money as the best solo acts. In actual fact, they were a treble act. We must never forget their writer, the superb Eddie Braben.'

SIDENOTE: I met Ray Galton and Alan Simpson just the once. Galton asked where I was living. My mother

194

Eddie Braben once said to me that all he ever did when
he was with my father and Ernie was laugh. Yes, I'm sure
they argued over the occasional line here and there with
the scripts Eddie provided – maybe even took him for
granted on occasion – but there was never a dark cloud
hanging over them. There was certainly no demoralised
Eddie toing and froing on busy trains with a case of notes
as he has sometimes been portrayed.

Eddie was reclusive from day one, and that altered little
over the years. He made few appearances at rehearsals, and
that didn't trouble him or my father and Ernie. Most of his
scripts were sent down by Royal Mail. But as soon as Eddie
was in their orbit, you could hear the laughs a mile away.

These unexpected screen adaptations of the M&W
story have always been a source of consternation. Even
the late, great Victoria Wood, in her film made of M&W's
early days, diluted facts for the sake of pace and drama.
But at least it was a good film, managing to capture the
fundamental relationship of Eric, Ernie and Sadie.

SIDENOTE: Victoria Wood, when visiting the family
home in 2009 to discuss her film project, quietly asked

me if my mother was okay bringing us tea and biscuits in from the kitchen 'at her age'. Fast forward to 2023, and my mother's still bringing in tea and biscuits on a tray – if a little less comfortably – while poor Victoria died over seven years ago.

While I'm writing about writing, and about script-writers, I'm pausing to mention that Eric and Ernie often received unsolicited scripts. One arrived on the doormat, and all it contained, much to my father's amusement, was all their 'bits of business', as he called it, linked together, and nothing else!

Eric joins Ernie in front of camera. He wiggles his glasses, and tells Ernie, 'You can't see the join, Ern. Best wig you've ever had.' He then slaps Ernie on the face, before looking at the camera and saying, 'This boy's a fool.' He puts his arm behind the curtain and begins to strangle himself. Eric turns to Ernie and says, 'How are the short fat hairy legs, Ern?' The author of the piece then suggested that he and Ernie 'can fill in the rest for yourselves'.

Eat your heart out, Sid, Dick and Eddie!

At this point in 1970, the BBC M&W team was Bill Cotton, head of light entertainment and therefore over-seer of all discussions, Eddie Braben on script duties and John Ammonds as show producer.

John Ammonds

John Ammonds was born on 21 May 1924 in Kennington, London. Bored with education, and after briefly working as a part-time civil servant at the London County Council, he gained employment at the BBC in 1941 as a sound effects operator. This led to him working in the Variety Department in London, Bristol and Bangor.

After being called up and joining the Army, Ammonds ended up in Army broadcasting in Hamburg. After being demobbed in 1947, he rejoined the BBC as a programme engineer and then as a studio manager. In 1954, Ammonds became a radio producer in Manchester. This was where he first met Morecambe and Wise and produced their series *YOYO* (*You're Only Young Once*).

Further training resulted in Ammonds becoming a television producer and director. His credits in the 1960s included *Here's Harry*, *The Dick Emery Show* and *The Val Doonican Show*.

John Ammonds was reunited with Morecambe and Wise at the BBC in 1968 and he worked with the double act until 1974.

The 1970s as a whole saw Ammonds helm television shows including *An Evening with Francis Howerd*, *Look, Mike Yarwood!* and *The Les Dawson Show*.

John was once again reunited with Morecambe and Wise at Thames Television. While there, he was also assigned shows including *Bernie* and *The Jim Davidson Show*.

In 1986, Ammonds become an executive producer at LWT. There, he oversaw programmes including the sitcom *Running Wild* and the comedy impressions show *Copy Cats*. Although he retired from broadcasting in 1988, he continued to give interviews about his life and career.

'I'd done a full series with Val Doonican,' recalled Ammonds in an interview a few years before his death. 'I was sitting in the BBC bar, and my boss, Bill Cotton, approached me ... He asked if I'd like to produce Morecambe and Wise.'

Due to a partly shared history through their years in radio, Eric and Ernie had decided in advance that John Ammonds was the man they wanted for the job. They knew how he worked, they felt comfortable with the idea of him being at the helm, and the three of them had good chemistry. There were no egos that could have derailed the new project they were embarking upon.

Personally, I always found Johnny Ammonds to be malleable. He was strong on getting across his own opinions, but in a calm way. And Eric and Ernie would listen and express their views, and Eddie Braben, when there – which was mostly on a Thursday for a read-through of his newest script – would join in, expressing his own opinions. And as I watched, I found it fascinating that slowly they would all start to see which one of them had the strongest idea – the idea that they needed to work with – and ultimately there would be collective agreement, and they'd move on until the next differing of opinion came along. It was all thoroughly civilised, and though it could occasionally get a little lively, it would be Johnny who would call for a tea break, and within

198

moments everyone was sipping tea and munching a biscuit and gagging about in near hysterical laughter. Then it would be back to the script and the disagreements, but calmer now, and a mutual acceptance of one specific idea would be reached – the decision made.

It wasn't an easy start for John Ammonds, for Eric and Ernie told him they needed the studio performing floor to be raised to deliberately create a theatre stage effect. Essentially, they were creating a proscenium arch so that it would feel to an audience they were in a theatre rather than a television studio. This would remain one of the strongest nods to Eric and Ernie's days of treading the boards.

'We had to crank the cameras as high as they would go so we weren't looking up their noses,' recalled Ammonds. But it all worked, and with the addition of the seemingly superfluous theatrical curtains – at least superfluous in Johnny Ammonds' mind – things began to formulate just as Eric and Ernie had hoped.

'A producer,' said Ammonds, 'would normally deal with the button pushing and the director would deal with the actors and cameras. I had to do both! I think it has its distinct advantage in comedy if you can think about the cameras during a rehearsal. Giving the artists direction, going for reaction shots, that kind of thing. You can find the best way of doing it. I also dealt with props and scenery and lighting.'

Morecambe and Wise had refined their personas now, and were finding great satisfaction in this new approach. As my mother once put it, 'Your father was a kind of straight man who was very funny, as opposed to Ernie, who became the comic who tried to be funny but wasn't.' And in a nutshell, that was how Eddie reconfigured M&W.

Eric, Ernie, Eddie and Johnny, and pretty soon Ernest Maxin on choreography, with Bill Cotton overseeing his big project while never directly interfering with the creative process. That was the team behind the amazing decade M&W would enjoy at the BBC.

SIDENOTE: During this golden BBC period, Eddie Braben began to feel the pressure of working on the Morecambe and Wise shows, notably their Christmas specials, and doing bits of material for other performers such as Des O'Connor and Bruce Forsyth. Eddie was constantly in demand.

'If he thought of a good idea for Eric and Ernie in the middle of the night,' recalls Dee Braben, 'he would have to get up and go and write it down. Although working on the shows and with Eric and Ernie was essentially fun, it was also a lot of hard work. A real strain.'

One day on a train in 1972, he all but collapsed. At that point he took three months off.

FIFTEEN

The shows were forward thinking in terms of how they were made. Former BBC top executive and now presenter Alan Yentob once told me that the Morecambe and Wise shows were crafted pieces, exactly worked out from beginning to end, supported by endless rehearsals.

My father would frequently shift a line here or there if it was too funny. 'Too funny' could damage the flow for the audience – it was important, in most situations, to have breathers and build up as the routine in question developed. Even choosing the right moment for a musical number or a guest star was integral to the finished product. This probably explains why the shows are still eminently watchable today, and frequently transmitted – each show is a piece of complete entertainment. The Two Ronnies, Messrs Barker and Corbett, have a similar legacy, but it's trickier for some artistes – absolutely great as they were – like Bruce Forsyth and Des O'Connor. You have in their case a medley of things they did which were excellent, rather than a pure forty-five-minute-to-one-hour crafted piece.

At Ernie Wise's funeral in 1999, Alan Yentob told me that he sees Morecambe and Wise and David Attenborough as the two cornerstones of what the BBC represents. Coming from him, that observation has stayed with me through the passing years.

Eric and Ernie were big fans of *The Two Ronnies*. Often considered rivals, they actually were not. They liked comedy too much, and respected other comedians too greatly, ever to view themselves as being in competition in some way. Indeed, my father and Ronnie Barker were building quite a friendship in the last five years of my father's life. They both had quick minds, and a funny line constantly on the end of the tongue. It was heart-warming to see the two of them together having a chuckle.

I think both the Ronnies took my father's departure badly. At the wake, which was back at my parents' house, I heard a downcast Ronnie Barker telling Ronnie Corbett that this would make him consider his own future, and what might or might not follow as a result of this loss. And Ronnie C was nodding in absolute agreement. It's worth noting that they ended their much-loved series two and a half years later. Also

Ernie with his parents, Harry and Connie. Despite him feigning that everything was wonderful, Ernie's childhood was in fact not a happy one, and he found himself the breadwinner from around the age of eight onwards. Doreen Wise referred to it as slave labour.

Doreen and Eric. This was snapped on their shared birthday, 14 May 1951.

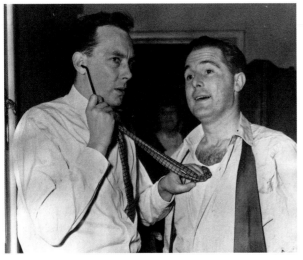

Eric examining Ernie's wallet!

Eric and Ernie, circa 1954. Durin the 1950s, many of their publicit stills had Eric holding a cigarette or cigar, and Ernie a pipe.

Ernie in a dressing room with singer Alma Cogan. Both Eric an Ernie were very fond of Cogan, who died tragically young.

Eric and Ernie on stage in the 1950s. At the start of that decade work was in short supply, but eventually it came along on a more regular basis

St Annes, Blackpool, 1957. Gary and Gail, with 'Uncle' Ern and 'Aunty' Doreen, plus their mum and dad. All in the name of summer season publicity.

Doreen, Ernie, Eric and Joan, with Gail and Gary at the front. Taken on a caravan park near Weymouth during a summer season in 1960.

Gary and Eric in 1965; Gary wearing a gold-plated guitar badge, given to him by his hero, the guitarist Bert Weedon.

Eric and Ernie, Joan and Doreen as they leave Heathrow for a week's holiday in Bermuda, before going on to New York to appear for the first time on *The Ed Sullivan Show* in 1963.

Doreen, Ernie, Eric, Joan, Gail and Gary and two naval officers at Portsmouth harbour in 1970. They flew in from Luton airport for one of the many events that M&W were invited to attend. Behind them is the Britten-Norman Islander aircraft in which they had just landed.

Eric and Ernie with André Previn, in arguably their greatest ever television moment, the Christmas show of 1971. Since then, whenever Previn visited London, taxi drivers would call him 'Mr Preview', much to the maestro's amusement.

Eric and Ernie alongside their wives, plus, from left to right: their scriptwriter Eddie Braben and his wife, Dee, producer Johnny Ammonds and his wife, Wyn. On this evening Eddie won the Writers' Guild of Great Britain award for Best British Light Entertainment Script for The Morecambe & Wise Show. One of many awards won by Eddie, Eric & Ernie.

Gary captures Eric and Joan in the garden of their villa in southern Portugal, circa 1977. It was at this villa that Eric would write the outline to the Tom Jones and Shirley Bassey routines that have since become part of entertainment history.

© Doug McKenzie

Ernie, Doreen and M&W's agent Billy Marsh. Billy brought them to television, and his greatest move came in 1960, when he convinced Lew Grade to give them their own TV series for ATV.

Eric and Ernie in Florida at the same time, which didn't occur very often, circa 1980.

Gary and Eric in the garden of the family home, August 1982.

'Hello sailor!' On the backwaters of the Thames around Maidenhead, Ernie was clearly a long way from his days shipping coal from Newcastle to Battersea during the war years.

Ernie and Doreen in later years, after Eric's death.

Gary, Joan and Gail at Luton Hoo, recording for the documentary
Morecambe & Wise: The Lost Tapes in October 2020.

Gary in Yorkshire in 2023, with his friend Tommy Cannon. Cannon and Ball fulfilled the prophecy made by Eric Morecambe shortly before his death that they would inherit Morecambe & Wise's crown.

David Bailey's 1970 shot of the duo captures the energy of their most successful decade.

interesting is that the pairing of Ronnies Barker and Corbett was Bill Cotton's idea. They were shown on the BBC from 1971 to 1987, though they did later come out of retirement to make a series called *The Two Ronnies Sketchbook*, which was a look back at their earlier work.

'Eric and Ernie did routines, whereas the Two Ronnies did sketches,' says comedian Steve Punt. 'So with Ronnie and Ronnie, they were two men teamed specifically to work as a television duo, and everything was cued. You knew where each of the sketches was going, and the gags were clearly posted and well defined. With Eric and Ernie, that wasn't the case. It was more about getting to know and understand their relationship, and waiting to see how that influenced what they were going to say or do. You couldn't pre-empt them. As a young kid, it was therefore much easier to watch and laugh at the Ronnies, but all the time I was growing more into Morecambe and Wise. Eventually I got it – I got who they were, and what they were about.'

Time drifted by. The shows came and went, and 1971 saw what would arguably become their most memorable Christmas show. This show would include guests such as actors Francis Matthews and Glenda Jackson, singer Shirley Bassey, and a certain conductor called André Previn.

It's a remarkable show, especially – though not only – for its guest stars. The Previn sketch has become something firmly stuck in the public psyche, a little like the Two Ronnies' 'Four Candles' sketch, and Monty Python's 'Dead Parrot' sketch.

André Previn

André Previn was reportedly born on 6 April 1929 in Berlin, Germany.

A musical prodigy, he was enrolled at the Berlin Conservatory when he was around the age of six.

Previn's family moved to Paris, where the young musician joined the Conservatoire de Paris. When their American visas finally arrived, they made their way to Los Angeles. André officially became a US citizen in 1943.

The various orchestras Previn worked with include the Houston Symphony Orchestra, Pittsburgh Symphony Orchestra, Los Angeles Philharmonic, Oslo Philharmonic, London Symphony Orchestra and Royal Philharmonic Orchestra.

Among Previn's many awards, he won four Oscars. They were for scoring the films *Gigi*, *Porgy and Bess*, *Irma La Douce* and *My Fair Lady*.

André Previn, who was awarded an honorary Knight Commander of the Order of the British Empire in 1996, died on 28 February 2019 in New York, aged eighty-nine.

John Ammonds was keen for some time to get André Previn on a Morecambe and Wise Christmas show. 'I'd seen him on a BBC Two programme talking to camera, and I knew he had a good experience with all kinds of entertainment,' Ammonds said. 'Eric said he liked the idea of using him for the Grieg sketch, but said I would never get him!'

Ammonds played amateur detective, and through the producer of the show he'd seen Previn on, managed to get the idea he had in mind through to Previn's agent.

'The following day,' said Ammonds, 'I got a call, and eventually spoke to the man himself. He was keen on the idea, and so it was up to him and me to put the plan together that fitted us both.'

Ammonds then had to tell them that Previn would be required for a week's rehearsal. 'I could almost hear a crash at the other end of the phone,' he recalled. André couldn't give up a whole week, so they agreed on three days.

'Eric was unhappy with the situation and expressed concern about how he [Previn] could learn the whole routine in that time . . .'

The read-through with my father, Ernie and Previn went very well. 'I was helpless with laughter,' said Ammonds. 'As Previn was reading it, he was also performing it, and we all knew it was going to be great.' But then Previn's mother became ill, and he had to fly back to America. 'Worse still,' said Ammonds, 'he wouldn't be back before the actual day the show was recorded . . .'

SIDENOTE: I knew for a fact that my father and Ernie were considering scrapping the whole routine from the show at this point. I was only fifteen at the time, but I clearly recall him back at home during this period and on the phone to Ernie. Previn's name came up a few times, and comments such as, 'Sod him! Let's do it without him', and, 'We can do something else we've been working on', came up. And, as Ammonds pointed out to me,

205

'When alone with him, he [Eric] was extremely keen to get across to me that the routine with Previn was not as funny as I was thinking it to be. Of course, the rest is entertainment history.'

Ammonds' final thought on this noteworthy time was a poignant one. 'A few months before Eric died, we were having lunch and I asked him if he remembered that moment. He smiled and said, "John, I have never been more wrong. It is the funniest thing we ever did."'

SIDENOTE: There is a well-known story about how André Previn learned his lines for *The Morecambe & Wise Show* with a torch and a copy of his script while in the back of a cab from London's Heathrow airport to his home. I told Lenny Henry and his studio audience this story on his series *Trust Morecambe & Wise*. Lenny mischievously interjected to ask if André Previn always travelled in a taxi carrying a torch! Much laughter from the audience, and much laughter from me. But in actual fact, Previn DID carry a torch for precisely this purpose. The great man was often catching up on work on the hoof.

Stephen Fry posted a message on Twitter after André Previn's passing in February 2019, paying tribute to his great achievements and ending with ' . . . and yet most of my generation will always think of him as André

Preview, conducting Eric Morecambe. He probably wouldn't mind . . .' -

It was down to Eddie Braben to update the Previn sketch from its original format, as written by Sid Green and Dick Hills, when it was Ernie who played the Previn role in a far less structured and amusing piece.

'Dad would start writing for the Christmas shows in something like March or April,' recalls Braben's daughter, Clare. 'I remember being on a beach on holiday one Easter, and he was making notes for Eric and Ernie's Christmas show on cigarette packets!'

Clare can also recall the times when writers' block was evident. 'I got ready for school one day, and as I passed his office door, I could see him sitting in front of a blank piece of paper in his typewriter, head resting on one hand. When I returned from school, he was in the same position, the blank piece of paper unmoved and untouched.' She adds, 'Equally, though, I can remember going to sleep at night to the sound of his typewriter clacking away.'

On Morecambe and Wise, Ernie said in the early 1970s, 'The art, we found, was in making it look easy, and indeed this proved to be the most difficult part.' He continued, 'The essence of our act is what we call the mutual trigger. Neither of us is the comic, nor the other the feed, though we may appear to some people to slot automatically into those two separate roles.'

Ernest Maxin had been helming the choreography for the M&W show, and in 1974, following John Ammonds' departure back to the Mike Yarwood show, Maxin took over as producer. In fact, the whole change came about because Eric and Ernie had wanted to pursue a more musical feel to their shows, which John Ammonds was happy about, but strictly speaking it wasn't his bag. He would rejoin them in future years.

Eric and Ernie had for so long been comics mostly operating around crosstalk comedy, but both men had long embraced the desire to inject their work with a more musical flavour, lavish in its delivery, and in keeping with their upbringing watching the big silver-screen stars of the day. Particularly for Ernie, this was a step into his past.

It's been said that John Ammonds and Eric Morecambe were made for each other, and Ernest Maxin and Ernie Wise the same. I can see some truth in that, but in terms of the musical direction the shows would take under Maxin, I know my father and Ernie relished the prospect equally, and both men were ready for this new development in their television shows. 'We want to give it a bit of Hollywood,' my father would say, referencing their future series.

GAIL: I would guess that in the early years, their act always did include song and dance, and anyway it was better than being out of work. It was fun, because they enjoyed each other's company. Ernie had been successful in show business from a young age, and he would have picked up great insights into what worked in the entertainment industry, and what didn't. So I don't think you can overstate the fact, as Sadie had originally failed to do, that Ernie really recognised that Dad was a uniquely special talent. And wouldn't you want to be close to that?

My father was trained to dance, perhaps not to Ernie's level, but it would give them a whole new avenue of comic possibilities to pursue. Ernest Maxin was a big fan of the 'shiny floor' show, as it was known. Essentially, big production routines, which is possibly why Eddie Braben nicknamed him Ernest Maximum!

Ernest Maxin

Ernest Maxin was born on 22 August 1923 in Upton Park, London. His formative years as a performer included appearing in revue at the Hippodrome Theatre in London. In 1959, he started the Ernest Maxin Orchestra. He moved to ABC in 1959 for a five-year engagement

In 1964, Maxin moved to the BBC and stayed there until his forced retirement at sixty. His various BBC credits as a producer, director and/or choreographer included *The Howerd Crowd*, *The Norman Wisdom Show*, *The Kathy Kirby Show*, *The Dick Emery Show*, *The Black and White Minstrel Show* and *The Les Dawson Show*.

Despite his many plaudits, Ernest is best remembered for his time as a choreographer and then taking over as producer of *The Morecambe & Wise Show* when John Ammonds left.

Ernest died on 27 September 2018 in Woodford Green, east London.

I have many happy personal memories of Ernest, who achieved so much as a choreographer and producer in his long life. Before and after Morecambe and Wise, he produced Dave Allen, Dave King, Dick Emery, Les Dawson, Jack Benny, Charlie Drake and many others.

In the early 1950s he was on stage with one of Ernie Wise's mentors, Arthur Askey. Everyone trusted Ernest because he was an old pro who had been around before the wheel and experienced so many facets of the business. He was consumed with sentimentality, and was brave enough to admit it.

I had lunch one day with Ernest and Martin Sterling, the latter later to become a *Coronation Street* writer just like my father-in-law, George.

After acting out some tearful moment from a scene Ernest had watched in a film – and he could cry real tears on demand – I jokingly told him he was an old ham. He looked at me astounded, smiled and said, 'You've only known me a short while. How did you work it out so quickly?'

His son Paul, with whom I remain in contact, described Ernest as 'half man, half kryptonite'. A lovely description of a man who always looked liked he was in his fifties, and always dressed like he was Cary Grant. I'm fairly certain Ernest saw himself as a cross between Gene Kelly and Burt Lancaster, both names that came up frequently in conversation with him, and even when with him in a restaurant, he would need the merest hint of an excuse to burst into his Gene Kelly dance routine, much to the surprise of other diners, if not the staff, who had not only come to expect it, but to crave it.

Paul told me that near the end of his father's life, Ernest asked Paul to remind him how old he was. 'You're ninety-five, Dad,' he replied. Ernest shook his head and said, 'I wish I hadn't asked!' Ernest always told people he was fifty-five, as it was 'better for business', he'd say with a knowing wink. He was seventy-odd when he told me that, and still doing daily runs through Epping Forest. You could almost believe his revised age because of the slim frame and toned condition he kept himself in. I'm sure, and certainly hope, he fooled a good many TV execs.

Being sentimental, Ernest had found the absolute perfect company in Morecambe and Wise, who carried their own sentimentality, especially when it came to the early Hollywood musicals.

Both Eric and Ernie, and especially Ernie, became more and more keen to present their own musicals as a pastiche at every opportunity. After all, it was watching these old films at the local flea pit that had driven M&W to have a go at getting into the show business world. Ernest gave them that opportunity, because he was the specialist of the big production number; he'd just never had the opportunity to work with a double act like Morecambe and Wise. And the BBC supported both him and the show to the hilt. When they took on Gene Kelly's 'Singin' in the Rain' – without any rain! – the production values were extraordinary. As you watch it, you half expect Gene Kelly himself to come dancing on to the set. The same with the dancing newscasters performing 'There Is Nothin' Like a Dame'.

Concurrent to this had been Eric and Ernie's slight fatigue with the repetition – however good, however well-received – of the current format of their show. My father especially voiced his feelings as early as 1973 that they needed to change their format. Both he and Ernie had thoughts of a sitcom of some kind, as the flat and bedroom sketches worked so well in the current M&W show format. That appealed to Eddie Braben, too. 'We've been kicking ideas around but not worked out a new format yet,' my father said in an interview. 'There's nothing we'd like to do more than get away from the old routine and make a complete switch . . .' One idea he liked was to play a butler to Ernie's character, living alone in a big country house.

My father was aware that he and Ernie had always survived by being a little ahead of the game. They saw the death of the variety theatres when others around them just ignored the elephant in the room, and that would cost those performers their livelihoods eventually.

Author Graham McCann, who published an excellent biography of Morecambe and Wise in 1998, also suggests that the writer Roy Clarke – *Last of the Summer Wine*, *Keeping Up Appearances*, *Open All Hours* and many other series – was commissioned to write Morecambe and Wise a sitcom. Clearly this was never executed. And maybe it was a good thing, for while Eric and Ernie were both men who tended to look to the next big thing for their act, I never for a moment felt the viewing public did.

I was once sipping coffee with my father in his Harpenden kitchen around this time – 1973–74. He told me that he'd had a 'sort' of fan letter from someone who enjoyed their shows but questioned whether it was sensible to continue with the same format. One of the tabloids had suggested the same thing at this time, and what with Eric and Ernie questioning it themselves, one can see how the idea for change was a developing theme.

My father asked me what I thought about it. It was kind of him to seek the opinion of his young son. 'Do you think the shows are too familiar in the format we've been doing?'

'Well,' I replied, 'we know there's a play, a flat routine, a musical number, guest stars and the opening bit in front of the curtains. But it all works.'

He looked a little doubtful. 'That sounds like it's getting too familiar,' he said.

Comedy actor Rowan Atkinson told me years later that it shouldn't have been a case of looking for a new direction so much as rarefying what they did. I think that is something M&W slowly began to consider for themselves. More effort went into their Christmas shows, and gaps appeared in their television series – though not too many, it should be noted.

I think Rowan was spot on in his observation, and it might have been not only better for their shows, but for their health, if they could have, for argument's sake, just done Christmas specials for two or three years – what we came to call 'event' TV. But a constant counter to this – and one that would come again when considering eventual retirement – was a genuine fear, possibly for both men, and definitely for my father, of being forgotten. They had travelled a long and hazardous path to find a level of popularity and stardom they could not have anticipated, so the idea of a break, while welcome, may have seemed unwise.

They were also men with northern roots and a strong work ethic. Both had fathers who had done physical labour to make a living. I know my father felt guilt over this whenever he thought of his dad, and whenever he himself took any time away from the studios.

SIDENOTE: Susan Belbin worked as an assistant floor manager with Morecambe and Wise on their BBC shows from 1973 to 1976. She was present at their rehearsals, including at the BBC Rehearsal Rooms (nicknamed the Acton Hilton), in North Acton, and their technical rehearsals, dress rehearsals and recordings at BBC Television Centre. She recalls, 'I remember Eric once asking me, "Do you think we have another ten years in us?" He meant professionally, not personally. I said, "Yes, of course I think you both have." But clearly he was very worried.'

SIXTEEN

The BBC were not looking for any change in what their prized double act were bringing to their shows. Things were working unbelievably well as it stood, and the 'if it ain't broke don't fix it' motto ultimately became the common expression in their camp. It's interesting to note that right up to the end their format remained almost entirely unchanged, despite the arrival of the alternative comedians, bringing what comedian–writer–broadcaster Arthur Smith described as 'comedy's version of punk'.

SIDENOTE: All at once we had shows like *The Comic Strip Presents . . .* and *The Young Ones* emerging on British television in 1982. These shows – and the stand-up clubs that were now getting into full stride, it should be remembered – produced a raft of alternative, and very talented, comedians: Ade Edmondson, Rik Mayall, Nigel Planer, Dawn French, Jennifer Saunders, Alexei Sayle, Keith Allen, and many others, all influenced by the first notable alternative, Billy Connolly. In their midst was writer-performer Ben Elton, a huge influence on new comedy at this time, yet one who has forever pointed to

Morecambe and Wise as his inspiration. As a child he sent M&W a script for them to consider. I wish I still had it.

'Comedy changes so fast,' says comedian, actor, producer and half of Armstrong and Miller, Ben Miller, 'the only place to really understand it is at the coalface, and I'm now somewhere in the office overlooking the pit!'

It's curious to note – and maybe it was the development of the musical side to Morecambe and Wise that prompted it – but post 1974, I never once heard my father mention that their show's format was tired or in need of reinvigorating. Perhaps in part it was the continued accolades that made them less determined to seek change. There had certainly been many accolades, not least an article by the pre-eminent critic of his time, Kenneth Tynan. To say he praised them in a big piece in the *Observer* magazine section in 1973 would be an understatement. He commented that Eric Morecambe 'has burgeoned into one of the most richly quirkish and hypnotic performers in the history of the box'. And he continued, 'How much of it is due to Braben and how much to the performers is hard to determine: but we know that the scripts are heavily modified in rehearsal and that most of the changes come from Eric.'

Tynan was, in part, confirming the successful combination of the team Bill Cotton had put together. Opportunity, timing, inevitability – perhaps all of these were in evidence. But the results would only continue to improve, especially with Ernest Maxin now bringing in increasingly outlandish musical routines for each successive Christmas show.

There was still, just about, a life away from the studios. It's hard to imagine, looking back at this crazy decade, that there was any time for Eric and Ernie to be apart from one another. But while Ernie and Doreen enjoyed boating and travelling to America, we spent either the Easter or June of each year as a family in Portugal. My parents had had a villa built outside Albufeira, when it was still little more than a fishing village. It's vast development was some way off in the late 1960s, and it wouldn't become a massive urban sprawl and major Brit tourist destination for another two decades.

GAIL: I have so many happy memories of our holidays in Portugal. The spade in the back of the hire car (the ubiquitous Mini) to dig us out of the sandy tracks posing as roads. The mules, the carts, the women with more than one black hat on their head (each one representing a deceased husband). But mostly, I remember Dad away from work. He loved Portugal, the villa, the Portuguese, the other villa owners around us, and being with his family. Strange that he enjoyed it so much, considering he didn't swim, so didn't use the pool, didn't really do sea and sand, and didn't do sunbathing. And he never took his socks off!

We would all head off to the beach after lunch, leaving Dad in the villa for a few hours. That was his creative time. He would play music (records on a record player driven over from the UK), and occasionally he would find a track

218

that had certain potential as a musical number for him and Ernie plus a guest star. Everything would get noted down, and if I was lucky, and he was keen enough, he would act out some of his ideas to me within seconds of my returning back to the villa. I say 'if I was lucky' because I recognise now that I truly was, which I didn't know at the time: getting a private viewing of something that would become universally loved, I expect I rolled my eyes before walking away, saying, 'Yeah! That might work. Now I need to take a shower.'

Back from the beach, Mum would go straight to the kitchen and put a kettle on for a pot of tea for us all, so no audience there, either. You, Gary, weren't really interested in anything that didn't involve kicking a football!

There would be more fun as afternoon turned into evening, when we would go out to a restaurant. Back in those days, hardly any waiters or waitresses spoke English at all. Dad relished going through what I've now come to recognise as his Restaurant Routine. They certainly didn't know who Morecambe and Wise were. He would get a real twinkle in his eye and a mischievous look, that said, 'I'm going to make you all laugh, whether you want to or not!' I think that getting laughs out of non-English-speaking people really pleased him. I guess they all thought he was a mad, likeable and funny eccentric Englishman on holiday. The embarrassment it caused us, the children, was off the scale, and I wouldn't change a single second of it.

Back then, the Algarve was often called Europe's best kept secret. That was used as a tourism slogan for a while to encourage visitors to the region. When we'd first arrived there, the international airport, akin to something out of Hergé's *Adventures of Tintin*, had only just been opened. Prior to this, you had to fly to Lisbon and drive or train down to the southern coast, as Paul McCartney had done with Jane Asher. En route, with Asher driving, he quickly wrote a little song he'd been toying with called 'Yesterday'. My wife, Tanya, and I still to this day tend to fly to Lisbon and drive down to the Algarve and make it part of the trip, and that piece of Beatles history always comes back to me.

I've written before how my father still had to make people laugh even if they didn't recognise him. That was his nature. But being able to do that on his own terms was as close to a real holiday away from Morecambe and Wise as he was ever going to allow himself. He said that if he switched off just the once, he might never be able to switch on again, and therefore you had a relaxed man on his holidays, but one easily able to up the pace at short notice if required – almost as if *hoping* it might be required.

Eric and Ernie had no contact at all during these annual excursions. It was deliberate, because it made the reunion a revitalised one. I wonder how things would have played out if the internet had existed back then. Would they have emailed through some gags and ideas for the shows to each other, perhaps? Would they have video-called? Had Zoom meetings with Bill Cotton, Eddie Braben, John Ammonds and Ernest Maxin, all from different parts of the world? That would have been irresistible, I'm sure.

Some of their most memorable comic moments developed while on holiday, including their backing Tom Jones for his number, 'Exactly Like You', and making things uncomfortable for Shirley Bassey in the footwear department. And it transpired, in more recent years, that Ernie had been keeping an abundance of notes throughout his working life – mostly gags and funny observations, some of which made it to their shows. It was Ernie who had come up with the idea of having breakfast to the stripper music, which Ernest Maxin would construct (quite literally) and choreograph in 1976.

SIDENOTE: In 1976, Eric and Ernie were awarded the OBE from HM the Queen at fifty and fifty-one years old respectively. In 2015, my mother, as Joan Bartholomew, collected her own OBE from HM the Queen, for extensive charity fundraising work. Eddie Braben, according to his widow, Dee, called the OBE One Boiled Egg!

I recall with fondness a trip around 1973 to Portmeirion – the Italianate village created in north Wales by Sir Bertram Clough Williams-Ellis, and made globally famous by Patrick McGoohan in his 1967 cult series *The Prisoner*. It was always good to spend time with my father away from his work, and the tranquil setting of Portmeirion offered him a lot of peace.

He was someone who couldn't easily switch off. He liked to say that the only thing worse than being constantly recognised was going unrecognised. Recognition kept him in tune with his working persona. It was simple reassurance rather than specific reward or gratification of any kind. His other favourite line – 'It's all based on fear!' – springs to mind.

For Eric and Ernie, the seventies rolled on as if the decade could never end, and they would always be with us as perpetually middle-aged men presenting series after series and Christmas show after Christmas show, transcending generations, their humour existing purely and simply to be enjoyed.

SEVENTEEN

I have a lovely memory of Scarborough in the mid-seventies. One of my jobs as an employee of Billy Marsh was to sell Eric and Ernie merchandise while they were touring the country doing one-nighters – their 'bank raids', as my father liked to call these brief visits. The show itself was made up of decades of collected pieces – the bits they'd come to feel the most comfortable with performing – some of which dated right back to the days when they were struggling to get work on the road. All of it had been cleverly honed and brought up to date to deliver an intimate performance of two great friends whose partnership spanned decades.

I recall sitting in the dressing room at the Floral Hall, Scarborough, with both men, just listening to them chat together. What was fascinating was how so much of their conversation was about other acts, most long gone, and many I'd never heard of. I thought it was rather wonderful that they'd probably been sharing these sorts of conversations when they were on the road as young hopefuls, a far from certain future ahead of them. How marvellous, it struck me, that whatever it had been that inspired them then hadn't somehow diminished into something more negative or disappointing. They had clearly retained their sheer exuberance for the business they were in, the skills of many who had gone before still mattering to them, indeed still exciting and motivating both of them despite most having passed.

It wasn't all joy in Scarborough. As it was customary for them to arrive excessively early at the theatre where they were working, their arrival was not always expected. At the Floral Hall, they were greeted by the sight of their show's producer and a young backstage hand *in flagrante delicto*, both half naked and sprawled drunkenly across the floor of Eric and Ernie's dressing room. 'There was booze everywhere, and it was clear what had been going on.'

My father could recount this type of event quite calmly, but at the time he was apoplectic, according to Ernie, and straight on the phone to their agent Billy Marsh, the producer being one of Billy's main people back in Regent Street. Apologies were made, the 'crime scene' cleared, and theatrical life returned to some kind of normality.

Ernie was great at simply brushing off these moments, and calming my father down. Ernie, as we know, had a strong aversion to any situations that involved heated exchanges, so was quite content to take the role of quiet appeaser.

SIDENOTE: By Scarborough, my father – and occasionally Ernie – had broken one of their own golden rules, which was never to drink alcohol before a performance. (Indeed, not until the mid-1960s did alcohol ever make a presence in our house, let alone his dressing room.) My father would now have a large whisky and water – his favourite tipple – about an hour before going on stage, and if cajoled, Ernie would join him with something like a glass of wine. Call this one of the earliest indicators of a growing over-familiarity with what they were doing: not just the live shows, but their whole careers in terms of length and direction. That this revealed a growing discontentment with what they were doing would be an exaggeration – perhaps a touch of reluctant acceptance of the repetition setting in would be more precise. Familiarity can clearly breed contempt in more than just personal relationships. Their live show, they both felt, had grown tired – corny was the word my father used to describe it – which is why after around 1977, they abandoned it altogether.

They'd been looking for new goals for their partnership for some years by the 1970s, but other than the occasional diversion, they never really moved on to anything else. And as a double act, they never would.

Thinking of those live tour dates they did during the seventies, I recall one quirky development. Eric and Ernie, right from the outset, had a strong and honest relationship with their fans. They never forgot that their success had only happened through those said fans.

My father strolled into the living room one afternoon, tutting away to himself. I was doing something useful, like watching television. The tutting continued and with occasional shakes of his head. In his hand he held around fifty A4-sized M&W photos. It was standard practice for either he or Ernie to sign a large wad of them, before passing to the other to do likewise, as quickly as Royal Mail would allow.

'I don't know what Ernie's thinking,' he said, a bemused smile on his lips.

'What do you mean?' I asked, half-listening.

'I think he must be having a mid-life crisis.'

'Ernie is?' Now I was suddenly curious. With Ernie, anything other than constantly reliable 'Little Ern' was unthinkable. It would have been the equivalent at that time of being told Margaret Thatcher, after much consideration, had decided to reverse her decision on the miners and keep all the coal pits up and running.

'Take a look at these,' he said, passing me a handful of the M&W photos.

Ernie, it was extremely clear to see, had signed each photo, 'Luv ya! Ernie Wise!'

'Well.' I laughed, perplexed. This was *Ernie Wise* we were talking about – the man who would often turn up to rehearsals wearing a suit and tie! 'It's certainly out of character.'

'It's what pop stars do, not comedians,' he said. 'It began on the tour dates after each show at the stage door.'

'Can't you say anything?'

'What can you say?'

Quite true.

'Well, *I* ain't signing 'em!' he said.

I think eventually, albeit reluctantly, he did sign that particular batch. But it came as a relief when the 'Luv ya!' phase became a brief 'Love you!', and finally was dropped

altogether. Perhaps, in a private moment, the ludicrous-
ness of it hit Ernie. Perhaps Doreen came across them and
advised him to stop.

A year or so later, apropos nothing at all, it came up
again in family conversation. 'Was anything ever mentioned about it?' I queried.

'No, nothing.' My father smiled. 'Thankfully, it all just
stopped as quickly as it started.'

I've long sensed with my father that much of his thinking
and his humour was all about acknowledging the slight
ridiculousness of life – the unplanned realisation of finding ourselves in it – and then accepting that and going
along with it accordingly, but always with an eye to the
funny side that this 'ludicrous' situation has engendered.
He often used the expression 'you'll miss me when I'm
gone', as my sister Gail once reminded me. Indeed, it was
so 'him' that I used it as a title for a book. But it is an
interesting line to regularly come up with. It suggests a
man who, perhaps because of his illness, recognised that
the 'when I'm gone' might be any moment soon, for any
of us. And when he considered legends of the past that
he'd grown up watching and respecting, you can be sure
he recognised his own brief mortality.

Alongside this, he often mentioned there was only
one way to go when you reached the top. I'm not for
a moment suggesting he had a vision of some impend-
ing collapse for Morecambe and Wise, but the greater
sense of something finite in what they were producing.
How many more live touring shows? How many new

Christmas shows? How many more TV series? How many more anythings, as the years ticked by at a seemingly increasing and relentless speed?

Achieving such an incredible level of success created its own kind of pressure. Dwelling on their stardom only got them concerned over what their next Christmas show would be like. And Eddie Braben was no less unaffected by such thoughts. As I've mentioned, Eddie got quite ill from the stress of it, having to take some time out from working on the shows.

Ernie, in fairness, never lost his cheerful approach to it all. I sensed he still came at his career as he'd done as a child prodigy working with Arthur Askey at the London Palladium. There was a mostly carefree side to Ernie's nature that rumbled merrily along, and guided him through all and sundry. If something came along that struck him as unpleasant, then he'd do his best to sidestep it.

Lenny Henry's *Trust Morecambe & Wise* had Hugh Dennis as one of the guests on one of the shows. He's no novice when it comes to double acts, partnering the aforementioned Steve Punt. He made a comment that comes back to me frequently. Confessing to being a huge Morecambe and Wise fan, he said that out of all their work, it's the recording of their 1973 live show (filmed at the Fairfield Halls, Croydon) that he loves the best.

'Why?' I asked, genuinely curious, as like most others my natural focus is on their BBC shows, and sketches with names such as Shirley Bassey and André Previn involved.

'It shows their relationship better than any other recording,' he said. 'It's a live show in which nothing much happens, yet everything happens. You can see their friendship, feel the warmth, the long history, and the trust they had in each other.'

SIDENOTE: This was the only recording of their seventies touring show. Billy Marsh made it as a gift to Eric and Ernie, and as a record of those touring years. Since then, it has been picked up by Thames, released on VHS, and more recently shown on Channel 5.

Steve Punt said to me: 'Today, of course, M&W would be touring with a whole reconstruction of their greatest hits, including, naturally, their "Andrew Preview" routine. But what Eric and Ernie did was to keep their theatre touring show completely removed from their television shows. In doing that, they created something retrospective, something that spanned the previous decades of their own history right back to when they first worked together as kids.'

Steve Punt is correct in his observation. My father often worried – unnecessarily, I always felt – that the material they were performing live was shockingly dated. But that never mattered, just as their television shows were never truly about the material – or not, let's say more honestly, the material alone. Of course Eddie Braben's material mattered, but it was always about their relationship, which Hugh Dennis found himself wholly connecting with.

Ultimately, Eric and Ernie brought the accoutrements of

the theatre into the studio to emphasise their shared history. The unnecessary curtains, the variety-era feel to both their live shows and their TV work: an opening introduction piece, a guest star, a musical number, a musical outro to the show (usually the 'Bring Me Sunshine' number).

Eric and Ernie's 'Bring Me Sunshine' has become their motif. The innocent, almost naive lyrics encapsulate the whole ethos of Morecambe and Wise. The song is not associated with anything remotely unpleasant or political – an ode to living life through nothing more than fun, sunshine and love. It remains relevant, as it perfectly counteracts the reality of today's life, in which the simple things of yesteryear become remote, not least through the bludgeoning evolvement of technology that makes quainter our relatively recent past.

It's often picked by guests on *Desert Island Discs* – from photographer Rankin to actor Daniel Radcliffe, and Dawn French to Richard Osman – and is in that programme's top ten chosen songs of the last decade. Radcliffe chose it above all others, because 'it's going to make me happiest when I need it', which perhaps sums up Morecambe and Wise's appeal to this very day.

And it wasn't even a song written with them in mind. It was composed by Arthur Kent and Sylvia Dee, the latter writing the lyrics, and first recorded by The Mills Brothers in 1968. It reached the top 20 of the Country Charts for Willie Nelson, which makes it all the more astounding that it should end up as the song forever linked to a comedy partnership. And it tied in nicely with the skip-dance they would do to make their exit at the close of each show.

Their producer, John Ammonds, came up with the idea for both the song and the skip-dance; the latter developed from a scene with Groucho Marx in a Marx Brothers movie.

'"The Groucho dance", I like to refer to it as,' John Ammonds told me when I interviewed him at his home in 1982. 'The evening before seeing the boys at rehearsals, I'd been watching the Marx Brothers movie *Horse Feathers*. I mentioned it to Eric, as he was a big fan of the Marx Brothers. I began to remind him of the scene where Groucho does a hilarious dance, and I showed him what I meant. Both Eric and Ernie fell about laughing at this. The following Sunday, after they sang "Bring Me Sunshine", they put it in the show and danced off to it.'

SIDENOTE: John Ammonds' wife, Wyn, who suffered from multiple sclerosis, had lunch with me and Johnny at the time of our interview. Her movements were highly restricted, and she couldn't speak with a clarity to anyone's ear but Johnny's. Watching him meticulously and lovingly spoon feed Wyn, while continuing to talk all things Morecambe and Wise, was not only touching beyond belief, but exhibited a dexterity I'd hitherto not believed possible. Not only was he in full interview mode, carer mode, chef and waiter mode, but with an ease I can't fully express. And through the centre of this occasion, he was calmly enjoying his own lunch, with no sense of rush or stress. And all with a smile, as if there was no effort required. And that was Johnny, at home and at the office.

But Johnny was a ferocious worker. He was always happy to work bank holidays, and genuinely chuffed to discover that Eric and Ernie shared the same work ethic. Eddie Braben once told me that if you sent Ammonds a Christmas card, you expected it to come back with suggested corrections!

Much as I loved Johnny, and miss his gentle wisdom to this day, he was prone to the same story retelling issues as my grandmother, Sadie. Yet there was always a large core of truth running through all he was telling you. The stories were just slightly tweaked with each rendition. Or maybe he told you all the right stories, but not necessarily in the right order!

GAIL: I remember Dad saying he asked Johnny [Ammonds], 'How are we going to get off stage, like in a theatre?' Apparently, when Dad said that, Johnny twiddled with his moustache, as he often did, and said, 'Well, you could dance off!' As he did this, he waved his arms about. That made Dad think of Groucho Marx, and thus the 'dance' was born! It was such a great device for them. Dad said that he loved how visual and simple it was. I'm sure neither he nor Ernie could have guessed just how iconic that moment would become.

As well as being connected through a musical motif, there is another similarity between Laurel and Hardy and Eric and Ernie: how they were loved by their fans. No matter how they aged, or how their shows fared, no one ever fell out of love with them. Few remain in the hearts and minds of the masses – transcending their work and continuing to resonate with the people – in the way these two duos have.

It's interesting to me that both Eric and Ernie were astute when it came to recognising their own worth in the entertainment industry, but when it came to Laurel and Hardy, they never failed to rank themselves behind them. And just as others would later take from them in terms of their creative work, they took from Laurel and Hardy. The looks to camera that Ollie so wonderfully did, and which my father took and developed for television audiences, and the whole slow-burn approach to delivering lines through bemused expressions and dialogue mostly consisting of the virtually nonsensical. And the shared bed idea, which I've touched upon, but will look at in greater detail later. I do wonder, though, if there would even have been a Morecambe and Wise without Laurel and Hardy.

GAIL: Without Laurel and Hardy, they would have been more like Fred Flintstone and Barney Rubble – another double act adored by Dad.

'Morecambe and Wise are a double-edged sword,' says Ben Miller. 'On the one hand, they show what is possible; on the other, they pull the drawbridge up after them, because you can't imitate them and get away with it. Xander [Alexander Armstrong] and I always thought carefully about anything "in front of curtain", because it felt like M&W were the masters of that, and we'd only come off worse. In fact, we thought carefully about ever appearing as ourselves, in case we got compared to them. We did love a pipe, though. Lots of our early characters smoked pipes, and looking back, I think that was our nod to them. Apart, that is, from just being funny, because twenty-year-olds in the 1990s didn't smoke pipes!'

Something I came to notice during the time I spent with them when they were on the road was how my father would wait a little while before joining Ernie on stage. The orchestra would burst into the opening bars of 'Bring Me Sunshine', Ernie would step out from the wings to applause, and my father would count to three or four, then step out and join him to increased applause. It some-how created a question mark.

As Steve Punt says, 'That's a clever device. It makes the audience wonder, "Has Ernie come on to cancel the show, because Eric couldn't make it here tonight?" Then when they realise that he's there, and all is good, it lifts the place even more.'

I asked Steve Punt what it was like starting a double act with the shadow of Morecambe and Wise hanging over them. 'We never really felt there *was* a shadow hanging over us,' he says. 'At least not to begin with, as we weren't talking to each other in that intimate kind of way that Eric and Ernie were. We were working with fixed stage mics, so projecting ourselves out to the audience. Radio mics came later, and when you're working with fixed ones, you're not in a position to be close and do the intimate dialogue stuff.'

When you think of double acts post Morecambe and Wise – and you've considered, in no particular order, French and Saunders, Smith and Jones, Fry and Laurie, Watson and Oliver, Hale and Pace, Punt and Dennis, Armstrong and Miller – you soon arrive at, and hover over for a lengthy period, Reeves and Mortimer. At least, *I* do! 'That was a media thing, that they were the new Morecambe and Wise,' says Steve Punt. 'One was shortish and one tallish and wore glasses and looked a bit like Eric. But that was where the similarity ended. Reeves and Mortimer had their own specific style that bore little resemblance to Eric and Ernie's. I do think much of that comparison came about due to Vic looking like Eric.'

235

SIDENOTE: I met Vic Reeves on the set of the Victoria Wood *Eric and Ernie* TV film. He was playing my grandad, George. He was working, so it wasn't the occasion to discuss his double act with Bob Mortimer, but I certainly came away that day thinking how irritating those continued comments about their similarity to M&W must have become for both men. They were even being used by the media as a reason for his divorce, with one paper stating that his wife could no longer live with him, because he was constantly watching Morecambe and Wise videos! Having said that, I came away from their earlier Channel 4 shows seeing the similarity to Eric and Ernie. Not in terms of material – I would agree with Steve Punt on that – but more in their chemistry and general interaction. Perhaps it is their sing-song voices, and speed of delivery, but they come across as Morecambe and Wise on stimulants – manically energetic, fast-talking, quick-thinking and very funny.

It's interesting to read that Vic and Bob don't really speak to each other much any more. 'Bob and I have never been ones for talking on the phone ... It's not a conscious thing. We haven't discussed it,' said Vic.

The important thing to remember here is that Vic Reeves is, or was, a comic creation of Jim Moir's: '... a character I invented at art school, actually. I put him on stage. And I haven't done him for a while ...' It's nice to note that he's back on TV as Jim Moir, and working alongside his wife, Nancy Sorrell, in a series that demonstrates his love of art.

While I think of modern comedy and comedians past and present, it's a tired old trope to say that it and they were better back in the day. It was different, and different chiefly because of technology and fashion. Eric and Ernie found only a few of the comedians that came before them that funny, and it was because they couldn't relate to the issues of that time, the clothes they wore, the things in general that were considered funny then but no longer translated to new audiences. And it was further undermined by the surviving grainy black-and-white images, and fractured, tinny sound that was the technology of that era.

'To begin any double act,' says Ben Miller, 'you each have to believe you'll be better off together than you would on your own. The first time I stood on stage with Xander in a sketch, people just started laughing, and the experience was so different from performing on my own that I forgot all my lines!' Miller adds with a laugh, 'As they say about double acts, it's like a marriage – except the sex is better!' He continues, 'When we were starting out, it was very important to create something that felt distinct from the theatrical feel of M&W, and to avoid just posing in suits!'

Ben Miller makes an interesting observation about how Morecambe and Wise came to set the bar so high. 'There's an argument to be made that the greatest achievements in any medium come from the artists who get there first. In modernist painting, say, it's hard to beat

Picasso. In television, M&W were in exactly the right place at the right time, developing their act just as music hall was ending and television was taking off. No other double act can ever be as successful again, because it will never be as fresh.'

Their former agent Jan Kennedy would agree with this (as did Eric and Ernie themselves), but adds that they are still unique in what they gave the public. 'Ernie was the greatest and most generous "straight man", if we call it that, and Eric had what Billy always called "funny bones",' she says. 'Theirs was the most amazing coming together of two separate – and very different – personalities, who created comic perfection.'

I would agree with this, at the risk of sounding biased. Morecambe and Wise would have still been the best in my opinion even if they'd come along second or third to television, mostly because the viewing public fell in love with my father in a way that was so utterly strong and unfathomable that I am unable to fully do it justice in words even now. I've noticed it's something my mother always says if asked what the main reason was behind Eric and Ernie becoming such great legends. 'Everyone just loved Eric,' she will say with a shrug. 'It was as if he was part of everyone's family.'

Ben Miller does add that there's more to it than just being first. 'Growing up in the 1970s, they were like members of the family. Eric was like your funny uncle, and Ernie – who was my hero – your slightly annoying uncle. You'd talk about them [Eric and Ernie], and crack their jokes, even when their show wasn't on. It wasn't like now, when everyone has their favourite comic.

Everyone in the country loved Morecambe and Wise. Understanding their surreal northern humour was part of being British.'

Also, it's worth noting that Eric and Ernie weren't entirely alone in trying to crack TV comedy as a double act. With greater success than they themselves were achieving – certainly to begin with – Mike and Bernie Winters were a big hit on the BBC show *Variety Parade* from 1955 to 1958. But Ben Miller is absolutely right about being in the right place at the right time. Eric and Ernie had the right agent, the right chief exec at ATV in Lord Lew Grade, the right writers for that time period in Sid Green and Dick Hills, and very little competition beyond those sporadic appearances of Mike and Bernie.

A further key to their longevity is the fact they had colour television, which burgeoned forth just as they themselves did. 'All of life is based on timing!' How often did my father say that? Very often, for sure.

'There will always be double acts coming through, I think,' says Ben Miller. 'It's that master–servant dynamic – two human beings stuck with each other, with all the petty frustrations that creates. I can't see that ever not being funny.'

Ben Miller knows how supportive that relationship can be. 'As well as keeping the faith when things weren't going well, we [Armstrong and Miller] were there to keep one another's feet on the ground when we found success ... The work will be the work, but the act is something bigger than that. It's a bubble of sanity in a completely bonkers world. A place where you can still be the person you were before all the crazy ups-and-downs.

I don't know how solo performers do it, frankly, without going completely mad.'

And of anyone going into comedy, he says, 'You have to be bold to do something no one else is doing, to pour every waking second into figuring out how to make the act the best it can possibly be. You have to find a way to let the audience in on the joke – for them to be the third corner of that partnership. And you have to stick with it when it's not working.'

EIGHTEEN

I would say that 1975 was the first of the absolute three peak years for Morecambe and Wise, which would culminate in their last Christmas show for the BBC in 1977. Their star wouldn't rise any higher – and arguably couldn't, such were the dizzying heights they had reached.

It was around this time that the author of *Paradise Postponed*, Sir John Mortimer, described Eric Morecambe as being possibly the most recognisable person in the country. Certainly, neither my father nor Ernie could go anywhere without an onslaught of love and/or interest from fans, which is hard to describe when you're living through it by proxy (always the natural role for loved ones, quite rightly kept to the periphery).

Let's take a moment to look a little more closely at the Christmas show of 1975.

There was no television series in 1975, giving a greater sense of anticipation to the year's festive special. It's worth noting that the 1975 Christmas show didn't contain the word Christmas in the title.

This special was written by Eddie Braben, with additional material by Eric and Ernie.

The show saw Ernest Maxin officially taking over the directing reins, as well as acting as choreographer.

Flick Colby choreographed Pan's People.
Orchestra directed by Peter Knight.
Special effects by Bill King.
TX: BBC One, 25 December 1975.

Running Order:
Staircase Gag:
Eric is standing at the top of a large
Hollywood-style staircase with members of
Pan's People standing at the bottom. The
staircase opens and appears to stretch Eric's
legs to an impossible degree. Ernie walks
underneath him.

Opening Titles:
A montage of footage from previous shows.
There are shots of Glenda Jackson, André
Previn, Shirley Bassey and Cliff Richard.

Opening Spot:
Eric gives Ernie a ballpoint pen. (Ernie
accidentally calls it a boil-point pen.) Ernie
gives Eric a Des O'Connor LP (*Des Sings Just
for Eric*) as a Christmas present. Gags included,
'If you want me to be a gonna, get me an LP by
Des O'Connor.'
Des then walks on and Eric backtracks and
says 'I like him' when he realises from the
sleeve photo that it's him.
Des has kept a list of the insults against
him. It is a huge long pink list that falls down

on to the stage with a flourish. On seeing it, Eric says, 'There's a whole series there!'

Eric lends Des his glasses at one stage as a joke, and Des asks, 'Are they for keeps or just for lenses?'

Des gets his own back and at one point is slapping Eric as he spells out some words like 'Tough', to which Des says, 'And I'm really enjoying this!'

Debbie Ash and Fiona Gray come on at the end and walk off with Ernie as they supposedly fancy him.

Des asks Eric if he's going to sing on the show. Eric says, 'You have my word.' They walk off together and Des has 'This boy's a fool' painted on the reverse side of his jacket.

Watching the Cricket:
Eric and Ernie at a cricket match. Use of stock footage of the cricket match. Eric ends up wearing a policeman's helmet that he steals when streaking on the pitch.

A Friendly Discussion with Robin Day:
Ernie and Robin Day have a heated discussion. Eric says sadly we've come to the end of Robin Day's friendly discussion. The next discussion will be with President Amin on the subject of how to make friends and influence people. Eric then joins in the fight.

A Gift for Annie's New Baby:
A sketch in which Eric and Ernie go to a
baby shop. The shop sketches were used quite
frequently. Originally they were considered
fillers, but they became quite a big part of
Morecambe and Wise's repartee. Ann Hamilton
plays the shop assistant. Ernie's sister is
having a baby and he's very upset. At one stage
Eric, who's smoking a pipe, puts said pipe in a
doll's mouth.

Quickie (as they called the brief inserts in their
shows, despite the innuendo – or because of it!):
Cut back to Eric and Ernie still fighting with
Robin Day.

Giddy-up:
Essentially, a routine involving Eric being
dragged off a sled by a horse while Ernie duets
with Diane Solomon. Ernie and Diane Solomon
are singing 'Somewhere My Love' – Lara's theme
from *Doctor Zhivago* – with his partner having
less success driving their sled, while wearing
a wonderfully false moustache. (Worth noting,
comedian–actor–writer Miranda Hart tells me
it's one of her absolute favourite pieces of their
comedy work, and I concur.)

Des Returns:
Des comes on and asks when he's going to sing.
This is followed by a staircase gag in which Eric

and Ernie remain in shot but Des disappears
out of shot.

The Lady Psychiatrist:
Eric and Ernie go to a psychiatrist played by
Diana Rigg. Eric tells Ernie at one stage to go
and look in a newspaper and see if they've split
up again! This is a bit of a filler sketch, but
it's setting Diana Rigg up for the main sketch
of the show.

Des Returns Again:
Des goes to sit and Eric and Ernie, dressed as
magicians, make him disappear.

Quickie:
Cut back to Eric and Ernie still fighting with
Robin Day.

Hey Big Spender:
Performed by Brenda Arnau, while Eric and
Ernie (dressed as female members of Pan's
People) perform a routine with Pan's People.
This includes using a ballet bar. There are slight
echoes of their Tom Jones number in this.

Des Returns Yet Again:
Des O'Connor attempts to sing 'Feelings' but is
thwarted by Eric and Ernie. He wants to sing
and he wants paying for it. Des tricks them
and he sings 'Feelings'.

Quickie:
Cut back to Eric and Ernie still fighting with
Robin Day. This time, Robin is wearing a crash
helmet and a floor manager tries to break
the fight up.

Diana Rigg:
Ernie introduces Diana Rigg in front
of the tabs.

Ernie's Play Wot He Wrote: Nell Gwynne
Eric is King Charles II and Ernie is Samuel
Pepys. Meanwhile, Diana Rigg plays the title role
in this rip-roaring parody of *Nell Gwynne*.
Eric memorably has a toy dog (a spaniel) and
he keeps making it whine throughout the sketch.
Gordon Jackson, who played butler Angus
Hudson in the popular LWT drama series
Upstairs, Downstairs, also made a cameo
appearance in this sketch.
This ended with a song-and-dance routine
to 'How Could You Believe Me When I Said I
Love You When You Know I've Been a Liar All
My Life?'.
It was a cold, blustery day when a film crew
descended on Broughton Castle near Banbury,
Oxfordshire.

Positive Thinking:
Eric and Ernie perform 'Positive Thinking' and
not 'Bring Me Sunshine'.

Robin Day is seen to stagger past in the
background with the aid of a walking stick.
Extra titles are shown over an old photo
of Morecambe and Wise and the other
cast members.

The show followed the successful formula – the one Eric
and Ernie had considered moving on from a few years
earlier, but which now had become not just the desired
format, but the expected one, especially with viewers.

This pretty much replicates in layout and delivery the
Christmas shows of 1976 and '77, adding credence to
what Alan Yentob refers to as the crafting of their shows.
There is a pitch-perfect delivery with these shows that
makes them eminently repeatable to this day.

SIDENOTE: Pauline Cox was a make-up artist at BBC
Television Centre. She has fond memories of Eric and
Ernie, and remembers the phone ringing in the make-
up room on one occasion, and my father picking it up
and saying, 'There's no phone here!' and hanging up.
Interestingly, Gail witnessed this at home on one occasion. It was one of his running gags.

'Sometimes when I was making up Eric,' recalls
Pauline, 'he would suddenly twist around and seize the
puff with his teeth!'

Pauline mentions that their warm-up act in the studio
was often as funny as the show they were recording

there. I couldn't agree more. Eric and Ernie tended to do around five to ten minutes of their touring ventriloquism act routine with Charlie the dummy. It always got big laughs, and it was slightly disappointing when the floor manager would interrupt to say they were now ready to record the show.

They still had a warm-up man ready to do his part. Jeff Stevenson was a young comic in the early 1980s and did audience warm-up for the M&W show at Thames. 'I watched them rehearse,' he says. 'It was a masterclass. Then I came down to the studio to watch the audience coming in and to my surprise, Eric and Ernie were sat at the edge of the stage. Eric asked me to join them. He asked me how I was doing and what I had coming up. He then told me he'd seen me on television and liked what I was doing. "I saw you do one of Freddie Starr's shows, and I'm guessing that wasn't a great night!" Absolutely right, I told him. "Don't worry about it," he said. "We did a series [*Running Wild*], and it was so bad the critics said: 'Definition of the week: The box in which they buried Morecambe and Wise!'"'

I love some of the online comments from people who still enjoy these shows:

I have asthma. I laughed at them so much one time and caused an attack.

Comedy geniuses, great family entertainment, and British icons. Christmas isn't the same without Eric & Ernie, my childhood heroes.

After watching them once, I laughed so much my willy dropped off. Well, it didn't really, but how funny would that've been . . .!

I've often been asked what life was like at home with Eric Morecambe. I've been able to truthfully say that for me and my sister, and later my brother Steven when he joined the party, it all seemed somewhat normal. That, of course, is based on the fact we knew no different. There were hints, however, such as staying over at friends' houses and seeing how their families operated. I did start to see a difference there, as most of my mates' parents – especially the male parent back in the 1970s – tended to function on much more well-defined working lines. A part of me slightly envied that. But then I'd go home and be told we were all going to the Grosvenor Hotel in Park Lane, London, the next evening for some function or other. You'd get there and find yourself flanked by Elton John and Ronnie Barker, momentarily feeling slightly in awe of the company yet simultaneously expecting it, and increasingly becoming used to it.

But between these fleeting events was a profound normality, which I've sensed was my mother's doing. While the mayhem of show business went about its way, the family, for the most part, was living life glued in Middle England.

GAIL: It is interesting to look back on these long-ago times, as there's clearly such a difference from the life we lived with Dad in it, and the one with him no longer in it.

When I was around five to eight years old, I accepted everything as normal. I thought, like you, Gary, that all families had similar lives to us. In reality, most of what we did was built around 'Eric Morecambe' — we just didn't discuss any of it like it was unique, and therefore we didn't recognise early on how different it was: the garden fêtes, the opening of homes, shops, shopping centres, buildings and countless fundraising events that all penetrated our lives. For Mum, having done occasional tours abroad with Dad, it must have all seemed endless.

By the time I was eight, I would say that I did conclude our family was unlike any of my school friends' families. Perhaps through a desire to fit in, my way of dealing with it was to never talk about it. The night before, we could have been with royalty, or a very famous performer, and I would never dream of mentioning anything when back at school the following day.

By around twelve, I did find all the events — the dressing up and being on show — started to bother me a bit. I guess it was becoming a little tedious. When do you take charge of your own life? I would much rather have been horse-riding with my mates. In my early teens, the press attention really got to me. I had gone from being invisible at any of these events we were attending, to a photo opportunity. Possibly I'd become someone of interest, as I might one day go off the rails and give them a good story.

I remember arriving home from school, and Mum saying that a photographer was coming to take photos of me by the swimming pool, and with my horse, and next to Dad's Rolls Royce for some article. I found all of that challenging, and could get quite steamed up. Dad labelled me, 'The Princess Anne of the family'. I would make the photographer's life as hard as possible by refusing to be photographed wearing a bikini while mucking out *my horse. And those headlines! Always ridiculous, and nothing to do with the article that followed. When I was at college in Windsor, I read that I was at a fashionable finishing school on the Continent.*

Dad looked at me one day, when I was letting off steam, and said, 'Look what you're doing to yourself, Gail. It's not worth it. Nobody remembers, and the journalists have a job to do.'

All pre internet, celebrity and reality TV. I can only imagine how tough it must be for today's kids of the famous.

The 1970s was a decade of career-defining work for M&W, with charitable interests for both Eric and Ernie running alongside, some separate, some joint. And also the many fête and shopping-centre openings Gail alludes to, which appeared to colonise that full-on era.

But for the most part it was a wonderful and untroubled decade. I know both Eric and Ernie loved going to the rehearsal rooms – the script discussions, the rehearsals both in the early stages then later stages, the whole build-up process to the actual recording of a show.

SIDENOTE: Conversely, this being the big decade of Morecambe and Wise's career, it would also see both my grandparents, Sadie and George, pass away, and Ernie's mother, Connie, too. Ernie's Dad, Harry – who had never, it later transpired, fully recovered from his career with his son coming to an abrupt end almost before it had really begun – had pre-deceased the others in the mid-1960s. He'd lived long enough to see his child protégé become a huge star.

I've often wondered how my grandfather George viewed his son's extraordinary success. It was one thing that he was able to separate his own life from my father's, insomuch as show business was of little-to-no interest to him personally, but was there also little-to-no recognition of what was going on with his son? Maybe that's what made him appear so unflustered about it all. As my mother says, 'You must remember that George worked very hard all his life – he was a labourer. It was physical work. All he would be able to think about at the end of each day was what he was going to eat for his supper! His life was very different from Eric's.'

While the 1970s ticked merrily along, we all somehow appeared to forget that my father had suffered a near-fatal heart attack some years previously. In fact, rarely was it ever even referenced. 'People would sometimes ask me how I was feeling,' my father said of this period. 'I'd have to think twice before realising what they meant.' Even he, too, had apparently forgotten.

With the benefit of hindsight, we should have been more aware that this shadow had retreated, not departed. Without realising it, the early seventies, with the more generous and gentle pacing instilled by Bill Cotton, had been supplanted by a treadmill.

It was a different treadmill than before – subtler – but

a treadmill all the same. Being Morecambe and Wise required so much external stuff that went way beyond the remit of their shows. It was less the rollercoaster ride of yesteryear, more a slow-motion fall from a great height.

I'm not sure Ernie recognised the warning signs at this time, either. Understandable, really, as he was on the same treadmill, no doubt with his own issues and daily strains to contend with behind the main focal point of the act.

Ernie had spent most of his life worrying about his partner, so there was nothing especially new happening in the 1970s to concern him. It's worth remembering, however, that, though he was sharing the same treadmill, he hadn't nearly died while on the previous one.

At this point they should have done what Rowan Atkinson suggested: simply rarefied themselves, said a big 'No' to almost everything except an annual Christmas show. But it's not what happened, because being in the moment is not the same as reflecting upon it.

What happened instead is that they became used to it all – it became familiar, as they had accepted the insanity of their work as normal in the 1950s and '60s: the sixty cigarettes a day and the toing-and-froing to America. Alas, a serious past illness plus the stress of being the country's top comedy act really don't make the best bedfellows.

In July 1977, now in their early fifties, Eric and Ernie performed one of their charity Royal shows. This time it was at the Theatre Royal, Windsor, for Prince Charles. Billy Marsh and his liaison man Andrew Neatrour – an independent producer and nothing to do with Billy's

London Management operation – would put on many charity Royal shows together during the seventies.

The wonderful and versatile blues, jazz and pop singer Madeline Bell – a friend of the Morecambe family to this day – was on the show, she being a personal favourite of Prince Charles and Morecambe and Wise.

I had the pleasure to occasionally work with her as a publicist at that time. I'd mentioned Madeline Bell to Billy Marsh, who then discovered how thrilled Prince Charles was on learning there was a direct connection with her, and so straightaway Billy put her on the Windsor show.

After the show wound up, I hitched a lift back to my parents' house with them, Mike Fountain as always driving us. My father said that around two-thirds of the way through their performance that evening – which was the usual touring act they performed for the 'bank raids' – he hadn't felt quite right. 'I came over a bit faint, after a while, and a bit short of breath. But it passed.'

I remember that striking me as bad. It wasn't as if it was winter and he had a cold or a virus of any kind. Perhaps these occasional moments should have been scrutinised more thoroughly – they weren't dissimilar in nature to the funny turn at Ed Sullivan's, or the severe pains in Yarmouth – but as I've said before, the whole family was on the frantic journey of M&W's career *with* them, and we just went where the current took us. Every observation was kept to the moment in which it was raised, and not mulled over later, because at any later time we were in the next moment of their frantic journey.

SIDENOTE: I remember as we drove past the front of the theatre after that Windsor show, we saw Bruce Forsyth and his then wife Anthea Redfern, who had attended the show, in a very heated exchange. My father got Mike to hoot, and Bruce and Anthea quickly glanced up and waved and smiled all very jovially. Bruce and Anthea would separate exactly two years later, in July 1979.

NINETEEN

The year 1977 was a big one insomuch as it was the first time since 1967 that Eric and Ernie decided to switch channels, feeling it was time to part company with the BBC and try pastures new at Thames Television. They executed this move because of a promise by Thames – a promise led by their old friend, the entertainment exec, Philip Jones.

Philip Jones was a charming man, with an honesty and integrity equal to that of Bill Cotton's. He made no secret that he wanted his bite at the Morecambe and Wise cherry, and a chance to persuade them to switch channels. Hence the promise of a film, which he knew as a genre both men, especially Ernie, were still really keen to have another crack at. He also knew that money wasn't the answer – the BBC could offer M&W any amount of money to convince them to stay – it had to be something the BBC could *not* offer. And that was making a movie through the Euston Films branch of Thames Television. It had proved a successful venture for John Thaw and Dennis Waterman with *Sweeney!* and *Sweeney 2*. So, as a carrot to M&W, it was going to prove a crucial one.

Eric and Ernie had always wanted to do something cinematic that went beyond the moderate achievement of the Rank Organisation outings of the mid-sixties. This appeared to be their big chance. But it never was, for Thames were not looking to give M&W a big-budget cinematic break with their full backing. Fundamentally, they were paying them lip service to get them to sign a contract to join Thames and produce almost exactly the same shows they were producing for the BBC.

Before getting to Thames, however, they had the small matter of the BBC 1977 Christmas show to rehearse and record. It's never been a favourite of mine, but it was still a highly entertaining show with great guest stars, and their biggest in terms of viewing figures. The figure varies according to the source, but it's widely regarded to have pulled in between twenty-five and twenty-nine million viewers. It's considered to be one of the highest audiences for one channel in British television history.

The show itself was a fond farewell to the BBC. We even get to see Eric and Ernie packing up their flat to move, which is rather a poignant moment considering the wonderful decade they'd spent in that fictional space.

Guests were Penelope Keith, Elton John, Angharad Rees, Francis Matthews, Arthur Lowe, John Le Mesurier, John Laurie, John Thaw, Dennis Waterman, Richard Briers, Paul Eddington, James Hunt, Stella Starr, Michael Parkinson, Richard Baker, Frank Bough, Angela Rippon, Barry Norman, Eddie Waring, Richard Whitmore, Philip Jenkinson, Peter Woods, Jenny Lee Wright and Valerie Leon. My apologies to anyone I've missed. This was a big cast, and unlike in the 1950s and early 1960s, when Eric and Ernie were often lost within a big cast, they were a completely different product by now, operating on their own terms.

They were never anything less than loud in their delivery, thanks chiefly to those early days of the variety halls, which created a wonderful energy, intensity, indeed almost madness to what they were saying.

And so an era ended. *The Morecambe & Wise Show* ran on BBC Two and BBC1 for a total of nine series and eight Christmas specials, between 1968 and 1977. While arguably it is the 1971 BBC Christmas show, with 'Burly Chassis' and 'Andrew Preview' that is likely to remain the most watched and remembered – as predicted by my father at the time – that whole wonderful decade of M&W shows was their magical era. And now the party had come to a fairly abrupt end.

SIDENOTE: The opening to the 1977 show wasn't, strictly speaking, a part of the familiar pattern of their other Christmas shows, it being filmed on location. It was a parody of the popular seventies 'buddy' cop series of the day, *Starsky and Hutch*, starring Paul Michael Glaser and David Soul. Eric and Ernie's version was 'Starkers and Krutch!' It was nice to see that David Soul recently caught up with the parody, and tweeted: 'Yeah. You got me. I would call this great parody. Bravo!'

Bobby Warans was working in the props department of the BBC, and did the Christmas special that final year. 'I was heading to the main lifts in reception with the set designer, Vic Meredith,' he recalls. 'In burst

Eric, and told both of us to enjoy ourselves that night. "We've just signed with Thames Television," he said. So we knew Morecambe and Wise were leaving the BBC before anyone else – before Bill Cotton and the other executives. We felt very honoured!' And Bobby Warans also recreated the Morecambe and Wise flat's living room for the *Trust Morecambe & Wise* series I did with Lenny Henry.

Their arrival at Thames Television bore similar hallmarks to the BBC years. They arrived full of enthusiasm, this being as near as they'd ever get to trying something new.

Eric and Ernie looked pretty much the same as they had in their last show for the BBC, and the Thames show's format wasn't dissimilar, either. Their flamboyant producer was Keith Beckett. He was quite nomadic in his work, and eclectic in his choices, ranging from producing the likes of *Opportunity Knocks* to six specials with Bruce Forsyth, and one-off shows with Janet Brown, Shirley Bassey, Freddie Starr and Mike Yarwood. He was also a guest producer for several of Benny Hill's shows.

Beckett did three M&W shows on their arrival at Thames TV – from 1978 to 1979.

I think that caught them slightly by surprise. Though with no real plan in mind on how a change would be orchestrated, they'd expected different ideas to be thrown their way. But Thames wanted what they had been doing for the BBC, but on Thames! Alas, what was missing was BBC clout and production values, and writer Eddie Braben. Eddie had a year or so left on his BBC contract so couldn't move with them. If Eric and Ernie had been looking for a fresh challenge – and according to my father, that's exactly what they *were* looking for – they had found it, if not quite in the manner they'd expected or wanted.

'I don't think those Thames shows were ever as good as the BBC ones,' my mother tells me. 'Repetition began to creep in. Older sketches were regurgitated with different guests playing those original roles. I think Eric picked up on this so much that he seriously considered retiring. They had had this immensely long run of success, that maybe now it was time to count one's blessings and call it a day.'

I've always been, at best, ambivalent about their move to Thames. I'm relieved to see my mother feels the same way. What one has to remember is that at the BBC they were at their peak, and they set the bar so high with such consistently wonderful shows that are still screened and enjoyed to this day. That was always going to be a tough act to follow. As my mother says, 'Some of the numbers and sketches they did for Thames were equally as good as what they'd been doing for years at the BBC. What was missing was the consistency. At Thames they were great in patches.'

To mark their arrival at Thames and deliver 'event' TV, there was absolutely no appetite to make a full series of shows. What they did instead was make a 1978 autumn special, where we literally see Eric and Ernie dumped by a van outside the Thames Television studios. It was a jokey nod to any animosity felt by the BBC at their departure.

And clearly there was animosity. When the BBC, soon after their departure, rapidly repeated some of their BBC shows, the announcer introduced it as, 'The *best* years of Morecambe and Wise'. Emphasis was deliberately placed on where they'd enjoyed their 'best years'. In truth, if a little cheeky of the BBC, that was pretty much the case and difficult to protest against.

Keeping Braben-esque in style, there was also one of the play's 'what' Ernie wrote. This time it was *Dr Jekyll & Mrs Hyde* – extremely funny and guest-starring actress Judi Dench, shortly before she went on to become one of the biggest stars on the planet.

Their first Christmas show at Thames, in 1978, was written by Barry Cryer and John Junkin, who often worked together as a writing team.

'One of you is prowling around the room, and the other one is tapping away,' said Cryer. 'I'd be sitting there typing, and John would be walking around the room, twiddling his glasses, being Eric Morecambe.'

Barry was an old friend of Eric and Ernie's. Actually, Barry was an old friend of everyone! I've hardly met anyone who hadn't at some point had a beer and a few laughs with Barry. As the writers for the show, they continued keeping faith to Eddie Braben's style, with the only notable change being in its conclusion, the show ending on a dance routine, rather than the 'Bring Me Sunshine' number we were all so familiar with. Cryer still insisted that Eddie Braben was the main writer for Morecambe and Wise. 'He saw how they bonded,' said Cryer. 'He turned them into Eric and Ernie, not Morecambe and Wise.'

Perhaps claiming the wheels fell off at this point is an exaggeration – the shows still had Eric and Ernie's comedic effervescence – but there was something missing. People were literally coming up to me in the street to say how much they love Morecambe and Wise, but not the Thames shows!

What was missing can't be fully defined; suffice to say that what might therefore have been missing was the something indefinable that the BBC itself brought to the shows. M&W looked out of place on Thames Television, as if they'd stepped into the wrong studio, but were given permission to do their show anyway before being sent home.

And just as they got into their swing, up would pop an advert. *The Morecambe & Wise Show* was something that for its duration required the viewer to suspend disbelief – one certainly shouldn't have to contend with the distraction of adverts for carpet cleaners and toothpaste. But I would say that the 1978 Christmas show was as good as it ever got during their time at Thames. There were enough similarities to their BBC work, plus the quality of the show itself, to create a general air of approval. And although their guest stars' star quality arguably would lessen in the coming months and years, they did have actor–comedian Leonard Rossiter, a huge star at that time, and former prime minister Lord Harold Wilson on board.

Generally speaking, Thames were a little cheeky when it came to the guest stars they'd encourage on to the M&W

shows. At the BBC, John Ammonds would work directly with the boys and Eddie on a script, then work out the biggest name they should get to play the necessary guest-star part. This was based purely on suitability. Or they would come up with a guest star they really wanted on their show, and work a script to suit that person. Thames didn't work like that – they looked down the list of their own entertainers and used the M&W show to showcase these artistes. There is absolutely nothing wrong in doing this, but for Morecambe and Wise it was a little constraining on what they could do.

SIDENOTE: Donald Sinden's son – actor, director and producer Marc Sinden – tells me that his brother Jeremy was working at the same rehearsal rooms as Eric and Ernie. 'He bumped into Eric there. They started chatting, and Eric asked what our father, Donald, was currently doing. Jeremy replied, "He's playing King Lear for the Royal Shakespeare Company." Eric said, "Good lord! Do they know?" Dad dined out on that comment for years! As a family we adored Morecambe and Wise. We had an annual black-tie party at home on Christmas Day, with a cast that would make the West End and Pinewood empty. But everything would stop for their Christmas special. We had about four television sets scattered around the house, and everyone would crowd around them to watch it, and then spend the rest of the party discussing and dissecting it.'

Jeremy's story reminds me of the time impressionist

> Mike Yarwood excitedly approached my father at the BBC to tell him that he had included an impression of him in his new series. My father smiled and said, 'Are you doing it now?'

Eric and Ernie were fairly optimistic in late 1978, as it quickly rolled into January 1979. Then my father had a second heart attack – right in front of me, as it happens. On a Russell Harty show three years later, he jokingly said I'd caused it. I *think* he was joking!

He was opening the fridge door – it could have been that breakfast routine to the stripper music – and fell backwards on to the tiled floor. I thought he'd slipped on something. But as he got up, he told me he'd momentarily blacked out. And now his heart rate wouldn't slow down, and he was perspiring profusely – or sweating like a pig, I think were the words he used in that moment. I reckon we both knew what was happening.

Back to hospital, back to recuperation, and this time the need for the then pioneering bypass heart surgery, which was carried out by Professor Magdi Yacoub.

> GAIL: It was a crazy time. Mum also went in an ambulance to the same hospital on the same day, as the evening before she'd slipped on ice walking the dog, and broken her ankle! It was quite surreal taking a cooked meal to them both sitting up in bed. Mum looked really fed up. Dad did his usual smile and said, 'Well, it was worth all that money on your cooking lessons, Gail!'

For Ernie, it was 1968 revisited. He said at the time, as his partner was back to making a slow recovery, that he really hoped Eric would be fit enough to begin a new Christmas Morecambe and Wise show. 'Everyone asks, "How's Eric?" and, "Are you going to do a Christmas show?"' recalled Ernie in 1979. 'Well, Eric has grown a moustache, and things are easing along. I'm sure everything is going to be all right, but we are not back on the treadmill.' It's an interesting choice of words, which sort of sums up how they were feeling about their careers now, if only on a subliminal level. It's hard to spot the difference between this and 1968, other than that both men were older.

This break from the 'treadmill' did create time for Ernie and Doreen to pursue other interests. Ernie had long been into what he called gourmet foods. 'I used to be a cook in the Merchant Navy, and I've always maintained an interest in cooking,' he said. 'I love good food. These days, I seem to be six pounds overweight. I do exercise, but not enough. The thing is, I should push myself away from the table sooner.'

In this same interview, he got on to talking about what the future would be if my father had to retire through health reasons. 'You are asking me if people would accept me on my own, instead of the two of us together?' he said. 'Well, I think if people knew the situation, they would accept it – if they knew Eric couldn't do the work.'

I find this observation fascinating in light of what would happen to Ernie when, years later, he did find himself on his own.

'You could spend all year just working on one Christmas

show,' he explained. 'But I'm not vegetating. I don't believe in retirement. If you're fit and well, you shouldn't retire. No one should retire if they don't want to.'

Like Ernie Wise, Thames were nothing if not patient, and always supportive of their two biggest stars, treating them as the Crown jewels of their programming. Any lack of knowing how to present them to their fullest potential bore no connection to their respect for them and their talent.

'It was a little unfortunate for Thames,' recalls my mother, 'as they had the latter part of their careers. And with Eric being ill, things began to pile up. Also, the continued repetition of material used in much older sketches wasn't ideal. Eric was very aware of this. I know both he and Ernie were at this point getting closer to retirement, even though they could be serenaded away from actually making that decision. But it was difficult as they felt, quite rightly in fact, grateful to Thames. However, because of all that had been going on in the background, they hadn't as yet been able to give them their best.'

When they came back in 1980, with my father supposedly – though questionably – fully recovered, that was when one or two of the wheels started to fall off.

TWENTY

Morecambe and Wise were suddenly looking older than they should have done for men in their mid-fifties. Maybe they hadn't aged overnight, but the hiatus from TV screens emphasised an unexpected ageing that we hadn't, at home at least, really noticed.

Every line of their long and fruitful journey was mapped across their faces, and Ernie, I felt, wore an almost haunted look. It was as if he wasn't quite there, and when Ernie wasn't quite there, his partner carried about an anxious air, and perhaps forced things more than he was used to just to get through the routines. Ernie, we must remember, was the glue to this double act. If Ernie wasn't one hundred per cent on song, then my father became partially unstuck. And 'cuddly little Ern' had a gauntness about him, accentuated by his now completely white hair.

The bits of business referenced earlier – the short fat hairy legs, the wig, his shortness – were no longer funny reference points, because you can't go around knocking someone who's suddenly looking much older than their age.

John Ammonds told me a telling thing, just after Ernie's own eventual passing. He confessed that it was less Ernie who was the problem at the recordings of the M&W

shows at Thames – Ernie had always had trouble remembering lines – but my father. After his heart surgery, he had emerged lacking his natural comic timing, according to John Ammonds. 'For the first time since we'd all been together on the shows, we had to edit Eric in the editing suite to get the timing back on track!'

Sticking with Ernie a moment, the ageing element I'm sure reflected on the shared suffering and success of being in a double act. The ups and downs are always shared, as Ernie pointed out in interviews throughout the years. And as we know, Ernie's early years had been tough compared to his partner's. Ernie had endured a difficult childhood where money had been scarce and affection barely demonstrated. He had been the breadwinner from late childhood to the end of his parents' lives. Ernie was possibly feeling utterly exhausted by it all.

Eric and Ernie, from 1980 on, looked diminished. A listlessness emerged in both performers and performances, which at that time none of us could quite fathom or express in words. Mostly because we weren't trying to. Family, and the full working circle of M&W, were living it in real time. All the questioning would follow much later. If we had any observations, it was about the paucity of decent material for them to work with.

It's easy to say the move to Thames from the BBC was the underlying cause of change, and it is true that their starting out again on a new adventure didn't help. But remaining at the BBC wouldn't have prevented either my father's illness or its on-going issues.

*

Eric and Ernie still worked hard at what they did, but as my mother points out, following his second heart attack her husband wasn't a well man. 'We all worried about him,' she says, 'but quietly you start to think he is indestructible. He mostly felt that way himself, and we went along with it.'

SIDENOTE: At this time, my father discovered a new-found interest in writing books. It started with a novel, *Mr Lonely*, and concluded with two children's books – *The Reluctant Vampire* and *The Vampire's Revenge*. Following a period of recuperation, this grew into something more than a passing interest, and was clearly engaging him more than performing comedy by this stage in his life.

I had the genuine pleasure and honour of turning his two vampire books into a trilogy with the publication of *The Vampire King*, and also, following on from *Mr Lonely*, I was able to work up his notes and some written chapters of the next novel he had been planning, *Stella*. Both these titles would be published posthumously, and I was always grateful to Ernie for the support he gave me on this, especially *Stella*, for which he did an upbeat review for a national paper. *Stella* more than *Mr Lonely* unexpectedly reflects my father's own background in Lancashire. He deliberately hid himself behind a female protagonist.

The first M&W special for Thames was in 1978. Also in 1978 we had *Eric & Ernie's Xmas Show*. It's interesting to note that my father didn't warm too much to the 'Eric and Ernie' tag, as it sounded too chummy and lacked the edge the BBC had given them by always branding them 'Morecambe and Wise'. I casually mentioned this to former head of light entertainment at Thames Television, the truly kind and affable Philip Jones. He was shocked. 'We only did it because we thought they would prefer it!'

Ernie and Doreen were great friends with Philip and Florence Jones, and would socialise regularly through the years, so little was ever going to be said that might impact on that relationship. Not at this point in their lives and careers. This was no Lord Lew Grade conflict bubbling away, and never could be. This was a different era and set of issues they were now negotiating their way through.

Christmas with Eric and Ernie in 1979 was a replacement for their standard Christmas show. It was too soon to contemplate the work required for one of those. So the '79 special was mostly the two men reflecting on their careers with host David Frost and guests Des O'Connor and Glenda Jackson.

SIDENOTE: Glenda Jackson appearing with them on David Frost's M&W replacement Christmas show emphasised the respect she had for the two comedians.

When I worked with Lenny Henry on his three-part series, *Trust Morecambe & Wise*, Glenda Jackson was again willing to appear on the sofa talking about them. I bumped into her in make-up, and she said, 'Gary. It's been a while since we last saw each other. When was it?'

'I was twelve, I think, and I'm now sixty-three!'

'Oh no!' She winced, sinking into her chair. 'Was it really that long ago?'

Things appeared to move forward at pace from this point on, as in we deluded ourselves that everything was fine again, despite Eric and Ernie looking older and more tired with each show.

Series one at Thames was transmitted in the autumn of 1980. They had a Christmas show in 1980 as well, the first 'proper' Christmas show since 1978. Series two was in the autumn of 1981. And Thames, still keeping the *Eric & Ernie's Xmas Show* title going, gave us another Christmas show that festive season of '81.

Series three was October through to December 1982. *Eric & Ernie's Xmas Show* followed that same year. Series four was autumn 1983, and my father, if not Ernie, was beginning to look very drawn. Ernie himself was complaining he was having more trouble than ever remembering his lines, though he also admitted with a chuckle that it wasn't exactly a new problem.

The 1983 Christmas show would be the last one Morecambe and Wise would ever present.

Had it not been for the determination of my father, this programme may never have been completed, as actress Gemma Craven, in conversation with author Paul Burton, still remembers.

'We did a *Mack and Mabel* "Keystone Cops" sequence

with Eric and Ernie both dressed as policemen,' she said. 'I was at the top of this ladder. One minute I could see both Eric and Ernie below, the next I could only see Ernie. Eric had collapsed and the paramedics had to take him to hospital. When Eric got better, he came back and, bless him, finished the show. I greatly admired him for that. He came back and carried on as if nothing had happened. I remember him saying, "Anything to give you a tea break!" They broke the mould when they made him. He was a one-off, a consummate professional, and I loved him so much.'

Discussing Morecambe and Wise reminded Gemma of a musical number she agreed to do for the duo. 'I had to jump into a tank of water. I am terrified of water! It was only four feet deep but I had to go under the water. I was really scared. I didn't tell them until afterwards. Eric loved that and gave me a big hug and burst out laughing. They then told me that no one else would agree to do it!'

I bumped into the actor Burt Kwouk in his later years. With Burt's usual exuberance, ubiquitous cigarette dangling from his lips, he couldn't wait to tell me how wonderful it had been appearing with M&W in that show, loosely reprising his role as Cato from the Pink Panther movies, a role that had given him a global presence.

It was an odd show, with all its repetitions from past years. And that despite Eddie Braben being on board as writer, perhaps suggesting his river was running a little dry, too. Eddie wasn't getting any younger, either. After a long gap away from M&W, was he still feeling the creative desire that he'd felt when they'd all first met back in the late 1960s?

I'd describe the 1983 Christmas show not just as being a poor entry, but in all honesty – and this is based on their own astonishingly high standards – as pretty dire. It lacks everything that made Morecambe and Wise Morecambe and Wise. Even at the time it didn't make comfortable viewing. They were going through the motions, while attempting to convince themselves and the viewing public that they weren't.

The actor John Thaw said, after working with them in the seventies, that it was the repetition of material more than anything else that was depressing both Eric and Ernie.

Nanette Newman's husband, the film director Bryan Forbes, once told me that Nanette was so proud to be in that final show. And actor Christopher Biggins told me he had been so looking forward to his own agreed appearance in their Christmas show for the following year, but of course that was never to happen.

Nevertheless, 1980 to 1983 represented a stable time for the double act, now in their mid to late fifties, and their families. I would say my father seemed on pretty good form, despite all I've just said above. As long as he had his writing and fishing, he had enough escape there to allow the M&W show to keep on rolling.

There had been one or two discussions, both with Ernie and also with the family at home, about retiring completely from television, but I sensed that he was just sounding us all out. I think Gail had a better insight into all of this – the idea of calling it a day for M&W once he had reached the magic sixty years of age.

But as we now know from Paul Merton, my father was quietly asking the question about a return to the BBC, which admittedly might only have been to do the one show a year – their famed Christmas special – but it was still M&W work being planned for future years. No one in the family knew of this secret plan ticking away inside his head. Did Ernie?

Their fame was so great by this point, and my father – all because of his health-related issues – was slightly more withdrawn than before. I can only imagine that just to go out and bump into the general public must have been a strain for him. It's true that he preferred to be recognised than go unrecognised, because without the recognition he would have felt they were doing something wrong. But this interaction with the public wasn't as enjoyable as it had once been.

My father enjoyed being famous and said that anyone famous who claimed otherwise was lying! It was enhanced pleasure, because their fame pre-dated the invasive world of social media, the paparazzi, Z-list 'stars', and general media intrusion. Back in the sixties through to the nineties, there seemed to be an unspoken under-standing that everyone would play fair, even if boundaries were slightly pushed.

I'm not sure my father would have been able to com-fortably deal with it all had he and Ernie been strutting their stuff now. There was a part of him that was very private – that same boy who had delighted in entertaining his friends was equally content to sit alone, staring out of the window of the school bus.

At this point, what my father loved most was being alone in his upstairs office at home, tapping away on his portable typewriter surrounded by Tipp-Ex. How would his life have been if it were the age of the internet and social media? Would he and Ernie have been exchanging jokey comments about each other and other entertainers? I can imagine Ernie taking people on a ride through his variety hall upbringing, and my father throwing in barbed comments about it at every opportunity. The world of social media might have done them both a lot of good. They would have realised how loved they were.

Doreen Wise related to me a time when she, Ernie and my mother were down on the beach near Torquay with Gail and me in the early 1960s, and my father stayed behind. She explained that my father could go into these quiet spaces where he would be distant and uncommunicative. I believe that to be true as I'd witnessed it for myself at home occasionally.

GAIL: Well, he really never was a fan of beaches! I do agree he could be quiet and introspective at times. I'm sure that's why he loved fishing so much. He was always happy to go on his own. I have always thought of him as an introverted extrovert. He was definitely a deep thinker, nothing shallow about him. I often say that he really 'got' life. Mum would describe him as a mass of

275

contradictions. For all the activity and the joking, there was also a remarkable stillness about him at times. He came across as both ridiculously frivolous and ridiculously grounded.

TWENTY-ONE

There is an anecdote, albeit apocryphal, about John Lennon and David Bowie, and it relates a little to my father and fame. Apparently the pair were once walking around Hong Kong some time in the late 1970s, when a child approached Lennon and asked, 'Are you John Lennon?'

'No,' Lennon replied, 'but I wish I had his money.'

The child went away.

Bowie was very impressed with how effective this retort was and began using it himself thereafter.

Some months later, Bowie was walking around New York on his own, when a voice behind him asked, 'Are you David Bowie?'

'No,' Bowie replied, 'but I wish I had his money.'

'You lying bastard,' said John Lennon, stepping up to him out of nowhere. 'You wish you had *my* money!'

The basic idea was one my father used on several occasions, particularly at airports where he was never keen to be recognised. Partly it was because he was, if not a nervous flyer, assuredly an uncomfortable one.

Entertaining the public was his *metier*, but that was in a more controlled environment where he had the curtains to disappear behind, and a dressing-room door to shut on the outside world. Not an airport lounge where the stares would follow indefinitely. I think he just felt mildly threatened, and understandably so. For a start, he had become one of the most recognisable people in the United Kingdom, and not everyone who recognises you is necessarily a fan.

The first time it happened was at Faro airport, Portugal, when a woman approached and asked him if he was Eric Morecambe. He just said no, but that he wished he was. She then said, 'I bet you wish you had his money,' chuckled and walked off. He clocked it, though, as he always did with good lines, and made it his own. Interestingly, this was also around the late 1970s when John Lennon was allegedly using a similar approach.

There were family trips, less frequent than in previous years, but still occurring. Portugal, particularly; but also now Florida, my parents having somewhat spontaneously decided to buy a condo over there. They knew Ernie and Doreen owned one, and had met up with them in the Sunshine State once.

'One came up for sale,' says my mother, 'and we went to see it. Your father took one look, and that was it. No negotiation, he just said we'll take it. He could be impetuous.'

SIDENOTE: Ernie and Doreen had been going out to Florida for some years, and Mike Winters, of the double-act Mike and Bernie Winters, had semi-retired out there to re-emerge as a novelist.

Once described as Morecambe and Wise-lite, you'd have thought there would have been little harmony between them all, but curiously Mike and his wife Cassie and Ernie and Doreen Wise became great friends.

I guess there was that feeling of having done the journey together – same venues, same peers, same triumphs and tribulations. Bernie and his dog Schnorbitz became their own double act. Mike Winters emulated my father as a writer, but arguably with greater success, as he was now done with both comedy and the UK, or as much as were possible, and fully ensconced himself with America and being an author.

There was a slight haze around us all during this odd period. The nearest we ever got to answering my father's repeated question: 'Do you think I should retire?' was to say that only he could make that decision. He would ask Ernie the same question, and just like us, Ernie would say, 'That has to be your decision'.

Were we therefore waiting for him to retire? Would we all be surprised if he had? I don't think we would have been surprised, because of all he'd been through with his health, and the fact he'd carved a secondary career for himself as an author, which he was genuinely enjoying as much as anything he had enjoyed in a career of comedy. But I'm not sure we were waiting for him to make some great pronouncement on retirement, as much as a reduction of his workload.

GAIL: I was waiting for him to retire. I would talk to him about it, and I would ask Mum about it. She always came across a bit stressed on the subject, and say something to the effect that the doctors thought he was fine to keep working, and naturally Ernie's name would come up in any conversation about retirement, as Ernie was fit and well.

I recall being in the back garden wandering around with Dad. Out of nowhere he said, 'Well, that's it, Gail. I'm retiring when I'm sixty! Giving up Morecambe and Wise.' And he looked really happy, as you do when finally you make a difficult decision you've been putting off. He'd become a grandfather in 1978, and again in 1980, and was thrilled to be 'Poppa'. Both of his parents had died in the late 1970s, and I think their absence, and his grandparent status, had made him start to think that it would be okay to consider retirement. I think sixty, psychologically speaking, sounded better to him; more legitimate than retiring in his fifties.

He and Ernie had discussions in early 1983 about rarefying their appearances. So now they were thinking that come 1984 they should consider only presenting Christmas specials. All well and good, but as my mother points out, 'He then would join Ernie for a meeting at the studios, have a great time catching up with Ernie, with the producer, with the director and everyone else involved, have a few drinks and come back home to announce they'd agreed to sign a contract for two more series as well as a special!'

Eric and Ernie were becoming a lot like ageing rock bands, such as the Stones, in that they seemed unable to quit despite the external warnings. The Stones certainly ignored the warnings, like heart surgery for Mick Jagger and the death of Charlie Watts. Perhaps this inability to stop is as awful as the determination to continue. Many applaud the 'never-say-die' approach of those, like Bruce Forsyth, who seem to continue to their last breath. I'm just not so sure it's the best path to take.

Despite my father's heart surgery and two prior heart attacks, and Ernie having trouble remembering his lines – and suffering a form of asthma – they carried on, because it is what they had done from the beginning of their journey together.

SIDENOTE: With hindsight, I would probably now say that in the last year of his life my dad wasn't seeking out 'funny' in the day-to-day in the same way, though he still enjoyed a laugh of course!

We should as a family perhaps have made more of this change at the time. But the natural transition of less comedy and more 'other interests' seemed acceptable in the moment it was occurring.

It was also notable that he wasn't as fast on the uptake as he'd once been: the 'Eric Morecambe' rejoinders and quick wit were starting to be minimised or misplaced. I put it down to ageing, which was ludicrous. He was fifty-seven!

I've wondered since if Ernie was aware of any changes in his lifelong partner. Having said that, I sensed Ernie was slightly reduced as a performer, too, just turning his energy output down a notch, quite possibly an effect of all the ups and downs with his partner over the years, plus his own tiring of the repetition of it all. When you've spent your life striving for something then acquired it, complaining of repetition is not something you're overly concerned about.

TWENTY-TWO

As both the television series and the 'special' shows continued with Thames, finally the Euston wing of the company got around to making the film Morecambe and Wise had been promised, and which had instigated their move away from the BBC.

Shot at Albury Park Mansion, with interior scenes taped in Studio 2 at Thames' Teddington Studios, it would be titled *Night Train to Murder*, and for both men would prove not worth having left the BBC for.

One thing that summarises the studio's ambition (or lack thereof) to make this film is that it was *not* shot on film, but on tape.

Originally, it had a laughter track, but this was discarded. Retaining it might have improved the final outcome, as the Rank Organisation films from the mid-sixties suffered, as we know, from Eric and Ernie lacking an audience reaction.

It was, chronologically speaking, the last time they would appear together as a double act. (There was some TV work recorded post filming.)

It was directed by Joseph McGrath, who they knew

283

and liked very much. He'd worked on two Beatles movies – *A Hard Day's Night* (1964) and *Help!* (1965). Known mostly for his collaborations with Peter Sellers and Spike Milligan, Eric and Ernie were aware of his comedy pedigree.

More than anything it was a pastiche of Agatha Christie and others of that ilk, and just writing that down makes me beg the question: why did they choose that direction? The Rank films they'd made in the sixties might not have been outstanding, but they were biggish-budget entertainment with colourful locations, such as the South of France, and put together with a lot of thought, enthusiasm and determination.

Now, however, we were to be subjected to an implausible 1940s country-house murder-mystery, its chosen period making it dreary before the comedy even began. There was also an air to the project – something that my father picked up on early on – that this was much more a fulfilment of a contract than a new and exciting opportunity for him and Ernie. An uphill struggle, therefore, from the outset.

'Your father's biggest disappointment,' says my mother all these decades later, 'is less how poor the film turned out, which it did, but how he had failed to recognise that at the time of filming. He prided himself on recognising what worked and didn't when it came to what he and Ernie did. But he failed to sense it on this occasion.'

He was probably a bit harsh on the Rank films as they have, if anything, improved with passing time, cropping up with regularity on television, and giving a beautiful glimpse of time and place. And while accepting that

Night Train really was third rate, it's an important part of Morecambe and Wise's canon, showing where they were at this period of their career.

Night Train to Murder, at my father's insistence on watching it through on its completion, was to be shelved for as long as possible. He was certainly vocal about that. His wish was followed through, and eventually, following his death, the film slipped out on daytime television. He would have been okay about that. It was a prime-time screening or, worse still, a theatrical release that would have concerned him. Ultimately, it was never good enough to achieve the originally hoped-for theatrical release, which had been the biggest pull in getting them across the River Thames.

In that moment, my father seemed happy – happy with his writing and with his various appearances here, there and everywhere, both with and without Ernie. And he was even making some short films with actor Tom Baker, which would be posthumously screened as one film: *The Passionate Pilgrim*, narrated by the dulcet tones of actor John Le Mesurier. This was a departure from his partnership with Ernie, and even, for a short while, a departure from writing books. Not that Eric and Ernie were completely unused to departure from their work together. In 1981, my father appeared with John Alderton, Beryl Reid and Susannah York in a short film of four poems by Sir John Betjeman, *Late Flowering Love*.

When my father wrote the novel *Mr Lonely*, shortly followed by his two children's books, he was writing without much effort to disguise who he was and how he was known. By the time he started his fourth book, *Stella*, there was less Eric Morecambe and more a detached voice to what he was producing. He was mastering a neutral tone – or starting to. There were still Morecambe-isms throughout the text, but they were reflex habits, not where his creative tone was now heading.

> GAIL: He also wrote *Eric Morecambe on Fishing*. I love reading it, as it really is his natural voice talking about his many experiences on the riverbank. In fact, it's not entirely about fishing – not a 'how to' book at all. You don't need to know anything about fishing, or even have an interest in it, to enjoy the book. And it has wonderful illustrations. I'm sorry that he never got to see the published item. I think he would have loved it, perhaps even more than any book he'd been involved with to date.

He was clearly enjoying these minor changes in his working life, and I believe it enabled him to keep going with Morecambe and Wise. It presented him with enough to sense he was now able to operate in a world separate from the one he had virtually been imprisoned in for the forty or fifty years prior.

These new pastures were not so much the chore of being endlessly funny, but a new and healthy way of life. You only had to compare the chat shows he turned up on as a new novelist to the myriad ones as a comedian to spot the difference. He went from being the mischievous comic with winks to camera, to the interviewee genuinely keener to discuss his writing than his comedy.

This, of course, must have proved a tricky juggling act – the novelist, detached from his partner, but still the comedian when back in the studios. Yet he enjoyed both careers enormously. He never complained about the endless shows he and Ernie were still doing, however unsatisfactory they might have begun to feel by now. Indeed, I believe he rather accepted the continued limelight, on the basis he was now able to escape into the insular world of the writer. Like his fishing, it was something he could do alone.

M&W delivered on raw energy, but that was beginning to stutter. Ernie told me that other than my father's new interest and distraction as an author, he too was finding issues with the continued work they were producing as a double act. We know that learning material was something Ernie had always struggled with – hence some of the memorable ad-libs from his partner – and it was becoming increasingly tricky for him.

Both Eric and Ernie were performing less as natural comedians and more as people carrying out the responsibilities of their job. My father was wholly professional to the end, but that didn't cover up the cracks. And I should add that I'm thinking as much of the man at home, and out and about mingling with the public, as the man in front of a camera.

There were now clear signs of my father's ill health at this point – early 1984. We were, in an unspoken way, putting it down to the mileage. But the shocking truth of the matter – something Gail recently reminded me – is that he was only fifty-seven pushing fifty-eight. That's not far off being ten years younger than I am while writing this book. Which begs the question: why didn't any of us realise that it must be serious? He shouldn't have looked like an old man. He shouldn't have puffed and panted his way up a couple of flights of stairs, when Bruce Forsyth and Lionel Blair were still dancing up them! I can only say that he genuinely seemed indestructible, using my mother's word. He'd already survived so much, we just assumed this was how life would be with and for him until he got older and finally did fully retire.

My father once told me that he felt he needed to end the double act, or risk coming to dislike Ernie. I was shocked by this. With the benefit of passing time, I've come to realise that this was a much bigger issue than anything about Ernie and their partnership, which was remarkable in its consistency right to the end. This was about my father's failing health, and where he wanted to be after decades of performing comedy. Maybe, to a degree, he'd just run out of laughs, or the need to provide them, at least.

Yet somehow he managed to keep up appearances, to summon the man the public wanted to see and hear. Standing beside him as he signed yet another autograph for a fan while walking down a street, my father's sheer engagement and energy to be the man they expected him to be never failed to impress me. On one occasion in the street near our family home, he was smoking a large Cuban cigar. As he went to sign his name for someone, he passed his cigar to the nearest child and said, 'Can you keep that going for me?!'

GAIL: After chatting with Dad on numerous occasions, I was left with the feeling that it was the responsibility of Morecambe and Wise he was exhausted by. He felt especially responsible for Ernie's career, and for making the shows funny. Ultimately, it came to the point where he felt that all those around him were just waiting for him to spin some magic. Do you remember, Gary, when in rehearsals he ran into a prop wall, and his heart went out of rhythm? Naturally, he had to have a few days off. He thought it would be fine, as there was plenty for them all to get on with, and he could turn up in time for the filming. When they reconvened at the studios, it was quickly apparent that they'd done nothing in his absence. Everyone had downed tools, so to speak, and decided to just wait for his return. He was upset and shocked by this.

To me, there are two types of performers: those for whom it is like a drug, and they can't fully function without it, and those for whom it is undeniably a job they adore, but who can happily function without it. Morecambe was the latter, and Wise the former.

Dad knew that Ernie was Mr Showbiz. Also, Ernie had never really been so ill that he'd required a single day off work. Ernie still had a lot left in the tank in his fifties, although learning lines had always proved a problem for him, and it was a worsening one by his own admission. Dad had always found learning lines simple. He would say that as soon as the show was in the can, he would forget them almost immediately.

On one of my visits back to the family home, he suddenly said, 'You will watch the shows when I'm gone, won't you? Because if you don't, then it's all been for nothing. I've done it all for my family, all of it!' I was taken aback, and other than confirming that of course I'd watch the shows, I didn't say much else. I've now come to realise that his home and his family were always his reason for getting out of bed and going to work at all. That isn't to say he didn't enjoy what he did, for he really did enjoy his career. But his motivation clearly came from somewhere else.

Night Train to Murder wasn't the only non-television project my father had been involved with. As mentioned, he had been busy working with actors Tom Baker and Madeline Smith on *The Passionate Pilgrim*. And there's something about it that is rather compelling. It has a *Carry On* movie feel to it, while simultaneously giving us a surprisingly invigorated Eric Morecambe. This might have been more the type of vehicle Euston Films could have provided for M&W. It certainly registered with a lot of people, as the film was released with the James Bond movie *Octopussy*, and another big theatrical release of the time, *War Games*, so it was seen by large numbers, and on the 'big screen'.

It interests me as to what Ernie was making of these occasional forays by his partner into solo projects. When I was with Ernie, I never felt there was any issue at all. On the contrary, I sensed he had always expected it as a natural development. And as mentioned, with Ernie finding lines difficult, just coping with the occasional M&W show was probably plenty for him to be getting on with. Also he was spending more and more time with Doreen at his condo in Florida, or hanging with friends in Maidenhead, where they lived. In any case, whatever was happening or not happening, being discussed or not discussed, it would all end on the night of 28 May 1984.

My father had agreed to do a Q&A show at the Roses Theatre, Tewkesbury, for his old pal Stan Stennett. It had been Stan, after all, who had got the ball rolling for Morecambe and Wise back in those quieter times of the 1950s, and both our families had stayed in contact during the years that followed.

It's true to say that my father hadn't been enjoying the best of health leading up to this show – enlarged heart being the heart specialist's diagnosis, which nowadays would certainly have put a stop to any thoughts of heading to do a Q&A performance on stage. But he was actually keen to try it out, as the format was something that appealed to him. It was a lively diversion from his new career as an author.

'The Q&A shows are easy for me,' he told me. 'I answer questions and talk about myself rather than have to perform any material. It's not hard work like a Morecambe and Wise show.'

> GAIL: It was impossible to be around Dad and think you were with a sick man. When Dad died, both Mum and I were angry with the doctors, whose advice Dad had always followed to the letter. Literally, the day after Dad died, his GP said it was wonderful he should have died while doing what he loved. But, of course, we the family knew that it was the last thing Dad would have wanted. And Tommy Cooper's very public demise had hung heavy on

291

him. I think our greater upset was in knowing how much he would eventually have enjoyed retiring, just stopping, being at home, writing more and having time with his grandchildren, who meant so much to him.

What Dad required was a doctor's note! If one single doctor had said he should stop working right now, he would literally have stopped the same day. But he needed that permission, and the doctors, like the public at large, erroneously assumed that working in comedy was his lifeblood.

With that doctor's permission, he could have, in all honesty, told Stan Stennett that the doctors had advised him not to do it. The lovely professor Magdi Yacoub, who had performed Dad's heart surgery a few years earlier, asked me why nobody had been in touch with him, as my father clearly needed a heart transplant.

In fairness, I soon came to realise that Dad might have died that night anyway, whether he chose to go to the theatre or stay at home. And I know that he would not have contemplated a transplant. He made that clear to me quite some time before. I think he would have settled for a couple of extra years pottering around the family home and seeing his loved ones.

We all know what happened next. Perhaps there was a certain amount of inevitability about it – certainly with hindsight – but he collapsed in the wings coming off stage and passed away in the early hours at Cheltenham hospital.

I know my mother felt guilt that she hadn't seen the signs; hadn't told him to just say no to doing the show.

However, his GP pointed out to us that he could have died at that moment just getting up from the sofa to switch the television off.

'I always think Eric had a premonition about himself,' says my mother. 'Often he would begin a conversation by saying, "Now, if anything happens to me ..."'

Ironically, he had gone through his life story on stage that night, talking about childhood memories that even my mother wasn't familiar with. 'It was a great show,' my mother recalls. 'The first half was the usual variety acts that you expected, and the second half was your father giving an extended interview to Stan. The biggest oversight was that no one recorded it for posterity, because it was absolutely brilliant. The audience was spellbound. You could have heard a pin drop.' But she adds, 'That said, it was a mistake to do it. He wasn't well a few days before the show. He was in pain but refused to cancel it. His health had been up and down, and I was scared of what might happen if he did this show.'

It seems my father wasn't as concerned as my mother. She says, 'Eric was actually quite excited about it. He had arranged for everyone involved to attend a small dinner party at a hotel after the show.'

And now began the nation coming to terms with the loss of their favourite comedian, the man who so many down the years have described to me as being like their favourite uncle, or a family member. It almost seemed impossible to digest the fact that he had gone.

I think, on an unconscious level, we all expected a Harry Houdini return: a triumphant reappearance somewhere unexpected, with a little smile and a tap of the famous spectacles: 'Evenin' all – I'm sorry I'm late. But that fooled you all, didn't it!' But unfortunately that just wasn't going to occur.

Our family remained in a state of shock that eventually ebbed into grief, then just plain sadness and emptiness for the following few years.

You never recover from the loss of someone you love; you eventually absorb it as having happened. That's about as good as it gets. And because it was Eric Morecambe, the sunshine seemed to have gone with him. We had entered my mother's childhood world of black and white. She had spent her early childhood out in Burma, as her father was an army surgeon. When she returned to England, still at school age, she couldn't understand where all the colour had gone. 'It was a black-and-white world I found myself in,' she says. '*Coronation Street* rooftops and London smogs.'

I honestly don't think she ever fully recovered from that shock, and now she'd lost that big ray of sunlight that had brought back the colour to her life like nothing before it.

TWENTY-THREE

And then there was Ernie.

Putting it mildly, Ernie was bereft. At the age of fifty-nine, he had not only lost his partner of four decades, but his job.

Doreen said of that time that Ernie didn't want to work again. 'When Eric died, he wanted to put down the shutters there and then. Professionally, it was hard for him. He did agonise about whether he should go on . . .'

Has anyone looked more tragic than Ernie Wise did the day after the loss of his partner? He looked shattered. Partly that was due to having not slept all night – there he was on the TV and news programmes that first morning post the conclusion of his career as half of the country's most revered double act. I seriously wondered if he would ever manage to secure some normality in his life – if he would ever emerge from that drawn, depressed state. Doreen wasn't in fact sure he ever did manage that. He had lost for ever the only other person he was married to, in a manner of speaking.

It all gets so maudlin when talking about funerals, if one is not careful, so I'm not going to linger here any more than is necessary. But there are a few interesting points to mention, if only as a nod to what was a difficult time not only for the family, but judging by the outpouring of grief, also for the nation.

Before my father's funeral took place, we had a family discussion and a consultation with Ernie and Doreen, and collectively decided it would be better for Ernie in the circumstances if he just read a suitable piece as a eulogy at the funeral service. It was my mother's idea, as she'd seen how destroyed Ernie was looking and sounding, and wanted to spare him any more pain than was necessary.

On the day, Ernie chucked the plan out the window – and quite rightly, in my opinion, for if he couldn't speak from the heart about my father, who could? – and went into describing his and his partner's aspirations as young lads, with this big, crazy idea of becoming stars.

Sitting there listening to these heartfelt words reminded me of their live tour work. Near the end of each show, and slightly changing the words with each performance, Ernie essentially would say, 'Do you remember how we had a dream of becoming comedians?' My father would glance at the theatre audience and reply, 'We should have given that a go!'

Inside St Nicolas Church, Harpenden, that day of 4 June 1984, the audience, who were now a congregation, had moments of laughter from words by comedian Dickie Henderson in his eulogy. But when Ernie slowly read out the words to their 'Bring Me Sunshine' song, there wasn't a dry eye left within or without the church.

SIDENOTE: In 2011, the BBC used 'Bring Me Sunshine' as part of a promotion for the seventy-fifth anniversary of its main channel. Its meaning is not adjoined to any specific time – it is a positive cry of hope for any generation coming through.

I know myself from various weddings and funerals I've attended that it crops up as the exit cue for both of those occasions with surprising regularity. So much so that between writing the last two paragraphs and editing them, I was informed by someone that he attended a wedding in Inverness, Scotland, recently, and they not only played it as the exit music from the service, but the bride and groom skip-danced down the aisle and out of the church to it!

Ernie was well placed to never have to work again should he so have chosen. He was fit, and he liked his swimming and boating, and regular trips out to Florida. But also he'd known little else since shedding his family home and leaving the pain and the gloom of East Ardsley Boys School. Doing 'something' was always going to beat doing 'nothing'. But venturing forth on his own certainly made doing nothing highly appealing.

For a start, Ernie knew that the British public – on a subliminal level at least, though on a conscious one with many – never forgave him for living. It's a harsh reality, and it's the truth. Ernie never denied it whenever it came up in conversation. He felt survivor's guilt, without a doubt.

Ernie also recognised that it was going to be tedious having people come up to him – not just the general public either – commiserating at the loss of his partner, when what they were chiefly commiserating with was the loss to the nation of a great comedian in Eric Morecambe. While not making Ernie reclusive, it made him reticent about putting his head above the parapet.

Add to this scenario that Ernie was someone, even in the good times, who welcomed peace and quiet, and we can appreciate how tricky was his situation. He wasn't cut out for people coming up to ask questions or ask for an autograph. He went along with it, but he didn't particularly do banter outside his working environment.

There was a time, perhaps up to the late 1960s, that he was more accommodating on that front, but with nearly losing his partner to a heart attack in 1968, plus the repetition that accompanies being permanently in the spotlight, I think he grew weary of attention.

Some people have told me they met Ernie and he wasn't that friendly. That to me means he was just trying not to engage in an effort to avoid what that involved, and what it took out of him, particularly once he was no longer part of a famed double act. Despite being naturally ebullient and amusing, he wasn't Eric Morecambe. And not being Eric Morecambe made him mildly inhibited when in solo situations. I sympathise with the public perception that he might have appeared misanthropic at times, and it might sound crass to say it wasn't deliberate. But it really wasn't.

Ernie was the gentle half of the double act – an easy, breezy smile and wave of the arm and off, just like when he'd first met Sadie and my father all those years before. But my father, in comedic terms, was more the blunt instrument, and more willing and able to take that tough comedian persona out into the big wide world. My father could be what the public wanted, because to all intents and purposes, that is who he had wished himself into becoming.

Ernie always had the hugest admiration for his partner's courage and self-confidence – possibly inherited from Sadie's approach to life that nothing shall prevent you from achieving your goals. And he was smart enough to recognise his own hesitancy in all decision-making. He'd spent half his working life allowing the decisions to be made by his colleagues, so to suddenly find himself in a large space, alone and free to call the shots was going to be difficult, if not impossible for him.

He once told me that what he admired the most about my father was his determination to make their double act succeed, even at the most unlikely of times, and his unwavering sense of belief in his comedic skills. He said something along the lines of how much he wished he'd had the same self-confidence in all he did.

Sensibly, he avoided all comedy projects involving any other partner. And the idea of forming another partnership was, of course, mostly a game being played out by the media. He knew the public would never accept that. It would have been tantamount to Stan Laurel finding a new partner after Oliver Hardy had passed away.

Ernie played it cannily by accepting a one-man tour of Australia, where he and my father had worked all those years back in the late 1950s. Morecambe and Wise have remained popular and well-respected in the Antipodes, including right up to the time of writing this book. Australia was also far enough away to separate Ernie from the harsher realities of the UK, where every move and comment he made was immediately scrutinised.

The UK was essentially waiting for Ernie to do something and fail miserably. Once that happened, they could throw up lines like, 'The curse of the straight man'. Or write how Eric was the funny one, thus implying that Ernie was destined to failure once his partner was gone. Whether such comments and scrutiny would have emerged or not we can't be sure, but it is likely.

Time went by. The Australian adventure was over, and by all accounts went well enough, and in 1987, now aged sixty-one, Ernie found himself back in London's West End, appearing in the musical version of Dickens' unfinished novel, *The Mystery of Edwin Drood*.

Although it received poor reviews, accepting the role was possibly a good move on Ernie's part. It was a departure from all that had gone before; all that had established him as a British institution. But the show required him to be on stage the whole time, something that Doreen believes brought about his first stroke.

I always wondered if that was really a possible link, but I'm beginning to see that it may have been, for each night Ernie was left utterly exhausted, barely able to move. The producers pulled the show after ten weeks, which in terms of his health was probably a relief. And at least Ernie had now been back performing, and he'd experienced plenty of knocks back in the day on the way up, so was immune to anything adjudged to be a failure.

One of the biggest strains for Ernie, which he reminded me of, was back to the old problem of remembering the lines. Barry Cryer told me that he went to see the *Edwin Drood* show, and said you could see every muscle in his face straining as he tried to recall each line. 'I couldn't go backstage afterwards,' said Barry. 'It would have been too difficult to be honest with him having seen the strain he was under on that stage. You could see him mouthing the other performers' lines before saying his own.'

Ernie told me a few years after *Edwin Drood* had ended, 'The atmosphere in theatres was giving me worse asthma than I'd had before.' But Ernie – addicted to show business and performing – was not going to leave the stage just yet.

Ray Cooney's hugely popular West End comedy, *Run for Your Wife*, was Ernie's next escapade in the world of show business, where he appeared as Detective Sergeant Porterhouse.

Ernie had seen it performed with actor–comedian–writer

Eric Sykes in the role and loved it, despite being back in the atmosphere of a theatre. I saw the show some time before Ernie was in it, and loved it just as much as he had. For Ernie, just hearing an audience laughing at the performers was enough to entrance him. It was possibly the nearest he got to the old days.

The winter escapes to Florida – they had their property in Boca Raton – gave Ernie somewhere to fully relax. Like many who are well known in the UK, escaping to somewhere you can be anonymous gave him and Doreen so much freedom. And Doreen pointed out that, 'Whenever we were in America and heard an English voice we would disappear.' Ernie and Doreen were never too crazy about small talk, and false congeniality, as they saw it. Ernie might have been missing his partner and his career, but at least now he was free from the whole tread-mill of work and the fame that accompanied it. Clearly he revelled in it. Both he and Doreen seemed to have their humour back in the 1990s.

While Ernie was showing some signs of ageing – and like my father before him, I'd say it was premature ageing, and perhaps a pre-cursor to the poor health await-ing him – he certainly had more of his old bounce back.

Around this time, I was with Ernie and Doreen at a BBC awards do. On one side of me was Doreen, and on the other side, television presenter David Frost. I was possibly the only unknown person in the studio audience. Sitting in front of me was astronomer Patrick Moore. He was slumped back in his seat, completely out cold. Doreen turned to me and said, 'All these stars and he still can't keep awake.'

I always liked Doreen's sense of humour. She was witty, and I can see why she was such a big fan of Morecambe and Wise, though whether it was their comedy that influenced her or her own humour gravitating towards the same, it's hard to know. I've always said that Doreen and I had a love–hate relationship – I loved her, she hated me! Actually, that's not true. We could disagree, sometimes a little too publicly, but it would always end in a phone call and lots of laughs. The big four of Eric, Ernie, Joan and Doreen had to stick together like glue for the whole thing to work, and us on the periphery – Gail and I and, later, Steven – had to quickly develop the same approach, and keep in step. I like to think that we did and still do. Morecambe and Wise is always our priority.

For my brother, it's been a little trickier. When my parents completed his adoption – 1973, I think – Morecambe and Wise were big stars. Steven hadn't been around during the earlier days of it all, so his memories are, by his own admission, limited. Fishing with his dad seems to provide the clearest memories. Gail and I have never been into fishing, so it was great to know that was something he and our dad shared.

In 1992–93, after a gap of a few years, I started to get back into closer contact with Ernie. We appeared on a BBC radio show together – me in the studio, and Ernie at his home in Maidenhead. We were both a little pumped and animated at being reunited after too long a gap.

Ernie reminded me of the time when I was a child, and I was sitting next to him at the premiere of their 1965 film, *That Riviera Touch*. I apparently turned to him and said, 'Is this live? Are you doing it now?' I was chuffed he remembered. Then we started talking about the antics of my father, particularly in his youth.

This all lasted around two or three minutes, then the presenter interrupted and said, 'Lovely! Okay, we'll do that again and start recording now!' I was furious, and I could tell that Ernie was bemused. What on earth was the point of reconnecting the pair of us after all this time and not recording the actual moment that it happened?

The retake was a damp squib, but we tried to sound spontaneous. I guess that's local radio for you, certainly back in the day. At least it marked the beginning of Ernie and me being back in reasonably regular contact again, and we would share quite a few phone calls over the next year or two.

Ernie mostly wanted to reminisce, and I'd laugh out loud as he described my father running around the place like a blue-arsed fly. Doreen would call out in the background, 'He couldn't get your dad out of the cinema,' which I can imagine.

The chief reason why Ernie and I reconnected following our odd radio moment was because I was keen to present a Morecambe and Wise stage play that would celebrate their life together. Alongside my talented co-writer Martin Sterling, I started working on various ideas.

Martin and I even wrote several potential scripts in a completely different way from the previous one we had written. We created one that was just my father's story. As soon as we had a few ideas knocked into something approaching a reasonable state, we started making enquiries about how this project, in whatever shape and form it would finally materialise, could be staged. The only problem in making 'a few enquiries' is that you end up letting the cat out of the bag. Quite soon I was fending off national media calls — and in a whirlwind week that literally ended up with me having to hide behind a hedge in my own back garden with my then wife and my kids, I ended up appearing on Richard and Judy's morning show.

I also found myself agreeing to some national press interviews. If nothing else, it gave me the opportunity to explain that this was a project in an embryonic stage. Naturally I hoped the publicity would then create interest behind the scenes so we could get something up and running. But right then, we had nothing to promote except the idea. We had shot our bolt, and in all honesty that was a mistake.

Little did I realise that the lull that then followed this momentary chaos would last exactly ten years. For Ernie it would be a posthumous project that eventually made it to a West End stage, and I wouldn't be involved in the creative process that took it there.

Ernie, Martin and I had got together several times to discuss the potential play, and Ernie had said early on, 'I always knew there would be interest in this as a theatrical production. But getting it right is the tricky part.'

To begin with, Ernie's enthusiasm for the project was good bordering on great. As Michael Grade once said, '[Ernie] was on a hiding to nothing really, but he just wanted to work and there was no way for him to work that wasn't hugely exposed and open to criticism and/or comparison. Also, in the public's mind they didn't want to be reminded that Eric was dead.'

With this in mind, Ernie being engaged behind the

scenes on a planned production about his partnership was ideal. He was the living connection, yet not required to perform or even be interviewed. He could even have used the opportunity as his directorial debut. How perfect would that have been? And with his 'theatre asthma', he wouldn't have to spend long hours in that environment. Perfect!

Then, in December 1993, Ernie suffered a minor stroke.

He then had a second stroke shortly after getting over his first one, which was a real hammer blow. There was no longer any talk of doing a play of Morecambe and Wise, and Doreen rang me up to emphasise as much. In fact, she went further and said that due to his health, she'd appreciate it if I just pulled the plug on it for the time being. That was fine, though I did point out that if anything, Ernie had been more interested than me and Martin Sterling. Doreen agreed, but explained that the strokes had left him confused, and it would worry him to hear any more about it. That made perfect sense. Doreen was protective to a fault with Ernie from beginning to the end, so there was no argument from our side.

Some months after his second stroke, and for a reason I cannot recall, I was having lunch with Ernie and Doreen, my mother and others (including Lord Lew Grade), at the Café Royale on London's Regent Street. This most likely will have been early 1994. The irony that we should be fine-dining in the street an unemployed Eric and Ernie had once bumped into each other just after the war wasn't lost on me; neither was the fact Lew Grade, Ernie's former boss at ATV, should have been there.

Ernie was on buoyant form that lunchtime, and he only

stopped for breath when deciding he needed a comfort call. As he left the table, I looked across to Doreen and said, 'Ernie seems on better form than I'd expected.'

She shook her head and pulled a grimace. 'Not really. He's on medication which helps, but he can't remember much from one day to the next. It's not easy for him now.' Or for Doreen, who without question dedicated her life to his health and career, just as my mother had done for my father.

In the summer of '94, I was on *Loose Ends*, a radio show hosted back then by Ned Sherrin. Actor Jon Pertwee – one of my heroes from his days as the Doctor in *Doctor Who* – was also on the show. While waiting to be called through, Jon said, 'I was with Ernie Wise the other day.'

'How was he?' I obviously enquired.

Another grimace, as was becoming familiar with those who were having recent contact with Ernie. 'Not great, to be honest with you, old boy,' he replied.

In 1995, Ernie had the most serious of his several strokes, though he courageously, if unadvisedly, talked about continuing to work. This was a defence, of course, against accepting where he was at. Despite the glass always being half full with Ernie, it can't have been easy for him to muster genuine enthusiasm for anything at this point.

Up to his illness, he had been appearing in panto in Windsor with actor Bryan Burdon, and still hoped they could perform together again. Burdon knew that just wouldn't be possible, having met up with him to have a chat about it. It was clear to Burdon by this stage that Ernie's vision and hearing were both severely impaired, and his speech had also deteriorated, with him now slurring a bit; this was all confirmed by Doreen.

I only talked once more with Ernie on the phone, and I tried to keep it as short as possible, as I knew he was finding it difficult.

Reality having to be accepted, on his seventieth birthday, 27 November 1995, Ernie announced his retirement. He would live a few more years – tough ones for both him and Doreen – before passing away in hospital from heart failure in the March of 1999.

The funeral took place on 30 March. I had a puncture on the way to Slough Crematorium, Bucks. Fortunately, I had allowed a lot of time to get there, as for me it was one of the most momentous events in my life, and I really couldn't have dealt with missing it on any account. It was as if I'd lost my father again, albeit in a watered-down sort of way.

It was all kept low-key, which neatly summed up Ernie's personality and the way he had lived his life. It was very moving. Michael Grade read a wonderful eulogy, which echoed the end-of-an-era feel to the occasion. One of his observations was: 'Let us be clear, they were equal partners in the comic genius department.'

From now on, Morecambe AND Wise would be talked about in the past tense.

Ernie was one of the good guys – one of the nicest people I've met, when I think about it. Always interested in you when in conversation, with lots of questions and responses. Nothing he said was just to fill in a silence. And always he was incredibly modest. Alongside my father, he was possibly the last of the 'gentleman' performers.

Despite their humble beginnings, they were never overly seduced by money flashed in front of them, completely sincere as performers who always put art for art's sake above all other needs. And they loved each other, and now had gone somewhere else. Perhaps they are together again. It's what all of us would want for them, and expect.

TWENTY-FOUR

We can't tell the story of Morecambe and Wise without acknowledging death, but the UK's most beloved double act live on and continue to thrive. This book is called *Forever in the Sunshine*, after all, so let's look at all the wonderful things Morecambe and Wise still bring to our lives.

We can always rely on our family friend Miranda Hart to say nice words about Eric and Ernie, as she did as part of the BBC's centenary in 2022: 'Watching Morecambe and Wise aged seven and deciding my life's aim was to "be silly" like them was my most vital, joyful and inspiring experience.' Thirty years later, she would be working at the BBC Centre herself. 'During one recording, I had to wipe away a tear that my comedy heroes had trod the same floor . . .'

In 2022, on the hottest day ever recorded in the UK, I bumped into presenter and show host Jonathan Ross. Quite literally, as it happened, in a hotel lobby in Whitby. My wife, Tanya, and I were escaping the city heat of Leeds – Whitby's coastline was a modest 29 Celsius that day – and he, poor man, was working in Whitby town centre, where it was around 37 degrees! Naturally, we got talking all things Morecambe and Wise because,

alongside Miranda Hart, there's been no more vocal supporter of M&W. Add Lenny Henry to that list, and also
Lee Mack. Both Lenny and Lee so often say wonderful
things about Morecambe and Wise, and I can add that
I've had the pleasure to work with the former.

Lee Mack I've met several times, and he always tells me
that my father is not only his hero, but the reason he felt
he could get into comedy. Lee for me is the nearest we'll
get to seeing Eric Morecambe in the flesh. It's something
that emanates from behind the eyes – a quiet confidence;
a smile that is more mischievous than humorous; a sense
that the intention for the day is fun. Plus, of course, great
comic timing, wonderful delivery, total self-confidence
and – as my father would have said – he's a lovely little
mover! And essentially, that was my father.

Back in Whitby. 'I like to do my bit for them,'
Jonathon Ross remarked, modestly. His 'bit' includes
several documentaries.

I was fascinated when Ross told me that one of his first
jobs as an interviewer/presenter came in the 1980s, when
he was sent to Hong Kong to cover the increasingly popular kung fu genre, led back then by the new kid on the
block, a young Jackie Chan. 'I was interviewing Maggie
Cheung, who plays Chan's girlfriend in the film they
were shooting, which was *Police Story*. I asked the usual
run of questions, then started struggling to think of what
else to ask her. Then I remembered she had spent time
in the UK. "What do you miss most about the UK?" I
asked her. "The Morecambe and Wise Christmas show,"
she responded. I really hadn't expected that reply.'

This neatly sums up where Morecambe and Wise's

journey would posthumously take them. People would watch them, remember watching them, want to talk about them with a slight air of nostalgia, express how much they related to them in their formative years, and generally see them as something comforting, which floats in the back of their mind, and usually comes to the fore around Christmas. That hasn't been confined just to the viewing public, but to programme-makers, too.

What became clear to our agent of that time, Jan Kennedy, was that Morecambe and Wise were unlike so many in British show business. They left such a large body of work, probably unequalled. On that basis alone, Morecambe and Wise weren't going to disappear any time soon. The human tale of two men on a journey was now unquestionably over, but the new tale of what they had come to mean was beginning. They've almost reached folklore proportions.

Occasionally it's something bizarre that comes along and surprises you. In 2021, and again in 2022, there were news pieces about a filmed interview Eric and Ernie did for a student circa 1970. In this interview, they discussed Monty Python – relatively new to our screens at that time, the show running from 1969 to 1974 – and made disparaging comments about their comedy. It was very much blown out of proportion, because Python was then the new kid on the block, and there was much wariness about what they were doing and what they were up to. And a couple of years after this interview, I know that my father came to admire Python – especially the films that followed – and got to know some of those involved quite well, like John Cleese.

On the back of this negative news story, I felt the need to contact ex-Python Michael Palin who, like me, had been drawn in to this news piece for comment. This was a huge plus as I got to sit down for lunch with one of my own heroes, though a hero much less for his Python work than for his travel films over the decades.

Palin, who is genuinely one of the nicest people I've ever had the privilege to meet, was wonderfully dismiss-ive of the whole thing, and even said that he and the others in Python would probably have agreed with my father's comments!

Back in 2002, about three years after Ernie Wise had left us, producer David Pugh, alongside Kenneth Branagh (on board as director), finally brought the stage play Ernie had been involved with at the outset to the West End stage.

To say *The Play What I Wrote* was a massive success would be an understatement. It transferred to Broadway in 2003, and returned to the UK to tour thereafter for some time to come, and it certainly helped the huge talent that is Toby Jones launch his remarkable career.

In 2022, it returned to Birmingham, and several other venues. In the revival, the biggest regular guest star was the actor and Hollywood A-lister Tom Hiddleston, but in the original production, Sir Roger Moore guest-starred the most. Moore said to me at the time, 'My biggest regret was not appearing with your father and Ernie in a Christmas show. I was always shooting the oh-oh-seven movies.' And he said it like that – each 'oh' being pronounced like a protracted 'oh dear'!

> SIDENOTE: Tom Hiddleston says that he was, like everyone else, quite depressed during the first pandemic lockdown, and would cheer himself up by watching Morecambe and Wise clips on YouTube.

The original production of the show also gave me and my family the chance to reunite with Eddie Braben. Dee Braben tells me that after my father passed away, Eddie would carry on writing down ideas that came to him for Morecambe and Wise shows. 'Eddie would say, "Oh, if only Eric were still alive we could have had such-and-such an actor for this role." He was still thinking of scripts for them.'

> SIDENOTE: Eddie sent me one of these scripts he was still writing after both the comics had died. It was one of their bedroom routines, and their voices just leapt from the page. It was so familiar in style from what he'd been producing with such great aplomb back in the day, that I honestly felt I'd already seen them performing it.

I believe that *The Play What I Wrote* played a major part in bringing Morecambe and Wise back to our attention. They had never fully gone away, but suddenly they were, as the expression goes, prime-time TV once again.

The TV show repeats have become a part of the Christmas Eric and Ernie 'hijacked', though they are not altogether limited to the festive season. And documentaries on M&W's double act have been plentiful, and several of them fascinating in content.

There have been many wonderful highlights involving M&W over the years. Victoria Wood's 2011 film of their early years, while not wholly accurate, was a wonderful tribute and insight, and certainly captured something of the era from which they emerged. I was fascinated by *Morecambe and Wise in America*, which had such amazing footage, and really took us outside the studio and into 1960s New York, when Eric and Ernie were working for Ed Sullivan over there.

What happens next? More of the same, I hope. My mother echoes my thoughts when she says, 'I think it's extraordinary how it's all continued after both Eric and Ernie have gone. It's beyond what any of us could have imagined. I only wish that Eric knew. He would have taken such enormous satisfaction over it. I think they recognised they'd always have a following of some kind, but not to the level that it has attained. They could never have dreamed of being as popular as they are all these years later.'

In 1999, a larger-than-life bronze statue was unveiled on Morecambe Bay of my father. Back to the spot where as a kid he'd fished with his dad. Now he is permanently there beside the shoreline of his youth.

The sculptor, as earlier mentioned, is the wonderfully talented Graham Ibbeson, a Barnsley boy with remarkable artistic skills. My mother and I went up to his workshop in Barnsley in 1998 to see the statue in development. Ever the perfectionist, he was nervous of our visit. But already we could see the extraordinary likeness to the man himself, leaving both widow and son lost for words. Other statues he's produced include Don Revie, Benny Hill, Fred Trueman, Cary Grant and Laurel and Hardy. Ibbeson's work is spread across the country – a bronze trail delighting millions.

In 1999, my mother rang me up saying, 'Guess who they've got to unveil Eric's statue?'

'Chris Evans?' I replied.

'No,' said my mother quietly. 'Her Majesty the Queen!'

This took a while to comprehend. The Queen didn't go around unveiling statues to comedians. I was lost for words yet again. This was more than just an honour; this was unique.

It was so pleasing to hear that, a few months before the death of the Queen, she had referenced the statue unveiling event to one of her household, saying how much she had enjoyed the occasion.

GAIL: Originally Mum was asked if she would unveil the statue, and of course she was delighted. I happened to be with her when she received a call to say that she was no longer required to do the actual unveiling. Well, Mum was miffed at this, and said, 'They've probably replaced me with Glenda Jackson!' Fast forward a few weeks, and purely by chance I was with her again when she answered

316

the phone, and this time was beaming ear to ear. When she put the phone down, she said in her usual understated way, 'That's all right, then. The Queen has said she would like to do the unveiling.' It was such a lovely moment that I've thought about much over the years.

The Queen and Prince Philip were making an appearance in Lancashire for another event, and it was at her suggestion they included the Eric Morecambe statue unveiling. I wonder if it was an acknowledgement of what Dad had come to mean to the whole country as well as to the royal family? He died before he could receive a knighthood – which he certainly would have done – but this was a perfect way of showing how much he, and Morecambe and Wise, meant.

In August 2013, Ian Ashpitel and Jonty Stephens took the homage to Morecambe and Wise they'd been quietly working on to the Edinburgh Festival. I tried not to prejudge it, as I'd made that mistake before with various things. But suffice to say, none of us in the family were too optimistic about how this would turn out.

In 2009, we had had the wonderful touring show of Bob Golding in the play *Morecambe,* a virtuoso performance by Golding, alone on stage for ninety minutes on a whistle-stop tour of my father's life from birth to death. It's curious that while doing the play, Bob captured Eric Morecambe in his private life as well as on stage! The persona rarely dropped. We'd often meet up for a bite to eat during this period, and it was like dining out with my father.

Ian and Jonty – Ernie and Eric respectively – were of course presenting something different. Theirs was an homage, incorporating material by M&W, Eddie Braben and Hills and Green. The problem the family always has is that not everyone is accurate when they 'do' Morecambe and Wise, and irritatingly they tend to go gung-ho, without consulting us or our agent, Suzanne Westrip.

I went to Edinburgh not even sure that I wanted to see them trying to be Eric and Ernie. But they were so good, there were times when I felt a shiver down the spine, like I was back in the auditorium with the real Eric and Ernie, watching it all again. I could almost picture myself selling T-shirts in the interval!

Here we are in 2023, and Ian and Jonty have more dates lined up, which speaks volumes. Both Gail and I have travelled to many a theatre to watch them, and even accompanied them on a cruise ship. Do we need actors recreating Morecambe and Wise? That's a grey area, as through modern technology we still have the real deal and in ever-improving digital quality. On the other hand, it is a theatrical experience that the likes of Ian Ashpitel and Jonty Stephens are offering us.

SIDENOTE: Jonty Stephens was brought into the world by a midwife who was the mother of Eric Idle of Monty Python. He's been in contact with Idle ever since he was born.

In 2016, Graham Ibbeson re-entered our lives with another wonderful sculpture, this time of Eric *and* Ernie.

Morecambe and Wise now stand proudly in bronze inside the aforementioned Winter Gardens theatre in Blackpool. It's a stunning work, and it feels so right to see them standing there together.

So much continues to happen on their posthumous journey that I honestly can't say what might be next.

The beat goes on. Documentary follows documentary, and Christmas is still alive to the sound of Eric and Ernie playing all the right notes.

Morecambe and Wise have become something beyond posthumous entertainers, more than any other British act, I would hazard. They transcend what they were and what they did: they've become a feeling, and one that is subliminally linked to plenty of sunshine, courtesy of Sylvia Dee and Arthur Kent's song, and all that is rose-tinted about the annual festive season.

SIDENOTE: American lyricist Sylvia Dee also wrote the lyrics for 'Too Young', a big hit for Nat King Cole. Born in 1914, she died in 1967, which means she passed away around two years before M&W made 'Bring Me Sunshine' their own. Arthur Kent, who composed the music for the song, lived till 2009.

While Ernie Wise spent much of his life in a boisterous, cheerfully excitable state, perpetually on the run from his childhood – and when not, then possibly reimagining it – Eric Morecambe spent too much of his own life having to discuss and consider his health. Prognoses, diagnoses, surgical interventions, dietary regimes, life-style, exercise routines. There was so much distraction for him in the business of being ill. It still catches me unawares at times that thought, unbidden, of how swiftly went his life's journey. My mother always says that the painful part is, 'He never was left any time to enjoy the fruits of his success.' That is without question true, but equally I'm confident that he enjoyed the journey, just as much as Ernie enjoyed his.

If you think too much about it, then you do start to wonder: wonder what if he had never been an entertainer and stayed in Lancashire, and followed as originally expected in his father's footsteps working for the council? Would he have lived a much longer life? Would it have been as satisfying to him? Would it have brought its own rewards and moments of great happiness?

And Ernie, too. What if he'd been stronger with Sadie and just out-and-out refused a return to the double act post Second World War during their unintended meeting in Regent Street? Would he have remained a singer and dancer? It's hard to know where that would or wouldn't have taken him, long term. But then the 'what ifs' are numerous in all our lives, and best discarded at the first opportunity.

My father assuredly spent too long perfecting his work at the expense of his life. His intensity for the former was detrimental to the latter. He emerged at a time when getting by on a daily basis was the priority, rather than personal wellbeing. Shiny big health clubs and extensive dietary information were nowhere to be seen, and there-fore never entered the daily discussions of the era. Not wishing to put too dramatic a light upon it, but life was about survival, not self-care or self-improvement. You only have to look at 1930–1950 film footage to get a sense of how tough and grim things mostly were. Leisure time back then seemed to be putting your feet up with a packet of fags and a cup of tea.

But the Morecambe and Wise story is about so much more than just their work. As the years go by, and I'm suddenly aware of being nearer seventy than sixty, when I think of Morecambe and Wise – which is every single day of my life, by the way – I more and more recognise how important their own personal relationship was to their output. Eddie Braben so brilliantly understood from the outset that the story of Morecambe and Wise's comedy was about the deepest of friendships, and he led them, and us, down that path of enlightenment.

I think we've now long passed the time when the public and the media alike somehow felt Ernie was worth less than his partner in their double act (something my father never felt for a second). Maybe it's taken time for the world to catch up with the idea that a double act, if it is to succeed, can't be anything other than exactly that.

The sunshine they generated certainly seems to have a forever shine to it, which I can't imagine will disappear any time soon. The world, and life in it, seems to get more complicated by the week. Morecambe and Wise remind us that there is still a silly way to look at things despite the daily chaos going on around us.

I've so enjoyed working on this final – for me – Morecambe and Wise book. It's been a real privilege. My yearning to present something unique and family-led, rather than solely reliant upon 'sources', had been a long-burning desire of mine. To actually turn it into a reality has been completely fulfilling.

Have I learned anything new as I've gone along? If not new, then absolutely it has reminded me of how integral Eric and Ernie each were to making the other one brilliant, and how important their childhood relationship was in cementing their success as a double act.

The whole idea of Eddie Braben's of having them share a flat and a bed while discussing who 'teacher' liked best at school was obviously a comic device. Yet it's one based on truth, which is where Eddie's thinking was so far ahead of our own. Their childhood days on tour squeezing into a bed together to save space; their year at Mrs Duer's in Chiswick sitting around the fireside; these were all real moments gently redesigned by Eddie to show the viewer how warm their long relationship was.

I certainly feel that I've come to realise without question that it was never about the comedy – or, at least, far less so – but about their friendship and battle through the eras. It is that which has made them endure in our hearts. We feel safe with them because they are clearly feeling safe with each other. And through wonderful scripts and performances, with their countless references to their semi-fictionalised past, we feel we've been on the whole journey with them.

I leave the final thoughts – mostly because my own thoughts are in exact alignment with hers – to my big sister.

GAIL: There was so much fun and laughter back then. That's what I noticed about other families — although perfectly happy and well functioning as they were, there was a lack of belly-laughs and hysterical giggles.

There is no doubt a price to pay for the partners and children of someone that is famous and constantly in the public eye, but I can honestly say I would not change a second of it.

Well done, Sadie, George, Ernie, Doreen, Mum and, my hero, Dad!

Didn't we have an amazing childhood? Can we do it all again, please?

SOURCES

Eric, Ernie and many others associated with them have been the subjects of fascination for decades, and they told their stories several times over to different people, privately and publicly. I personally heard most of them, from the horses' mouths as it were, at some point over the years. It is often impossible to pin down the original sources of many of the quotations contained in this book, but the publications listed below are an excellent starting point for those wishing to read more on these subjects.

Cook, William, *Eric Morecambe Unseen* (HarperCollins, 2005)

Cook, William, *Morecambe & Wise Untold* (HarperCollins, 2007)

Hogg, James and Sellers, Robert, *Little Ern* (Sidgwick & Jackson, 2011)

Holman, Dennis, *Eric & Ernie* (WH Allen, 1973)

McCann, Graham, *Morecambe and Wise* (Fourth Estate, 1998)

Sterling, Martin and Morecambe, Gary, *Morecambe and Wise: Behind the Sunshine* (Robson Books, 1994)

Sterling, Martin and Morecambe, Gary, *Memories of Eric* (Andre Deutsch, 1999)

Wise, Ernie, *Still on My Way to Hollywood* (Duckworth, 1990)
Burton, Paul, *Two of a Kind* (Fantom Films, 2020)
MorecambeandWise.com, Paul Jenkinson and Gideon Chilton

ACKNOWLEDGEMENTS

My sincere thanks to all those who contributed to this book by way of interview. Your contribution was invaluable.

Huge thanks as always to our family agent, and agent for Morecambe and Wise, Suzanne Westrip. Your friendship, support and understanding of Eric and Ernie have never been less than remarkable.

Thanks also to writer and entertainment historian Paul Burton, for his last-minute research and interviews. I don't know how you manage to track down information so quickly!

My warmest thanks and deep appreciation to the late photographer Alan Jubb. Alan took great photos of great performers over many decades, and helped me enormously on more than one occasion.